CAMBRIDGE TEXTS IN THE
HISTORY OF POLITICAL THOUGHT

DAZAI SHUNDAI
Writings on Political Economy

DAZAI SHUNDAI (1680–1747) is a critical figure in Japanese political thought who developed his philosophy in response to a perceived crisis in the status of the ruling samurai class, of which he was a member. This volume introduces sections from his most significant work of political thought, *Keizairoku* (1729), and its addendum *Keizairoku shūi* (1744). Extracts present Shundai's program of political and economic reform as he grappled with the upheavals and opportunities accompanying the breakdown of feudal agrarianism and the emergence of a modern commercial economy. While Shundai accepted the inevitability of this economic transition, his vision of political economy remained conservative, with a focus on strengthening samurai-class supremacy. Peter Flueckiger offers a critical introduction to Shundai's ideas, exploring the nuances of his engagement with Confucian thought, and extensive annotations provide further textual and historical context. This volume thus demonstrates how Shundai's writings prefaced increasingly ambitious theories of state-managed economic growth in early modern and modern Japan.

PETER FLUECKIGER is Professor of Japanese at Pomona College. His research focuses on literary theory and political and ethical philosophy in eighteenth-century Japan. He is the author of *Imagining Harmony: Poetry, Empathy, and Community in Mid-Tokugawa Confucianism and Nativism* (2011).

CAMBRIDGE TEXTS IN THE HISTORY OF POLITICAL THOUGHT

General editor
QUENTIN SKINNER
Queen Mary University of London

Editorial board
MICHAEL COOK
Princeton University

HANNAH DAWSON
King's College London

ADOM GETACHEW
University of Chicago

EMMA HUNTER
University of Edinburgh

GABRIEL PAQUETTE
University of Maine

ANDREW SARTORI
New York University

HILDE DE WEERDT
Leiden University

Cambridge Texts in the History of Political Thought is firmly established as the major student series of texts in political theory. It aims to make available all the most important texts in the history of political thought, from ancient Greece to the twentieth century, from throughout the world and from every political tradition. All the familiar classic texts are included, but the series seeks at the same time to enlarge the conventional canon through a global scope and by incorporating an extensive range of less well-known works and previously marginalised voices, many of them never before available in a modern English edition. Where possible, the texts are published in complete and unabridged form, and translations are specially commissioned for the series. However, where appropriate, abridged or tightly focused and thematic collections are offered instead. Each volume contains a critical introduction together with chronologies, biographical sketches, a guide to further reading and any necessary glossaries and textual apparatus. Overall, the series aims to provide the reader with an outline of the entire evolution of political thinking on a global scale.

For a list of titles published in the series, please see end of book

DAZAI SHUNDAI

Writings on Political Economy

EDITED AND TRANSLATED BY
PETER FLUECKIGER
Pomona College, California

Shaftesbury Road, Cambridge CB2 8EA, United Kingdom

One Liberty Plaza, 20th Floor, New York, NY 10006, USA

477 Williamstown Road, Port Melbourne, VIC 3207, Australia

314–321, 3rd Floor, Plot 3, Splendor Forum, Jasola District Centre,
New Delhi – 110025, India

103 Penang Road, #05-06/07, Visioncrest Commercial, Singapore 238467

Cambridge University Press is part of Cambridge University Press & Assessment,
a department of the University of Cambridge.

We share the University's mission to contribute to society through the pursuit of
education, learning and research at the highest international levels of excellence.

www.cambridge.org
Information on this title: www.cambridge.org/9781316510322

DOI: 10.1017/9781108225243

© Peter Flueckiger 2026

This publication is in copyright. Subject to statutory exception and to the provisions
of relevant collective licensing agreements, no reproduction of any part may take place
without the written permission of Cambridge University Press & Assessment.

When citing this work, please include a reference to the DOI 10.1017/9781108225243

First published 2026

Cover image: Gokcemim/Getty Images

A catalogue record for this publication is available from the British Library

A Cataloging-in-Publication data record for this book is available from the Library of Congress

ISBN 978-1-316-51032-2 Hardback
ISBN 978-1-316-64972-5 Paperback

Cambridge University Press & Assessment has no responsibility for the persistence
or accuracy of URLs for external or third-party internet websites referred to in this
publication and does not guarantee that any content on such websites is, or will remain,
accurate or appropriate.

For EU product safety concerns, contact us at Calle de José Abascal, 56, 1°,
28003 Madrid, Spain, or email eugpsr@cambridge.org

Contents

Notes on the Texts and Translations	*page* vii
Major Periods of Premodern Japanese History	x
Major Dynasties and Periods of Premodern Chinese History	xi
Introduction	xii

ON POLITICAL ECONOMY (KEIZAIROKU)

Preface	3
Introductory Notes	7

Volume 1
A General Discussion of Political Economy	16

Volume 2
Ritual and Music	38

Volume 3
Bureaucratic Offices	61

Volume 4
Heavenly Patterns	72
Pitch Pipes and Calendars	76
Geography	79

Volume 5
Food and Goods	83

Contents

Volume 6
    Celebrations   119
    Educational Systems   123

Volume 7
    Regulated Dress   129
    Ceremonial Guards and State Processions   130
    Military Preparations   132

Volume 8
    Laws and Edicts   137
    Punishments and Penalties   143

Volume 9
    Institutions   147

Volume 10
    Non-Action   164
    The Way of Changes   172

AN ADDENDUM TO "ON POLITICAL ECONOMY" (KEIZAIROKU SHŪI)
    Addendum to "Food and Goods" (Volume 5)   185

Character List   195

Bibliography   207

Index   211

Notes on the Texts and Translations

Keizairoku (*On Political Economy*) was originally published in 1729 in an edition printed with wooden moveable type. The translations of *Keizairoku* in this volume are based on the full, unannotated text included in volume 9 of the *Nihon keizai taiten* (*Essential Works of Japanese Political Economy*), published by Shishi Shuppansha in 1928 and edited by Takimoto Seiichi; this is in turn based on a manuscript copy in Dazai Shundai's hand that was passed down by his student Mizuno Genrō (1693–1748) and later held in the collection of the politician Inuzuka Katsutarō (1868–1949). I also made use of the 1729 wooden moveable type edition, as well as the partial, annotated text (made up of the preface, introductory notes, and volumes 1 and 10) included in *Sorai gakuha* (*The Sorai School*), volume 37 of the *Nihon shisō taikei* (*Compendium of Japanese Thought*), published by Iwanami Shoten in 1972 and edited by Rai Tsutomu. The *Nihon shisō taikei* text is based on the 1729 wooden moveable type edition and also makes reference to a manuscript copy held by the Sakai family of Tsuruoka in Yamagata prefecture (descendants of the daimyo, or feudal lords, of Shōnai domain) and the text in volume 6 of the *Nihon keizai sōsho* (*Library of Japanese Political Economy*), published in 1914 by the Nihon Keizai Sōsho Kankōkai and edited by Takimoto Seiichi, which is based on the same manuscript copy as the *Nihon keizai taiten* text.

Keizairoku shūi (*An Addendum to On Political Economy*) circulated in manuscript form in the Tokugawa period. It was first published in 1914 in volume 6 of the *Nihon keizai sōsho* cited above. My translations are based on the full, annotated text included in volume 37 of the *Nihon shisō taikei*

Notes on the Texts and Translations

cited above; this is in turn based on a manuscript held by the Keio University Library and also makes reference to the *Nihon keizai sōsho* text.

The texts translated in the present volume are written in a formal but accessible form of Japanese, which was typical of Tokugawa works on political economy. This language stands in contrast to the more difficult literary Chinese often used for more purely philosophical works by Japanese Confucian scholars at the time. The texts in this volume do, however, assume familiarity with the Confucian classics and a wide range of other Chinese works, indicating that they were directed at an educated, elite audience.

Portions of *Keizairoku* have been translated into English by Richard J. Kirby and published in the *Transactions of the Asiatic Society of Japan* between 1900 and 1913. The much shorter *Keizairoku shūi* has been translated in full by Tetsuo Najita and included in *Tokugawa Political Writings*, published by Cambridge University Press in 1998. These translations include no annotations, with the exception of the very minimal annotations included in one section of Kirby's *Keizairoku* translations. The annotations included with my own translations are designed to make the density of allusions and references in Shundai's works more accessible to the modern reader, as well as to show how he is positioning himself in relation to various historical and textual traditions.

In order to keep the volume to a manageable length, I have produced abridged translations of both works, translating about half of each. I translate at least part of each volume of *Keizairoku*, so as to provide a sampling of the full range of topics Shundai writes about (Kirby's translations contain no selections at all from four of the ten volumes of *Keizairoku*). Shundai typically begins each section of *Keizairoku* with a general discussion of a particular aspect of government, including an analysis of key terms, then presents specific examples from Japanese or Chinese history, before moving on to policy proposals for the present. The omissions from my translations are mostly from Shundai's historical examples and policy proposals. Both of these are often very lengthy and detailed, and briefer excerpts are sufficient to give the reader a basic idea of his approach to a particular aspect of government. With *Keizairoku shūi*, I translate the "Addendum to 'Food and Goods'" in its entirety, as this has been by far the most influential section of the work, while omitting the "Addendum to 'Institutions,'" which is a rather minor addition to his discussion of the same topic in *Keizairoku*.

Notes on the Texts and Translations

In my translations I have tried to keep Japanese terms to a minimum, generally limiting such use to terms that appear in standard English dictionaries as foreign loanwords (such as "samurai" and "shogun"), or terms for such things as Japanese musical instruments, currency units, and units of weight and measure. At the first appearance of key terms that I render in English, I provide the Japanese (and where relevant, Chinese) equivalents if these may be useful to readers familiar with the original Japanese or Chinese; for subsequent appearances, I only provide the English, except where a reminder of the Japanese or Chinese is particularly relevant. Similarly, when titles of Japanese and Chinese works first appear in the text, I provide both the original title and an English translation of it, and then for subsequent appearances generally only give the English.

Shundai sometimes presents arguments based on analyses of words themselves, such as by explaining their etymology. In these sections, I try to replicate his explanations using comparable English terms, but I include the original Japanese words as necessary to convey his arguments. His choice of terminology is also often designed to explicitly map Japanese examples onto Chinese precedents, which is significant given his view that Japan should be governed with the Way of the Chinese sages. In these cases, I try to convey the parallels he is drawing by using the same English terms for the Japanese and Chinese phenomena that Shundai himself describes with the same terms, even if this requires departing from more conventional English translations of certain terms.

Japanese names, with the exception of scholars who write primarily in English, are given in the Japanese order, with family name first, followed by given name or pen name. These names are given in full at their first appearance in the text; when given in abbreviated form in subsequent appearances, I follow the Japanese scholarly convention of referring to modern figures by family name and premodern figures by given name or pen name.

Major Periods of Premodern Japanese History

Asuka 飛鳥	592–710
Nara 奈良	710–784
Heian 平安	794–1185
Kamakura 鎌倉	1185–1333
Muromachi 室町 (Ashigaka 足利)	1336–1573
Nanbokuchō 南北朝 (Northern and Southern Courts)	1336–1392
Sengoku 戦国 (Warring States)	1467–1568
Azuchi-Momoyama 安土桃山	1573–1603
Edo 江戸 (Tokugawa 徳川)	1603–1868

Major Dynasties and Periods of Premodern Chinese History

Xia 夏	c. 2100–c. 1600 BC
Shang 商 (Yin 殷)	c. 1600–c. 1100 BC
Zhou 周	c. 1100–256 BC
Western Zhou	c. 1100–771 BC
Eastern Zhou	770–256 BC
Spring and Autumn	722–481 BC
Warring States	403–221 BC
Qin 秦	221–206 BC
Han 漢	206 BC–AD 220
Former (Western) Han	206 BC–AD 8
Latter (Eastern) Han	25–220
Six Dynasties	220–589
Sui 隋	581–618
Tang 唐	618–907
Five Dynasties	907–960
Song 宋	960–1279
Northern Song	960–1126
Southern Song	1127–1279
Yuan 元	1271–1368
Ming 明	1368–1644
Qing 清	1644–1912

Introduction

When Dazai Shundai (1680–1747) describes the goals of Confucian government in the pragmatic terms of "enriching the country and strengthening the military" (*fukoku kyōhei*), he calls for an alternative to the ineffectual moral idealism he finds in other Confucians of his time, which he sees as a betrayal of the true Confucian tradition and unable to solve the pressing issues of his day.[1] At the core of his political thought is a sense of crisis arising from the uneasy position of Japan's ruling samurai class in his time, whose status and wealth were rooted in a feudal agrarian model of society, but who increasingly faced challenges from urbanization and the emergence of a commercial economy dominated by the rising merchant class. Shundai was typical of samurai intellectuals in perceiving these changes not only as a threat to the financial well-being of his class, but also as a source of cultural fragmentation that undermined the organic wholeness of feudal agrarian society. His proposed solution, which set him apart from both samurai who hoped to restore an agrarian ideal and merchants who unapologetically celebrated their own commercial activities, was to accept the expansion of commerce, but have the samurai wrest control of it from the merchant class. In this way, he promised to harness the potential for increased prosperity offered by a commercial economy, while at the same time preserving existing hierarchies and inoculating against the disruptive effects of commercial culture and values. Similar visions of commercial growth encouraged but closely supervised by elites would continue to play a prominent role in

---

[1] Dazai Shundai, *Keizairoku*, p. 490 (references to *Keizairoku* are from the *Nihon keizai taiten* edition); translation, p. 87.

Introduction

Japan after Shundai, down to the varieties of state-managed capitalism that arose in the modern period.

The works translated in this volume address the topic of *keizai*, a term that in modern Japanese is equivalent to the English "economy" or "economics," but in the Tokugawa period was intimately tied to the practice of government and was not limited to strictly commercial or financial matters, as Shundai describes when he defines *keizai* as "managing society and giving relief to the people."[2] The shifting usage of *keizai* over time resembles the emergence in the West of the modern discipline of "economics" out of an earlier "political economy," so to reflect this parallel development as well as the range of topics covered in Shundai's writings, *keizai* is translated as "political economy" in the present volume.

The works in this volume, *Keizairoku* (*On Political Economy*, 1729) and *Keizairoku shūi* (*An Addendum to "On Political Economy"*, 1744), stand out for their presentation of economic prosperity as a key goal of government, including through forms of commerce that were traditionally considered unbefitting of the samurai class, as well as for their ambitious vision of an all-encompassing government management of society, manifested in a state-directed Confucian ritualism that regulates everything from musical performances to the adoption of heirs. To the modern reader, Shundai's combination of practical economic proposals with a fixation on minute matters of ritual may come across as an odd mixture of unrelated policy prescriptions. Within the intellectual framework of his time, though, these elements combine to form a coherent theory of *keizai* in the broad sense of an overall ordering of society, in which economics in the narrow sense is necessarily intertwined with culture and politics.[3]

---

2 Dazai Shundai, *Keizairoku*, p. 394; translation, p. 16.
3 The idea of such a mismatch is expressed by Tetsuo Najita in "Political Economism in the Thought of Dazai Shundai (1680–1747)," where he argues that Shundai's importance lies in his "provocative concept of economic well-being in society as the central aim of politics" (p. 821) and comments that "[Shundai's] descriptions of marriage ritual, rank, and costume are frightfully tedious and his comments on who should (Buddhist monks) and should not (all others) shave their heads, mean little to the reader today. By incorporating these disparate items within the framework of 'political economics,' he obscured some of the main lines in his thinking" (p. 830). A perspective closer to my own is presented by Tessa Morris-Suzuki when she comments that for Tokugawa period writers, "*keizai* was a philosophical system inescapably bound up with questions of justice, law, and morality. It is entirely consistent with this tradition, therefore, that Shundai's [*On Political Economy*] should contain sections on crime and punishment, geography, and education, for these matters were all integral parts of *keizai*" (*A History of Japanese Economic Thought*, p. 14).

Introduction

In Shundai's case, for example, the hierarchy and state-imposed order he seeks in ritual are also central to how he conceives of economic problems and their solutions.

Shundai's embedding of economic well-being in these broader frameworks is evident not only in his works on political economy themselves, but also in the wide range of his scholarly oeuvre, which spans Confucian philosophy, linguistics, literature, and other topics. His most prominent publication prior to *On Political Economy* was *Wadoku yōryō* (*A General Outline of Reading in Japanese*, 1728), a linguistic study that explains proper methods of reading Chinese characters in Japanese. In addition to producing studies of the *Analects* and other core Confucian texts, he offers explications of Confucian philosophy in *Bendōsho* (*A Treatise on the Way*, 1735), which argues for the superiority of Confucianism over Buddhism and Shinto, and *Seigaku mondō* (*Dialogue on the Learning of the Sages*, 1736), where he presents his views on such matters as human nature and self-cultivation through an analysis of the Confucian classics. In *Bunron* (*A Discourse on Literary Writing*) and *Shiron* (*A Discourse on Poetry*), published together posthumously in 1748, he evaluates historical changes in Chinese prose and poetry, which he sees as having degenerated over time from authentic expression into empty formalism. He turns to a critique of contemporary Japanese culture in *Dokugo* (*Solitary Words*), an unpublished work that circulated in manuscript form, where he targets popular poetry, music, and theater for their vulgarity and their corruption of public morals.

In Shundai's time, Japan was governed by a system that had grown out of a process of political consolidation in the late sixteenth and early seventeenth centuries that put an end to a long period of civil war. The final leader of this process, Tokugawa Ieyasu (1543–1616), acceded to the position of shogun in 1603, a position that was occupied by members of the Tokugawa clan until the Meiji Restoration of 1868. In theory the Tokugawa shoguns were military officials appointed by the emperor, but as with most shoguns since the establishment of the Kamakura shogunate in the late twelfth century, this arrangement, while having a certain symbolic significance, was a transparent fiction when it came to the actual exercise of power, with the shogun serving as the de facto ruler of Japan. The Tokugawa regime was a decentralized form of rule, though, with approximately one quarter of the country held by the shogun and his direct vassals, and the remainder held in fief by over two hundred feudal lords known as daimyo. Daimyo were largely autonomous in governing

Introduction

the internal affairs of their domains, but ultimately held these territories at the pleasure of the shogun. In addition, the shogun kept close watch over the daimyo through a policy known as "alternate attendance" (*sankin kōtai*), in which daimyo were required to divide their time between their own domains and the shogunal seat of Edo (present-day Tokyo).

Shundai was born in 1680 into a samurai-class family in Iida domain in Shinano province (present-day Nagano prefecture), but his family was forced to move to Edo in 1688 after his father offended the daimyo of Iida.[4] With his father reduced to the status of *rōnin*, a term for members of the samurai class who lacked a salaried position with a liege lord, Shundai took the low-ranking post "supervisor of pages" under the daimyo of Izushi domain, which he held from 1694 until he resigned in 1700. Angered by his resignation, his employer issued a ten-year ban on his employment by any domain. During this period of banishment, much of which he spent in Kyoto and Osaka, Shundai devoted himself to his studies. After his ban was over, he returned to Edo and was hired in 1711 as a secretary to the daimyo of Oyumi domain. He resigned from this position in 1715, after which he declined further offers of official employment, instead relying on his private academy in Edo as his main source of income. Although he corresponded with members of the governing elite and offered his opinions on public policy, he carefully guarded his independence as a scholar.

Upon his return to Edo in 1711, Shundai enrolled in the academy of Ogyū Sorai (1666–1728), whose controversial reinterpretations of the Confucian textual canon revolutionized the Japanese intellectual world of the time. In opposition to the metaphysical theories and emphasis on personal moral purification that had dominated Tokugawa Confucianism up to that point, Sorai portrayed Confucianism as a pragmatic doctrine of governance grounded in the historical practices of the sage kings of ancient China, which must be accessed through a careful philological analysis of ancient texts. Most of Sorai's disciples used his focus on Chinese linguistic and textual studies as a springboard for literary composition, particularly poetry in Chinese, but Shundai insists on holding fast to Sorai's emphasis on governance when he cautions, "The Way of the sages has no application apart from governing the realm and state …

---

4 Provinces were older territorial divisions that by the Tokugawa period had lost their original administrative role, but still functioned as geographical designations. Typically, there were multiple domains within the area of each province.

Introduction

Those who abandon this and do not study it, instead pointlessly spending their entire lives occupied with literary writings, are not true scholars."[5]

Shundai's professed mission of "governing the realm and state" was a topic of heightened relevance when he published *On Political Economy* in 1729, as the shogun Tokugawa Yoshimune (1684–1751, r. 1716–1745) was in the midst of a wide-ranging overhaul of governance known as the Kyōhō Reforms (after the Kyōhō era of 1716–1736).[6] These reforms were motivated in large part by issues that arose from the urbanization of the samurai, not only in Edo but also in the castle towns of each domain. The samurai, who by this time had transformed into more a class of civil servants than actual warriors, were supported primarily by taxes levied on agricultural production. Samurai received stipends from their liege lord denominated in fixed quantities of rice, but the monetary value of these stipends varied based on fluctuations in the rice market; rice prices plummeted by roughly half, for example, in the three years leading up to the publication of *On Political Economy*.[7] Apart from the peasants and samurai, there were urban commoner classes of artisans and merchants. A prohibition on commercial activity among the samurai, whose class identity dictated an aloofness from the pursuit of profit, prevented them from taking advantage of the economic opportunities through which the merchant class was becoming ever more prosperous. In order to maintain their lifestyles, samurai often went into debt to merchant-class moneylenders, leaving them financially beholden to those they regarded as their social inferiors.

Many of Yoshimune's reforms were aimed at improving the financial position of the samurai and suppressing the power of the merchants, such as by disallowing the courts of the *bakufu* (shogunal regime) from being used to enforce debt collection. Since its early days, the Tokugawa *bakufu* had not only directly administered major trading cities such as Osaka, but also monopolized such areas of the economy as mining and foreign trade. It allowed merchants to practice a certain degree of self-regulation

---

5 Dazai Shundai, *Keizairoku*, pp. 394–395; translation, pp. 17–18. I capitalize "Way" as a translation for the Chinese *dao* or Japanese *michi* when these are used to indicate some kind of philosophical or religious doctrine or systematic body of techniques or knowledge.
6 A traditional system for giving dates in Japan is the *nengō* ("era") together with the year within the era. In modern Japan, a new era is declared for the reign of each emperor, but before the Meiji era (1868–1912), new eras would be declared for a variety of reasons and did not necessarily correspond to imperial reigns.
7 For data on rice prices in this period, see Kozo Yamamura, *A Study of Samurai Income and Entrepreneurship*, pp. 49–53.

within guilds, but Yoshimune brought these guilds under closer *bakufu* control with the creation in 1721 of ninety-six officially licensed oligopolies, which paid the *bakufu* for this privilege and were expected to police their members so as to stabilize prices and assure the quality of goods. He promoted improved tax collection procedures among daimyo and an expansion of agricultural production, to be achieved by bringing new land under cultivation and developing new crops. The promotion of knowledge and learning was another aspect of Yoshimune's reforms, including such things as *bakufu* sponsorship of new educational institutions and a liberalization of the importation of foreign books. His reforms also extended to practices for appointments to official posts, loosening the role of hereditary status in order to better match officials' qualifications with their duties.

Shundai addressed a similar set of concerns to Yoshimune and presented a number of similar solutions, but envisioned a more comprehensive overhaul of governance rooted in the methods of the sage kings of ancient China, one that would go beyond piecemeal reforms to create a coherent institutional structure he found lacking in the Tokugawa regime. Portraying the samurai class as custodians of the Way of the sages, he strove to maintain their ruling-class status, while at the same time responding to changes in the economy that threatened this dominance. The resulting paradigm of political economy was a kind of adaptive authoritarianism, which would go on to appear in different forms in Japan throughout the Tokugawa period and beyond.

Reforming Tokugawa Japan with the Way of the Sages

Shundai's proposals for reform stress the role of governmental institutions in shaping society, an approach tied to his interpretation of the Confucian tradition as centered on the civilizing function of the state. Confucian teachings had been introduced to Japan no later than the sixth century, but came to particular prominence in the Tokugawa period, when Confucian scholars took the place of the Buddhist clergy as the preeminent scholarly figures. Tokugawa Confucians shared an ideal of a hierarchical society united through beneficent moral or cultural forces, but they took a variety of stances on such matters as the essence of human nature, the relation of the human world to the cosmic or natural order, and the basis of effective rulership. In the preface to *On Political Economy*, Shundai situates his work as a corrective to the errors of later Confucians, who

Introduction

he claims have abandoned Confucianism's original focus on governing society and devolved into the self-absorbed pursuit of "heart methods" (*shinbō*), a term he uses for practices of inner moral cultivation. Although Shundai's claim that later Confucians have lost interest in governing is a polemical exaggeration, he is pointing to a broad trend in Song and Ming dynasty Confucianism, inherited by many Tokugawa Confucians, in which the highest goal of self-cultivation is defined as the attainment of sagehood through the perfection of personal virtue. Shundai's critique then builds on certain earlier Tokugawa Confucians who gave attention to more practical techniques of governance, such as Kumazawa Banzan (1619–1691) and, most notably, Shundai's mentor Ogyū Sorai.

Shundai describes state-enforced cultural norms as necessary to give order to a chaotic human nature, a view he develops in opposition to versions of Confucianism that are premised on the innate goodness of humans. He particularly targets the Song dynasty philosopher Zhu Xi (1130–1200), who equates the Confucian Way with a universal moral principle (Ch. *li*, Jp. *ri*) inherent in both the natural world and our original human nature. According to Zhu Xi, our innate moral nature becomes obscured by immoral desires, but through practices of self-cultivation that tame these desires, we can access our original human nature and unite with the all-encompassing moral order of the cosmos. Shundai draws on the critique of Zhu Xi made by Sorai, who maintains that the Confucian Way is a cultural creation of specific rulers of ancient China, not a timeless metaphysical principle, and who portrays this Way as socializing the self through standards external to human nature. Zhu Xi's doctrine of innate virtue promises a powerful basis for individual moral autonomy, but Sorai argues that such a view of human nature is not only false but dangerous. When people are convinced that they possess the Way within themselves, Sorai cautions, they end up treating their own personal prejudices as universally valid. Shundai echoes this sentiment when he criticizes those who would attempt to find the normative "mean" (*chūyō*) by looking within the self: "Scholars of today err greatly when, relying on the theories of Song Confucians, they try to establish the mean by using their own individual hearts. They commit the great transgression of considering themselves to be sages."[8]

Among the cultural products that make up the Confucian Way, Sorai and Shundai particularly value ritual and music for their ability

---

8 Dazai Shundai, *Keizairoku*, p. 412; translation, p. 43.

Introduction

to affect people in a way not possible through discursive teachings, as Sorai describes when he writes, "Why is it that even though ritual and music say nothing, they are superior to language in instructing people? The reason is that they transform people. When people practice these and become fully immersed in them, then even though they may not understand them, their hearts and bodies have been quietly transformed by them."[9] Shundai similarly notes that "Teachings expressed in language enter people on a shallow level, are effective within a narrow range, and achieve things slowly, but teachings of ritual and music enter people on a deep level, have a broad range of effectiveness, and achieve results extremely quickly."[10] They depict the same kind of transformation as occurring through a government's "institutions" (*seido*) more broadly, which they describe as shaping "customs" (*fūzoku*); it is only when customs are transformed, they argue, that people will follow a government of their own accord. The political vision that emerges from this picture of ritual, music, and institutions is one of governance through cultural frameworks that structure people's behavior and consciousness in ways that are invisible to them, but are essential to their formation as members of a community.

Shundai attributes the problems of his age to a lack of the proper institutions needed to give order to society, which in his view must be enacted by governing authorities. Following Sorai's assertion that the origins of civilized society and good government lie in the methods of the sage kings of ancient China, Shundai presents his program of reform as creating the institutions that will align Japan with the methods of the sages. Prior to contact with Chinese traditions that transmit the Way of the sages, Shundai claims, ancient Japan was a barbaric country with no systematic methods of government. He locates the key foundational event of Japanese history in the civilizing process brought about by the introduction of Confucian culture from China, which he traces to the adoption of Chinese court practices and administrative structures by Prince Shōtoku (574–622). It is by looking back to this original Confucian transformation of Japan that he finds the basis for his program of reform in the present, commenting that "[Japan] is a country where the Way of the sages has

---

9 Ogyū Sorai, *Benmei* (*On Distinguishing Names*), p. 92.
10 Dazai Shundai, *Keizairoku*, p. 409; translation, pp. 39–40.

been used to govern since ancient times, so even though we may be in a later age, there is no reason why it should not be possible to revive it."[11]

Shundai situates institutional creation within the Chinese historiographical framework that takes the dynasty as the main unit of history, with the eventual decline of dynasties and their replacement by new ones seen as an inevitable historical cycle. The foundation of a new dynasty, according to Shundai, must be accompanied by the establishment of ritual, music, and other institutions of governance informed by the models of the sages. Even if it is impossible to create an eternal dynasty, he argues, the skillful establishment of institutions at the time of dynastic foundation can ensure stability for hundreds of years. Through this historiographical lens, he portrays the Tokugawa shogunate as one of a series of regimes in Japan analogous to the dynasties of China. He was not alone in his depiction of the essential role of Confucian civilization in Japan or his division of Japanese history into a series of distinct regimes, but these views put him at odds with those who adhered to ideologies of imperial rule rooted in Shinto mytho-history, where political legitimacy is equated with a single unbroken lineage of emperors descended from the Japanese gods.[12]

In assessing the institutions of the Tokugawa period against the larger background of Japanese history, Shundai uses the methods of the Chinese sages as a yardstick for evaluating Japan's historical regimes. He divides these broadly between the period of rule by the emperor and court nobility, lasting until the Genpei war of 1180–1185, and the subsequent period of political dominance by the samurai class. He praises Japan's warrior governments for the similarity of their decentralized rule to the feudal (*hōken*) system of the sages, in which the highest ruler directly administers a limited territory, with the remainder of the realm divided among semi-autonomous vassal states. He notes that in the Qin dynasty China abandoned feudalism in favor of a centralized system of "districts and prefectures" (*gunken*), meaning that Japan's first encounter with Chinese methods of government came at a time when these had already fallen

---

11 Dazai Shundai, *Keizairoku*, p. 386; translation, p. 5.
12 After his death, Shundai came in for harsh criticism from scholars of Kokugaku (National Learning). Attacks on Shundai's view of the role of Confucian civilization in Japan, particularly as expressed in *A Treatise on the Way*, came from such National Learning scholars as Kamo no Mabuchi (1697–1769) in *Kokuikō* (*Reflections on the Meaning of Our Country*, 1765), Motoori Norinaga (1730–1801) in *Naobi no mitama* (*The Spirit of the Gods*, 1771), and Hirata Atsutane (1776–1843) in *Kamōsho* (*Rebuking Absurdities*, 1803).

Introduction

away from the pure Way of the sages. Japan's warrior regimes reversed this trend, according to Shundai, culminating in Ieyasu's system of shogun and daimyo, in which "the realm finally became a true feudal system and thus generally resembled the Zhou dynasty of China."[13] He faults Japan's warrior elites, though, for failing to practice the ritual and music that the imperial aristocracy had learned from China, while commenting approvingly that "even though the court nobles have now suffered extreme decline, they still use the ritual and music of old."[14] Shundai's praise for the court nobility did not translate into support for a restoration of imperial rule, but he uses the court's accomplishments as a way of expressing a critical stance toward the Tokugawa regime and underlining the need for reform.

Shundai concludes that despite certain successes, such as the system of shogun and daimyo, the Tokugawa rulers have failed to create appropriate institutions in their role as dynastic founders, leaving government and society aimlessly adrift. He envisions reform as a top-down process of giving order to chaos, as expressed in his frequent distinction between proper cultural forms deliberately instituted by rulers and degenerate forms that arise from the general populace. He laments that people of his own time confuse these, commenting that "what people believe to be institutions of the state are in fact mostly things that originated from below."[15] Drawing on the dichotomy between the *ga* ("refined") and the *zoku* ("vulgar, common, popular") that was a cornerstone of Tokugawa literary and artistic discourse, Shundai comes down firmly on the side of the former, while depicting the latter as not merely aesthetically inferior, but also morally and politically corrupting. Running through his various proposals, from the reform of kinship relations based on Confucian ritual traditions to the promotion of the "refined" music of the sages and suppression of the "vulgar" and "licentious" music that arises from common society, is a paternalistic vision of the people being molded by civilizing mechanisms created for their benefit by rulers, who themselves look to the ancient Chinese sage kings for their models.

Sorai presents Confucian paternalism as a benignly nurturing force by clarifying that even though the Way is an external force that acts upon human nature, the norms of the Way are not merely an arbitrary

---

13 Dazai Shundai, *Keizairoku*, p. 400; translation, p. 28.
14 Dazai Shundai, *Keizairoku*, p. 409; translation, p. 39.
15 Dazai Shundai, *Keizairoku*, p. 625; translation, p. 148.

imposition on human nature, but are attentive to and draw out its intrinsic qualities. He explains this interplay of nature and artifice when he writes, "This can be compared to cutting down trees to build a palace. You build it by following the innate qualities [*sei*] of the wood. How could a palace, though, be considered the natural state [*shizen*] of wood?"[16] Carpenters must keep in mind the inherent qualities of the raw materials they use for building, while at the same time forming these materials into something more than what could arise spontaneously from the materials themselves. In the same way, raw human nature is not infinitely malleable and thus puts certain limits on the systems of governance that rulers can impose, but the Confucian Way provides a structure that develops this human nature above and beyond what people would be able to achieve on their own.

Shundai remains within Sorai's basic paradigm of portraying the Confucian Way as tied to but not identical with human nature, but emphasizes the friction that occurs when raw human nature is made to conform to the external norms of the Way. For Sorai, the Way of the sages is a gentle force that builds on a natural human instinct for sociality and cooperation, as he describes when he declares that "all people have a heart of mutual love, nourishment, aid, and accomplishment."[17] Shundai gives a bleaker picture of humans in their natural state, claiming that without the teachings of the sages, "As a matter of course, it would come to be that the wealthy neglect the poor, the lofty lord it over the lowly, and the strong tyrannize the weak."[18] Shundai presents the Way as forcefully disciplining human nature in a manner that Sorai does not, a distinction reflected in Shundai's exploration of the limits of Confucian cultural transformation and his articulation of methods of governance that, while never leaving behind such transformation as an ideal, find ways to adapt to barriers to its practice.

Shundai's Pragmatic Authoritarianism

Shundai combines his appeal to the precedent of the ancient Chinese sage kings with an insistence that rulers must apply the techniques of the sages with an eye to the circumstances of the present. As he puts it, "just

---

16 Ogyū Sorai, *Bendō* (*On Distinguishing the Way*), pp. 14–15.
17 Ogyū Sorai, *Benmei*, p. 54.
18 Dazai Shundai, *Keizairoku*, p. 411; translation, p. 42.

Introduction

because one should learn from the past and take the past as one's teacher, this does not mean that one should practice the government of the past in its entirety in the present, as there are many cases where the government of the past is difficult to practice in today's world."[19] For Shundai, the methods of the past are translated into present-day practice through the judgment and discretion of rulers, who are charged with studying the Way of the sages as recorded in the Chinese classics, observing the reality of the world they govern, and formulating appropriate policies. In this way, he promotes a flexible and pragmatic approach to governance, but one in which power remains firmly in the hands of ruling authorities.

Shundai finds support within the Confucian tradition itself for the idea that the Way, although rooted in the past, necessarily changes with the times. Discussing the differences between dynasties, he writes that "'continuities' refers to following the government of the previous dynasty, while 'changes' refers to revising its government. There is also what is known as 'subtraction and addition'; 'subtraction' refers to eliminating institutions of the previous dynasty, while 'addition' refers to adding new ones. The *Analects* refers to this when it says, 'That which they subtracted and added can be known.'"[20] Here he cites *Analects* 2.23, which states that the rituals of the Yin dynasty "relied on" those of the Xia, while making "subtractions and additions," and that the rituals of the Zhou did the same in relation to those of the Yin.[21] Such changes are adaptations to present circumstances, but must remain within what Shundai describes as the same "basic outline" (*daitai*) inherited from the past: "When one fails to take the ancient Way as one's root, one will be unable to understand the basic outline of government."[22] Another way he explains the creation of new institutions within an existing framework is through the relationship between ritual and "rightness" (*gi*): "rituals are created based on rightness. If one has virtue and rank and establishes rituals by pondering the past, why should this not be permissible? Confucius said, 'Ritual is the realization of rightness. If one arrives at it by bringing together various examples of rightness, then even though a ritual may not have existed among the ancient kings, it may be adopted based

---

19 Dazai Shundai, *Keizairoku*, p. 406; translation, p. 35.
20 Dazai Shundai, *Keizairoku*, p. 397; translation, p. 22.
21 Section numbers for citations from the *Analects* are taken from the James Legge translation.
22 Dazai Shundai, *Keizairoku*, p. 406; translation, p. 35.

Introduction

on its rightness.'"[23] For Shundai, rightness itself must be learned from the sages, and cannot simply be derived from personal reasoning or one's inner moral nature, but familiarity with this rightness allows rulers of later times to create new rituals beyond the specific creations of the sages.

Shundai's demand that rulers engage with the contemporary world is reflected in the prominent place he gives to defining the varieties of empirical reality and their relationship to the practice of the Way of the sages. This is a main focus of the first volume of *On Political Economy*, which, under the heading of "A General Discussion of Political Economy," describes four aspects of reality that rulers must grasp in order to govern: the "times" (*toki*) in which they live, the "principle" (*ri*) of things in the world, the "force" (*ikioi*) that can temporarily overcome principle, and the "human feelings" (*ninjō*) of the people they govern.

Just as important as empirical knowledge itself for Shundai is that rulers understand the limits of what they can possibly know, as he explains in volume 4 in relation to the ultimate unknowability of heaven. Shundai's analysis of reliable knowledge and its limits builds on Sorai's critique of the epistemology of Zhu Xi, for whom knowledge of external things is equated with knowledge of their underlying moral principle. For Zhu Xi, it is the presence of an identical principle within our own original human nature that allows us to know the principle of external things, meaning that the uncovering of our original nature through practices of self-cultivation results in the perfection of not only virtue, but also knowledge. Sorai faults Zhu Xi's theory for its hubristic claims to absolute knowledge, even of heaven itself, as well as for its reduction of the complexity of empirical reality to a moral binary of virtue and vice. He denies the existence of the morally perfect original nature at the root of Zhu Xi's theory, and argues that faith in such a nature as the source of perfect knowledge merely encourages people to project their personal prejudices onto the outside world: "The Song Confucian practices of 'investigating things' and 'extending knowledge' involve deciding for oneself that such-and-such must be this way and such-and-such must be that way, and that this must certainly be the Way of the sages. But this is just personal opinion."[24] From the perspective of Sorai and Shundai, Zhu Xi promises perfect knowledge but ends up falling into ignorance and distortions, whereas they have more modest goals but

---

23 Dazai Shundai, *Keizairoku*, pp. 412–413; translation, pp. 43–44.
24 Ogyū Sorai, *Sorai sensei tōmonsho* (*Master Sorai's Responsals*), p. 477.

at least offer reliable knowledge, applicable to governance, within this more limited sphere.

For Shundai, it is impossible to derive social and political norms from nature, in contrast to Zhu Xi's view that the natural world is imbued with the same universal principle that guides proper ethical and political relations among humans. This normative emptiness of nature does not, however, render it irrelevant to governance for Shundai, as he presents the empirical reality of nature as both a set of constraints within which the Way of the sages must operate and a set of resources that it can cultivate in the service of a cohesive and prosperous society. This portrayal of the relationship between the Way and the raw material of the empirical world echoes Sorai's description of how the Way shapes human nature, but Shundai adds a new element by emphasizing the role of the Way in extracting the economic potential of natural resources.

In his discussion of empirical reality in the first volume of *On Political Economy*, Shundai focuses on how the raw facts of the world circumscribe the actions of rulers. He interprets "principle," for example, in terms of inherent qualities of things that cannot be ignored or contradicted, which he distinguishes from Zhu Xi's idea of "principle" as a normative moral standard inherent in all things: "This principle is not the 'principle' of 'principles of the Way' [*dōri*], but rather the 'principle' of 'principles of things' [*butsuri*]. 'Principles of things' refers to the principle that necessarily exists in each thing. Examples of this are the grain in wood and the other various patterns in things."[25] He argues that much as one cannot effectively plane against the grain of wood, "Although the common people are lowly, they will never comply with government that runs contrary to principle."[26] He takes a similar approach to human feelings as an aspect of reality that rulers must respond to: "If one is in accord with human feelings when conducting governmental matters, then it will be easy for the people to follow. If one runs counter to human feelings, then the people will not follow."[27]

Elsewhere in *On Political Economy*, Shundai turns to the role of the Way in productively cultivating both human talent and the world of physical nature. In the section of volume 6 on "Educational Systems," he discusses the role of government-sponsored education in nurturing

---

25 Dazai Shundai, *Keizairoku*, p. 400; translation, p. 28.
26 Dazai Shundai, *Keizairoku*, p. 401; translation, p. 29.
27 Dazai Shundai, *Keizairoku*, p. 402; translation, p. 30.

Introduction

the full range of human talents and putting these to use in official posts. The promotion of talented officials is a rather commonplace idea in Confucian governance, but Shundai's focus on economic matters comes through when he applies a parallel framework to maximizing the productive potential of the land, arguing that when rulers recognize and develop the distinct potential of all types of land, even that which may appear useless, "such benefits as exist in the land will emerge without leaving anything behind, and they will moreover not be exhausted even after being used. This is called the 'inexhaustible storehouse' [*mujinzō*]."[28] He also describes such methods, supplemented by trade with other regions that extract their own distinctive natural resources, in terms of "leaving no unexploited benefits," where "unexploited benefits" are defined as "when things that are of benefit to the country are left untaken and remain hidden."[29]

The image of the ruler as a skillful manager of human and natural resources stands in contrast to Zhu Xi's portrayal of the ideal ruler as one who has successfully achieved the moral perfection of the original human nature, which then emanates outward to transform the realm. A typical expression of Zhu Xi's view in Tokugawa Japan can be seen in *Ji kokka kongen* (*The Basis of Governing the State*), a treatise on governing attributed to Honda Masanobu (1538–1616), a top advisor to the first two Tokugawa shoguns. This text declares that "If one attempts to govern the state but does not have the proper basis to do so, then one will not be able to govern. This basis is the heart of the daimyo."[30] It goes on to explain the process through which the morally purified heart of the ruler leads to good government: "To remove the clouding from the heart and purify it can be compared to polishing a mirror … When there is nothing that the heart does not reflect, then one's person will be well governed. When one's person is well governed, then in governing the state there will be nothing that is difficult to achieve."[31] In the preface to *On Political Economy*, Shundai derides this kind of faith in the power of rulers' personal

---

28 Dazai Shundai, *Keizairoku*, p. 495; translation, p. 93.
29 Dazai Shundai, *Keizairoku*, p. 495; translation, p. 93.
30 Honda Masanobu, *Ji kokka kongen*, p. 8.
31 Honda Masanobu, *Ji kokka kongen*, p. 8. This draws on the passage of the *Great Learning* that states, "When one's heart is correct, one's person will be cultivated. When one's person is cultivated, one's house will be ordered. When one's house is ordered, the state will be well governed" ("The Text of Confucius," Section 5; section numbers for citations from the *Great Learning* are taken from the James Legge translation).

Introduction

moral purification, citing examples of deposed Song dynasty rulers who devoted themselves to cultivation through "heart methods," rather than taking practical measures to regain power.

Shundai's combination of pragmatism with a strong ruling authority can be seen in his defense of the figure of the "hegemon" (Ch. *bazhe*, Jp. *hasha*). Historically this term referred to a series of rulers of the Spring and Autumn period in China who maintained systems of alliances among former vassal states of the Zhou dynasty, which was not formally deposed but exercised little real power at that point. In Confucian political thought, the term indicated more generally a form of rulership that, although not resorting to mere tyranny, relies on pragmatic techniques of administration rather than the moral force of the true "king" (Ch. *wang*, Jp. *ō*). Although the hegemon was typically seen as an inferior form of rulership, some Confucians, such as Zhu Xi's contemporary and rival Chen Liang (1143–1194), challenged the distinction between the king and the hegemon.[32]

Shundai follows this more positive assessment of the hegemon by repeatedly singling out for praise Guan Zhong (c. 720–645 BC), who served as prime minister under Duke Huan of Qi (685–643 BC), the first of the historical hegemons. He acknowledges that Guan Zhong's methods do not attain the level of the government of the sages, but notes that Confucius himself often praised him and that the goals of his government are compatible with the Way of the sages: "Guan Zhong's government put utility [*kōri*] first, striving to enrich the country and strengthen the military ... Enriching the country and strengthening the military are the duties of a hegemon, but they were not originally outside the bounds of the Way of the Two Emperors and Three Kings."[33] The phrase "enrich the country and strengthen the military" appears in texts of the Warring States period produced by rival schools to Confucianism that emphasized the practical aspects of wielding power, such as the Legalist School and the School of the Military, so Shundai's use of this phrase suggests

---

32 For a discussion of the relationship between Zhu Xi and Chen Liang, see Hoyt Cleveland Tillman, *Confucian Discourse and Chu Hsi's Ascendancy*, pp. 161–186.
33 Dazai Shundai, *Keizairoku*, p. 395; translation, pp. 18–19. The "Two Emperors" are Yao and Shun, legendary rulers of ancient China. The "Three Kings" are Yu, Tang, and Wen, the founders of the Xia, Shang, and Zhou dynasties, respectively.

Introduction

a less sharp division between Confucianism and these other schools of thought.[34]

Many Japanese Confucians noted a parallel between the hegemons of Chinese history and Japan's own shoguns, who similarly governed in the name of an essentially powerless emperor. Arai Hakuseki (1657–1725), for example, who advised the shoguns Tokugawa Ienobu (1662–1712, r. 1709–1712) and Tokugawa Ietsugu (1709–1716, r. 1713–1716), called for the transformation of the shogun from a hegemon into a true king to fully take the place of the emperor.[35] Shundai does not advocate that the shogun replace the emperor, but he blurs the distinction between the "hegemon" and the "king" by defining the shoguns as de facto kings already simply due to the power they wield, without reference to any notion of kingly virtue, commenting, "The shogun of today possesses the entire land, making him the king of Japan."[36]

Shundai's pragmatism also comes through in his prioritization of ends over means when situating other "Ways" in relation to Confucianism. He dismisses Buddhism and Shinto as irrelevant to Confucianism's mission of governing, but presents certain historical opponents of Confucianism, such as those described above in relation to "enriching the country and strengthening the military," as alternative means to the same end. Comparing Confucian methods of ruling to the five grains that normally nourish the body and non-Confucian methods to medicines one takes when ill, he writes, "Although they are not the ordinary Way for governing the realm and state, in a later age when various illnesses arise in the state, the Ways discussed by the various philosophers, such as the non-action of Laozi, the universal love of Mozi, and the punishments and legal techniques of Shen Buhai and Hanfeizi, all have their respective uses. When one uses them well, they are all good medicines and will not fail to treat the illnesses of the country."[37] He qualifies this elsewhere by pointing out that their shortcoming, when contrasted with the Confucian Way, lies in the fact that "because they all dispense with ritual and music, they only go as far as achieving a temporary tranquility."[38] When it has

---

34 The phrase appears in *Shang jun shu* (*The Book of Lord Shang*) of the Legalist School and *Liu tao* (*The Six Secret Strategies*) of the School of the Military.
35 For Hakuseki's views on the hegemon and its relation to shogunal rule and the reform of the Tokugawa shogunate, see Kate Wildman Nakai, *Shogunal Politics*, pp. 275–294.
36 Dazai Shundai, *Keizairoku*, p. 388; translation, p. 8.
37 Dazai Shundai, *Keizairoku*, p. 663; translation, p. 171.
38 Dazai Shundai, *Keizairoku*, p. 440; translation, p. 60.

become impossible to effect the deeper and more lasting transformation promised by Confucian ritual and music, though, these other methods offer at least a provisional solution that responds to contemporary reality.

The most radical "medicine" that Shundai embraces is the non-action (*mui*) of Laozi, which he describes as treating the illness of a governing dynasty that has declined to a point where further attempts to shore it up will only exacerbate its problems. At such a time, he argues, it is best to stop trying to forcibly repair things and instead simply let them run their course. This is where he sees Tokugawa society as having arrived in his own time, as expressed in his provocative declaration that "ever since the Genroku era [1688–1704], the samurai and common people in the land have been destitute and the vital force of the state has been in decline, so the present age is a time when one should stop everything and exclusively practice non-action."[39] *On Political Economy* comes to an ambivalent conclusion, then, following up its extensive proposals for political reform with a pessimistic stance toward the possibility of actually carrying out such reform in the Japan of Shundai's day.

Commerce and the Way of the Sages

In *An Addendum to "On Political Economy"* an area where Shundai deepens his push for reform is in the state management of the economy, which in *On Political Economy* he already presents as a way to counter the destructive effects of unfettered markets dominated by merchant-class interests. A negative view of merchants was typical of Tokugawa Confucian scholars, who came largely from the samurai class, with one reading of Zhu Xi's philosophy justifying such a stance by associating profit with the desires that obscure people's innate virtue. Members of the merchant class themselves, however, sought to legitimate their role by reconceptualizing the Confucian discourse that others used against them, asserting that it is only excessive and unjust profit, not profit per se, that compromises virtue, and that commerce in fact contributes to the public good. Shundai too finds a potential positive role for commerce, but only if its management is removed from merchants and put in the hands of the samurai class. Many of his specific economic policy proposals are extensions of existing practices and not original to him, but he is notable for developing a vision of samurai-class supremacy that explicitly addresses

---

39 Dazai Shundai, *Keizairoku*, p. 663; translation, p. 172.

and overcomes the conflict between commerce and a state-centered Confucian ideology.

Merchant-class intellectuals rose to prominence during Yoshimune's reign as shogun and were often critical of Sorai, whose samurai paternalism ran counter to their own ideal of the independent pursuit of virtue by commoners. A key center of merchant-class learning was the Kaitokudō, a Confucian academy in Osaka established in 1724 that was operated by and for merchants, but had also received a land grant and official charter from the *bakufu* as part of Yoshimune's promotion of education during the Kyōhō Reforms.[40] Also significant was the Shingaku (Heart Learning) movement founded by Ishida Baigan (1685–1744), which integrated Zhu Xi Confucianism, Buddhism, and Shinto into a system of practical moral teachings.[41]

In *Tohi mondō* (*Dialogue of the City and the Country*), Baigan writes of the benefits merchants bring to society: "Merchants circulate wealth and bring peace to the hearts of all the people, so this accords with the statement that 'Heaven and earth and the four seasons run their courses and the myriad things are cultivated.' In this way, even if wealth were to pile up as high as a mountain, one should not speak of there being a desirous heart."[42] He furthermore rejects any dichotomy between the profit-seeking of merchants and the supposedly selfless service ethic of samurai: "The profit that merchants obtain from sales is the same as the stipend of a samurai. To forgo profit from sales would be like a samurai serving without a stipend."[43] In a version of the kind of moral metaphysics we find in Zhu Xi's philosophy, Baigan defends the merchant class by presenting commerce as seamlessly integrated with both human morality and the nourishing forces of nature.

In keeping with his focus on the cultural frameworks through which people are formed, Sorai's critique of merchants is centered on the broader changes in social structure he associates with the emergence of

---

40 A seminal study of the Kaitokudō in English is Tetsuo Najita, *Visions of Virtue in Tokugawa Japan*.
41 Two important English-language studies of Shingaku are Robert N. Bellah, *Tokugawa Religion*, and Janine Anderson Sawada, *Confucian Values and Popular Zen*. Bellah contrasts Baigan and Sorai in "Baigan and Sorai: Continuities and Discontinuities in Eighteenth-Century Japanese Thought."
42 Ishida Baigan, *Tohi mondō*, p. 391. Here he alludes to *Analects* 17.19: "The Master said, 'Does heaven speak? The four seasons run their courses and all things are produced, but does heaven speak?'"
43 Ishida Baigan, *Tohi mondō*, p. 423.

Introduction

commercial culture, where he contrasts the organic wholeness of a feudal agrarian society governed by the Way of the sages with the fragmentation and atomization of commercial society. He finds his ideal social wholeness in the familial type of relationship that exists between rulers and ruled when they live in close proximity over many generations, a connection that he claims has been severed in the Tokugawa period by the policy of removing the samurai from the land and concentrating them in Edo and other castle towns. In these urban environments, he maintains, people interact as isolated and deracinated individuals bound by nothing more than momentary relationships of financial exchange. His solution, which had also been proposed earlier by Kumazawa Banzan, is to resettle the samurai in the countryside, where he argues they will develop bonds of affection with the ruled and return to a more frugal lifestyle.

In *On Political Economy*, Shundai advocates a similar agrarian ideal and suspicion of commerce to Sorai, but instead of trying to withdraw from and suppress the commercial economy, he concentrates on preventing merchants from monopolizing its benefits, which he claims they are currently able to do by forming cartels that manipulate prices and markets for private gain. He defines "interests and privileges" (*riken*) as "the right to freely pursue profit in things," and goes on to assert that "Those who practice government well hold on to interests and privileges at the top and do not allow the common people to possess them."[44] He is quick to acknowledge the superiority of merchants to samurai when it comes to matters of calculation and profit, but he sees merchants as using these skills to the detriment of society, necessitating corrective action from samurai-class rulers.

Shundai gives economic prosperity a central role in the Confucian Way when, as discussed earlier, he describes the government of the sages as serving to "enrich the country and strengthen the military." He presents the government's role in the economy partly in terms of promoting agricultural productivity, but also as including measures to reduce economic volatility and prevent merchants from exploiting this volatility for private gain. One such policy is "leveling" (*heijun*), in which the authorities stabilize prices by buying or selling goods to create additional demand or supply as needed. He specifically advocates such "leveling" for the rice market, which he proposes to carry out through "stabilization granaries" (*jōheisō*), in which surplus rice would be stored and then

---

44 Dazai Shundai, *Keizairoku*, p. 534; translation, p. 117.

Introduction

released to the market when prices rose or in the event of bad harvests and similar disasters. This role would be shared by a separate system of "public welfare granaries" (*gisō*), which would also serve as a source for people to borrow from at a modest interest rate to cover personal expenses, thus bypassing the high rates of merchant-class moneylenders. Although he describes public welfare granaries as serving the population at large, Shundai particularly focuses on their role as a source of loans for the samurai class, who would fund these granaries with a percentage of their annual stipends. Both of these types of granaries had existed in the past in both China and Japan and were in use in Japan in Shundai's time, but he envisions an expansion of these systems to give them a more prominent role in the management of the economy.

In *An Addendum to "On Political Economy"* Shundai extends the scope of his proposed government involvement in the economy by advocating that the daimyo initiate their own profit-making ventures. In order to solve their fiscal problems, he argues, daimyo should encourage the production of commodities to which their own domains are most suited based on geography, soil, and climate, and then strive to enrich themselves by exporting these products to other domains. He points out that by making use of economies of scale and the infrastructure already in place with domanial properties in Edo and elsewhere, domanial officials can gain an advantage over merchant-class traders. As evidence for the benefits of such a policy, he cites a list of domains that are already engaged in the kind of production and trade he calls for, noting the gap between the officially rated agricultural output of these domains and the effective wealth they enjoy as a result of their commercial ventures, which in his examples is anywhere from double to ten times their rated output.[45]

Shundai expresses some ambivalence about these daimyo-operated commercial ventures, as he sees such profit-seeking activities as less than ideal from the perspective of the Way of the sages. He offers a resolution

---

45 Luke Roberts, in *Mercantilism in a Japanese Domain*, argues that Shundai's ideas derive from a discourse on *kokueki* ("prosperity of the country") that originated among merchants, who sought to legitimate their own activities by stressing their contribution to the prosperity of the domain as a whole. He dismisses Shundai and other samurai intellectuals, claiming that "the dialogue between the intellectuals on economics was too bound by the discourse of old texts to be innovative" (p. 200 n. 4). I agree that merchants were generally ahead of samurai in articulating the benefits of commerce, but I hold that Roberts' judgment of samurai intellectuals overlooks the distinctive views on economics that they developed through their engagement with contemporary economic realities as well as their creative interpretations of textual traditions.

Introduction

to this dilemma through the same kind of medical metaphor he uses in *On Political Economy* to uphold the provisional use of non-Confucian Ways, commenting, "Just as how in an emergency doctors treat the symptoms, one should look at what is critical in the current illness and seek salvation from this."[46] Despite his presentation of this policy as a reluctant departure from his ideal, it shows continuity with the framework established in *On Political Economy*, in which the pursuit of prosperity requires that the samurai take control of commercial activities currently dominated by merchants and reorient these to serve the public good. Unlike Sorai, then, who imagines Confucian political reform as a return to a seamlessly harmonious feudal agrarian society, Shundai arrives at a kind of equilibrium in tension, where the vigilance of samurai authorities allows for a carefully supervised growth of commerce that keeps in check its tendency to undermine feudal social relationships.

Shundai's Legacy in Political Economy

In the later Tokugawa period, an expansion of the kind of domain-level commercial initiatives promoted by Shundai was accompanied by calls for the shogunate to respond to the challenges posed by Western powers, not only through a strengthening of Japan's military defenses, but also through the pursuit of new commercial and trade policies. This growth in involvement of the samurai class in commerce was accompanied by efforts on the part of intellectuals to define such activities as an essential component of good government. These figures carried on Shundai's pairing of commercial growth with a consolidation of state power, as well as his vision of the natural world as a source of tradable commodities, while going beyond his ambivalent pragmatism to advocate for state-sponsored commerce as an unalloyed good. Even when critical of Confucianism, they were often not so much rejecting its role in ordering society as claiming that alternative means, particularly those inspired by the West, were more effective in fulfilling this role.

In *Keiko dan* (*Reflections on the Past*), Kaiho Seiryō (1755–1817) defends commerce by linking it to the workings of nature, an approach similar to what we saw in Ishida Baigan, except from a samurai rather than a merchant perspective. Seiryō criticizes the way that Japanese elites disparage the pursuit of profit, contrasting them with the king of Hol-

---

46 Dazai Shundai, *Keizairoku shūi*, p. 47; translation, p. 189.

Introduction

land, who engages in commerce without the slightest hint of shame.[47] He counters the claim that commerce conflicts with the feudal ethic of the samurai: "The lord provides a stipend to the subject and has him work, and the subject sells his labor to his lord and collects rice. The lord buys from the subject and the subject sells to the lord; this is buying and selling. Buying and selling are good; they are not something bad."[48] Paralleling his depiction of commerce as embedded in feudal social relations, he portrays the world of nature as financial and commercial at its very core:

> As a general rule, all the things that exist within heaven and earth are goods. That goods then give birth to other goods is an example of principle. The way that paddies give birth to rice is no different from how money gives birth to interest. It is the principle of heaven and earth that mountains give birth to lumber, the sea gives birth to salt and fish, and things like money and rice give birth to interest.[49]

By declaring the productivity of the natural environment and the reproduction of money through interest to be manifestations of the same principle, Seiryō thoroughly rejects the idea that the financial economy is a corruption of nature.

In *Seiiki monogatari* (*Tales of the West*, 1798), Honda Toshiaki (1744–1821) rejects Confucian learning as useless and praises European learning for its ability to grasp empirical reality through such disciplines as navigation, geography, and astronomy.[50] Despite his repudiation of Confucianism, he frames his proposals within a discourse on civilization similar to what we saw in Sorai and Shundai, where governments must employ man-made "institutions" (*seido*) to shape the raw material of both the natural environment and human nature. He writes of how the "Way of humans" must be taught through institutions, which in turn shape "customs" (*fūzoku*); left to their own devices, people exist in a state of untutored barbarism that gives rise to destructive customs.[51] Through a similar logic, he emphasizes that even though the wealth of a country makes use of the inherent qualities of its land, this wealth is not a mere outgrowth of these qualities, as it ultimately relies on the country's institutions and teachings.

---

47 Kaiho Seiryō, *Keiko dan*, p. 239.
48 Kaiho Seiryō, *Keiko dan*, p. 222.
49 Kaiho Seiryō, *Keiko dan*, p. 222. Here he is referencing the use of rice as a commodity on which interest would be charged when lent.
50 Honda Toshiaki, *Seiiki monogatari*, p. 98.
51 Honda Toshiaki, *Seiiki monogatari*, pp. 142, 144.

Introduction

Toshiaki applies this view of institutions and natural endowments to explain the unequal development of countries and to imagine a place for Japan on the world stage. Writing at a time when Russians and Japanese were beginning to come into contact in such places as Sakhalin and Hokkaido, he sees the uncultivated natural environment and native people of these areas as open to transformation by either Russian or Japanese institutions. His goal is then to secure these areas for Japan and bring them to their full potential. He comments that Russian Kamchatka Peninsula and England lie at the same latitude, so they should have similar climates and agricultural potential, and yet one is a wasteland while the other is a great power. He writes of Kamchatka that "It ought to be a great country just like England. However, the wise and the ignorant are differentiated based on teachings and institutions. It is the rule of heaven that the wise use the ignorant as their servants. In this way, there come to be master countries and dependent islands and countries, and the Way of lord and subject is established."[52] Setting aside Toshiaki's questionable reliance on latitude as the measure of a region's potential, his approach to economic development is significant for the way it situates different regions within a globalized system of trade and colonialism, where the great powers are engaged in a contest to exploit the natural potential of undeveloped areas by bringing them within their own sphere of civilizational influence.

Satō Nobuhiro (1769–1850) presents similar ideas to Toshiaki in an even more extreme form by advocating a centrally managed national economy and a large-scale invasion of Asia. Going beyond Toshiaki's idea of developing Japan's periphery, Nobuhiro opens *Kondō hisaku* (*A Secret Plan for Unification*) with a bold declaration on the supremacy of Japan and its proper role in the world: "The August Imperial Land is the first country to come into being on the earth and is the foundation of all the myriad countries of the world. For this reason, when one manages this foundation well, then the entire world ought to become its districts and prefectures, and the rulers of all the myriad countries ought to become its subjects."[53] Like Toshiaki, Nobuhiro draws on European examples to argue that proper government management of the economy is more important than the innate endowments of a country. In *Keizai yōryaku* (*An Outline of Political Economy*), he notes that England and Russia have cold climates and lie between fifty and sixty degrees latitude, making it

---

52 Honda Toshiaki, *Seiiki monogatari*, pp. 141–142.
53 Satō Nobuhiro, *Kondō hisaku*, p. 426.

difficult to grow grain, but as a result of effective policymaking, "these countries have gradually grown rich and their militaries have grown strong, so that now they have become wealthy and flourishing countries unmatched in the world."[54]

The ideal of "enriching the country and strengthening the military" promoted by Shundai and Nobuhiro took on a distinctive meaning in the Meiji era, when it became a rallying cry among the leaders of Japan's push to modernize. In this Meiji context, the phrase was associated with an active government role in industrialization and economic development, through both the public sector itself and government guidance of the private sector, together with the creation of a modern military based on Western models. These economic policies were pursued alongside the consolidation of an emperor-centered national polity and the promotion of State Shinto and so-called "national ethics" (*kokumin dōtoku*). Although these developments went beyond what Shundai envisioned or would likely have supported, they show continuity with the paradigm of political economy that emerged in his writings and was continued by his Tokugawa period successors, where economic development guided by a governing elite is paired with a normative vision of society as an organic whole.

---

54 Satō Nobuhiro, *Keizai yōryaku*, p. 526.

On Political Economy

Preface

The Way of Confucius is the Way of the ancient kings. The Way of the ancient kings is the Way of governing the realm and is present in the Six Classics.[1] To read the Six Classics and study the Way of the ancient kings, and yet fail to become accomplished in techniques of political economy [*keizai*], is like being a doctor who studies diagnoses and treatments but is unable to actually cure people's illnesses. Although one may have extensive knowledge and impressive powers of memory, possess many talents, and master many arts, these will be of little benefit to the realm and state.

Scholars of the Han dynasty all cultivated techniques of the classics and strove to explain the Way of governance.[2] People like Jia Yi [200–168 BC] and Dong Zhongshu [179–104 BC] are superb examples of this.[3] This was possible because the Han dynasty was not far removed from ancient times. From the end of the Han dynasty, those who discussed techniques of the classics were fewer than in ancient times, but up until the Tang dynasty, theories about "heart methods" [*shinbō*] had not yet

---

1 The "Six Classics" are a set of ancient Chinese texts traditionally considered to have been edited by Confucius. There are different versions of the list of these works, but they conventionally include the *Shi jing* (*Classic of Poetry*), *Shu jing* (*Classic of Documents*), *Li ji* (*Record of Ritual*), *Yue jing* (*Classic of Music*), *Yi jing* (*Classic of Changes*), and *Chunqiu* (*Spring and Autumn Annals*). Because the *Classic of Music* is lost, the surviving works are often referred to instead as the "Five Classics."
2 Shundai explains the phrase "techniques of the classics" in *Rikukei ryakusetsu* (*A General Outline of the Six Classics*, 1745): "In the Han dynasty, the term 'techniques of the classics' referred to studying the Six Classics and applying them to the government and political economy of the state" (p. 306).
3 Both of these were state scholars during the Han dynasty who promoted the role of Confucianism in government.

arisen.⁴ This is because people had still not completely lost sight of ancient times.

In the Song dynasty, Cheng Hao [1032–1085], Cheng Yi [1033–1107], and Zhu Xi [1130–1200] explained the Way of the sages entirely in terms of heart methods. When the two emperors Huizong [1082–1135, r. 1100–1126] and Qinzong [1100–1161, r. 1126–1127] were captured by barbarians, neither lords nor subjects considered this shameful, nor did they seek out any stratagems for taking revenge on their enemies; instead, they merely expounded theories of achieving sincere intentions and a correct heart.⁵ Later, it is said that when the realm was seized by the Mongols and the son of heaven was sent adrift on the seas, on their boat Lu Xiufu [1236–1279] and his followers spent every day explicating the *Daxue zhangju* [*Sentence and Section Annotations on the "Great Learning"*] while weeping profusely.⁶ The level of ignorance this displays is pitiful and ridiculous, and their fate is nothing less than retribution for the heart learning [*shingaku*] of their ancestors.⁷ Discussions of heart methods are found in the teachings of the Buddha, but are nowhere to be found in the Way of the ancient kings and Confucius.

4   When Shundai refers to Confucian theories about "heart methods," he is referring broadly to views that see Confucian practice as rooted in the moral cultivation of the inner self.
5   Huizong and Qinzong were the last two emperors of the Northern Song dynasty. They were taken prisoner when the Northern Song capital of Kaifeng was captured by Jurchen invaders in 1127.
6   Lu Xiufu was a high-ranking official and military commander at the end of the Southern Song dynasty. The *Song shi* (*History of the Song*) recounts that when the Southern Song court fled on ships from Mongol invaders, Lu Xiufu gave daily lectures to the child emperor Bing (1271–1279, r. 1278–1279) on the *Sentence and Section Annotations on the "Great Learning"*, Zhu Xi's commentary on the *Daxue* (*Great Learning*) (*History of the Song*, vol. 451). When the Song forces met their final defeat at the Battle of Yamen in 1279, Lu Xiufu jumped into the sea with Bing, drowning them both. Zhu Xi's interpretation of the *Great Learning* played a key role in the Song dynasty formulation of Confucianism as a method for morally perfecting the heart, a stance that Shundai here, as in the preceding discussion of Huizong and Qinzong, criticizes as politically useless.
7   Sometimes "heart learning" (Ch. *xinxue*, Jp. *shingaku*) is used to refer to the philosophical current represented by Lu Xiangshan and Wang Yangming (see n. 8 below), in contrast to the "learning of principle" (Ch. *lixue*, Jp. *rigaku*) of the Chengs and Zhu Xi. Here, though, Shundai is using "heart learning" in a broader sense to refer to all these forms of Confucian cultivation that focus on the moral perfection of the self. Another use of "heart learning" specific to the Tokugawa period refers to a popular religious movement founded by Ishida Baigan (1685–1744) that incorporated Confucian, Zen Buddhist, and Shinto ideas. This movement is usually referred to in English by its original Japanese name of either Shingaku or Sekimon Shingaku; the latter term, which translates as "heart learning of the Ishida school," is used to distinguish it from other uses of "heart learning."

Preface

At the same time as Zhu Xi there was Lu Xiangshan [1139–1192], and in the Ming dynasty there was Wang Yangming [1472–1529].[8] Although their theories differed from those of Zhu Xi, they were the same in emphasizing heart methods. After these figures, the Way of the ancient kings became obscured. Techniques of political economy declined, the followers of Confucius came to an end, and the occupation of Confucians became no different from the practices of beggar Buddhist monks. For the past hundred years, Japanese scholars too have all been followers of Song Confucianism, and without exception they reduce the Way of Confucius to discussions of heart methods.

Wise people certainly existed during these times, from royalty and nobles on down, as did people who aspired to pursue political economy, but there was no means for them to study its Way and learn its techniques, so they merely practiced government by using bits and pieces of vulgar knowledge. Political economy differs between past and present when it comes to a consideration of the times and between China and Japan when it comes to customs. Nevertheless, the techniques for practicing it do not differ in the least. If something is appropriate for the past but not the present, or appropriate for China but not Japan, then it cannot be called the Way of the sages. Whether the Way is successfully practiced or not depends on those who are responsible for practicing it. In all the countries of the four directions, as far as the sun and moon shine, there should be no place where the Way of the sages is not practiced. This goes all the more for Japan; it is a country where the Way of the sages has been used to govern since ancient times, so even though we may be in a later age, there is no reason why it should not be possible to revive it. If there were heroic and exceptional people who were employed by the ruler, grasped the times, and carried out the techniques of the Way, then we would be able to count the days until the Way of the ancient kings and the teachings of Confucius were practiced throughout the land and all the people enjoyed their benefits.

It is said that in ancient times there was a man who spent a thousand gold pieces to learn the technique of slaying dragons, but there were no

---

8 Lu Xiangshan was a major contemporary philosophical rival of Zhu Xi. He equated the human heart (Ch. *xin*, Jp. *shin/kokoro*) itself with the Way (Ch. *dao*, Jp. *dō/michi*) and principle (Ch. *li*, Jp. *ri*), as opposed to Zhu Xi's view that the human heart is a mixture of the Way/principle with a "material force" (Ch. *qi*, Jp. *ki*) that potentially draws people away from the Way. Lu Xiangshan's philosophy emphasized innate moral intuition, in contrast to the moral rationalism of Zhu Xi. Wang Yangming inherited Lu Xiangshan's views on moral intuition, as well as his rejection of Zhu Xi's dualism of principle and material force.

dragons to slay, so he ended his days having accomplished nothing.[9] People like me are similar to him. However, if I were to end my days with things just as they are, it would be regrettable that the dragon-slaying art I have succeeded in learning would end up pointlessly buried in the ground, so I have written this with my clumsy brush and stored it away in a box, and I hope that if there are any people in the wide world who have dragons they wish to slay, they will secretly obtain it and use it to aid in their mission. This is my life's humble ambition. If within what I have written even the smallest part is taken up and put to use, then even though I may die, it will be as if I am still living. When Jia Yi of the Han dynasty heaved a deep sigh and presented his proposal on governance to Emperor Wen [202–157 BC, r. 180–157 BC], this was because he was included among the ranks of court officials.[10] Today I am a commoner who holds no office. Why, then, do I dare to take after Jia Yi? It is simply because I am unable to hold back my pent-up indignation, and so I give vent to the thoughts that have accumulated within my breast.

Fourteenth year of the Kyōhō era [1729], Yin Earth Rooster year,[11] second month, eighth day
Written by Dazai Jun,[12] non-officeholder in the Eastern Capital, original surname Hirate,[13] fifth-generation descendant of senior assistant minister of the Ministry of Central Affairs Masahide [1492–1553][14]

---

9 This is a reference to a passage from the "Lie Yukou" chapter of *Zhuangzi*: "Zhu Pingman learned from Zhili Yi how to slay dragons, exhausting his house's wealth of a thousand gold pieces. After three years his technique was perfected, but he never found a use for his skill."
10 The "Shuning" chapter of volume 1 of the *Xin shu* (*New Writings*), a work attributed to Jia Yi, talks of him prefacing a petition to Emperor Wen with the words, "I humbly find that there is one development that one should severely regret, there are two that one should shed tears over, and there are six that one should deeply sigh over."
11 "Yin Earth Rooster year" is the designation of the year 1729 within the Chinese sexagenary (or "stems and branches") cycle, in which each year in the cycle is referred to as a combination of one of ten "heavenly stems" (each of which corresponds to one of five elements and either the yin or the yang force) and twelve "earthly branches" (made up of the twelve animals of the Chinese zodiac). Half of the possible combinations are not used, resulting in a total cycle of sixty years.
12 "Jun" is Shundai's *na*, or given name ("Shundai" is his *gō*, or scholarly name). When writing about him, I follow modern Japanese scholarly convention in referring to him by his scholarly pen name.
13 Shundai's father was born with the surname Hirate, but changed it when he was adopted by Dazai Ken'ō, whose granddaughter he married.
14 Hirate Masahide was a samurai who served as a senior retainer to Oda Nobuhide (1510–1551) and later his son Oda Nobunaga (1534–1582), the first of the three great unifiers

Introductory Notes

- When it comes to techniques of political economy, the Way of the ancient kings of China is the pinnacle. The "ancient kings" refers to the Two Emperors, Yao and Shun, and the illustrious kings of the Three Dynasties, the Xia, Shang, and Zhou.[15] The Two Emperors and the founding kings of the Three Dynasties were all great sages and governed the realm with marvelous wisdom. The regulations they established are without exception mirrors for the ages. Among the kings of the Three Dynasties, there are many who are labeled "rulers of revivals." Although they are not at the level of great sages, they upheld the Way of the sages who were the founders of their dynasties, employed wise men, and established undertakings of a revival, so their achievements are no different from those of sages. For this reason, they are venerated in the same way as Yao, Shun, Yu, Tang, Wen, and Wu, and all of them are referred to as the "ancient kings."[16] The Way propounded by Confucius is this same Way of the ancient kings. In the Qin and Han dynasties, and later, there were many things that differed from the Way of the ancient kings, so it is difficult to indiscriminately adopt these things. Moreover, just because something is in the Way of the ancient kings, it does not necessarily mean that it should be practiced unchanged in the Japan of today. That being said, when it comes to the governance of the realm, if one does not ponder the past in all matters and reflect on these matters using the past as one's basis, it will be easy to be dragged along by the vulgar wisdom of later ages, which causes great harm. In the present book, I always strive to clarify that the basis for things lies in the affairs of the ancient kings. One should understand that the term

---

of Japan during the latter part of the sixteenth century. Masahide committed suicide by seppuku; the reason for his action is not entirely clear, but it is commonly explained as having been a loyal sacrifice to caution Nobunaga to reform his poor behavior. The official title that Shundai uses for Masahide here is his ceremonial title within the imperial bureaucracy.

15 Yao and his successor Shun are legendary rulers of ancient China, traditionally dated to around the twenty-fourth/twenty-third century BC.

16 King Yu is the founder of the Xia dynasty and King Tang is the founder of the Shang. King Wu was the first actual ruler of the Zhou dynasty, but King Wen, his father, began the process of conquering the Shang dynasty and was later honored as the founder of the Zhou.

"ancient kings" refers to the illustrious kings of the Zhou dynasty and earlier.

- The "age of court nobles" refers to the period up until the Genpei War, when the court nobles governed.[17] The "age of warriors" then refers to the period that began with Minamoto no Yoritomo [1147–1199], the Kamakura major captain of the right.[18] The "Muromachi" refers to the age of the Ashikaga shoguns of Kyoto.[19] "Oda" is Oda Nobunaga [1534–1582].[20] "Toyotomi" refers to Toyotomi Hideyoshi [1536–1598] and his son.[21]
- In China, during the Han dynasty they valued the office of generalissimo [*taishōgun*] and made it of equal rank with the three excellencies.[22] The barbarian-quelling generalissimo [*seii taishōgun*, commonly shortened to "shogun"] of Japan is an office of the third rank, so it is considerably lower in status than the generalissimo of China.[23] The shogun of today possesses the entire land, making him the king of Japan. For this reason, in the Muromachi period the Yongle [1360–1424, r. 1402–1424] son of heaven of the Ming dynasty sent a letter in which he addressed Ashikaga Yoshimitsu [1358–1408, r. 1368–1394] as the "king of Japan." In the present

---

17 The Genpei War, fought between the Minamoto and Taira clans, lasted from 1180 to 1185. As Shundai describes, it resulted in the decline of the emperor and court aristocracy as a political force and their replacement by a series of warrior regimes.
18 Yoritomo was the leader of the Minamoto during the Genpei War and became the de facto ruler of Japan after the Minamoto victory. He formally acceded to the position of shogun in 1192, which he occupied until his death. "Major captain of the right" is the office Yoritomo held in the court bureaucracy; this bureaucracy was divided into right and left divisions.
19 Ashikaga was the shogunal clan during this period and Muromachi was the name of the area of Kyoto where they had their palace. The Ashikaga shogunate officially lasted from 1336 to 1573, but the power of the Ashikaga shoguns declined precipitously after the Ōnin War of 1467–1477.
20 Oda Nobunaga was the first figure to make significant progress in unifying Japan during the period of civil warfare known as the Sengoku (or Warring States) period.
21 Toyotomi Hideyoshi was a former vassal of Nobunaga and the second main unifier of Japan during the Sengoku period. Hideyoshi was succeeded by his son, Toyotomi Hideyori (1593–1615), who was defeated by Tokugawa Ieyasu (1542–1616).
22 The three excellencies were the three highest-ranking ministers and served as advisors to the ruler.
23 The office of "barbarian-quelling generalissimo" in Japan dates back to the early Heian period, when its holder was charged with subduing "barbarians" in northeastern Honshu on the periphery of the territory controlled by the emperor. The shoguns of the Kamakura period and later technically continued to hold this imperial office, even though its role had changed to become the de facto ruler of Japan, with greater power than the emperor to whom it was formally subordinate.

age, Tokugawa Ieyasu [1542–1616, r. 1603–1605], the Light of the East, hesitated before the emperor [*tennō*] of Yamashiro and in an excess of humility did not call himself king [*ō*].[24] Although humility is truly an illustrious virtue, when the honorific title of the ruler of a state is not correct, there is no appropriate way to express it in writing and record it in books. There is the term "great lord" [*taikun*], but this is a presumptuous title, since "great lord" refers to the son of heaven, whereas "shogun" is not of such a lofty status.[25] Another term for the shogun is the "large tree" [*taiju*].[26] From the Muromachi period there was the title "public officer" [*kubō*], but this is a meaningless term. When one considers the ritual systems and precedents of Japan and China, there is no appropriate title other than "king." However, when the title of "king" is not proclaimed from on high, it is not right for the people below to use it without authorization, so I dare not use it in what I write. Left with no other choice, I use "prefectural official" [*kenkan*]. "Prefectural official" is a term that can also be used to refer to the son of heaven, but today it is in reality like speaking of the "public authority" [*kōgi*]. It is a term with a much broader application than "great lord." There are also places where I refer to the "state" [*kokka*] or the "court" [*chōtei*]. These two are also broad terms and, depending on where they are used, they can refer to the ruler. All of these are circuitous terms, but readers of this book should not be wary of this. I again recall the words of Confucius that state, "When names are not rectified, then language will not follow reality."[27] Therefore, when the shogun Tokugawa Ienobu [1662–1712, r. 1709–1712]

---

24 "Light of the East" (Tōshōgū) is the name under which Ieyasu was posthumously deified. The "emperor of Yamashiro" refers simply to the Japanese emperor; Yamashiro was the province in which the imperial capital of Kyoto was located. The emperor at this time was Go-Yōzei (1571–1617, r. 1586–1611), who formally appointed Ieyasu as shogun.

25 *Taikun* was the title used in diplomatic communications by Tokugawa Yoshimune (1684–1751, r. 1716–1745), the reigning shogun at the time Shundai was writing. The "son of heaven" (Ch. *tianzi*, Jp. *tenshi*), in its original Chinese context, was considered the universal ruler of "all under heaven" (Ch. *tianxia*, Jp. *tenka*). The term was adopted in Japan, however, to refer to the Japanese emperor. When China and Japan are each considered to have their own "son of heaven," then "realm" is a more appropriate translation for *tenka*, so this is what I use throughout the translations in this volume.

26 An abbreviation of *taiju shōgun*, or "large tree general." This derives from the nickname given to the Han dynasty general Feng Yi (d. 34), who would modestly retreat to sit alone under a large tree while others proudly spoke of their own military exploits.

27 *Analects* 13.3.

wrote a letter responding to the king of Korea in which he called himself "king of Japan," this was the correct usage and was not a presumptuous term.[28]

- People in Japan use the character *gyo* ["honorable"] incorrectly. This character comes from the term for driving [*gyosuru*] a chariot. "Driving a chariot" refers to the way that people rode ancient chariots by harnessing four horses to them, creating what were called "four-horse chariots"; there were also chariots with five or six horses. The person who takes the reins of a chariot and handles the horses is called a "driver." The way the son of heaven governs the realm resembles the way a driver handles his horses, so a ruler is sometimes called a "world-driver," meaning one who drives the entire world. Based on this term, the character "honorable" is appended to all things pertaining to the son of heaven; examples include referring to his clothing as "honorable clothing," his food as "honorable food," his seat as an "honorable seat," and his things as "honorable things" or as items for his "honorable" use. Such terms as "honorable excursion," "honorable entrance," and "honorable return" all pertain only to the son of heaven. One should never use the character "honorable" unless it is in relation to the son of heaven. In Japan, though, from ancient times it became the custom throughout the land for both lofty and lowly to use this character. People did not realize that this was presumptuous. Particularly in the current age, not only are people more and more disordered, but there are words to which the character "honorable" is appended and, because this character is used to show reverence for something, these end up revering things that are not suitable objects of reverence. There are a great many examples of this, such as people referring to their own night-watch duty at the palace as an "honorable watch," or their own official service as "honorable

---

28 Ienobu used the title "king" in diplomatic communications based on the advice of the Confucian scholar Arai Hakuseki (1657–1725), in place of the use of *taikun* by earlier shoguns, to which Yoshimune later reverted. Within an East Asian world centered on Chinese hegemony, the Chinese emperor alone was considered "son of heaven" in a diplomatic context, while the rulers of countries on the periphery of China such as Japan and Korea went by the title of "king" in diplomatic communications (even if they used other titles domestically). In this usage, "kings" are recognized by the son of heaven as the rulers of their own territories, while ultimately remaining subordinate to him.

service."[29] This is beyond laughable. In this book, I omit all uses of the character "honorable." I do so by no means for the purpose of treating those of high rank lightly. Rather, my intention is to do away with presumptuousness and dispel ignorance. I would be greatly pleased if my readers did not accuse me of the offense of disrespect.

- In China, from the Xia, Shang, and Zhou dynasties onward, a new name for the country was always established each time a new dynasty arose. In cases like the Qin, Han, Wei, Jin, and Song dynasties, the name of the country that the founding king came from was used to refer to the realm as a whole during that dynasty. The founder of the Yuan dynasty was a Mongol who took control of the realm, but because Mongolia is a barbarian land, he was embarrassed about it and did not use the name of his country of origin to refer to the dynasty.[30] Instead, he established a different name for the country, calling it the "Yuan." After that, the founder of the Ming dynasty followed this example; he was Chinese, but he did not use the name of his country of origin for the dynasty, instead establishing a new name and calling it the "Ming." In the case of the Qing dynasty of the present, a Tartar took control of the realm, so following the precedent of the Yuan, he established the name "Qing."[31] The names "Yuan" [lit. "origin"], "Ming" [lit. "clarity"], and "Qing" [lit. "purity"] all have the sense of a necessary renewal of the realm. In Japan during the age of the court nobles, they simply used the original name "Nihon" for Japan and did not establish any other name for the country. With the advent of the age of warriors, people spoke of the "Kamakura" period or the "Muromachi" period; these are names for the country under

---

29 Shundai is indicating that it is inappropriate to use "honorable" for things pertaining to oneself, since proper etiquette dictates that one humble oneself and honor others.
30 The Yuan dynasty was founded by Kublai Khan (1215–1294).
31 The rulers of the Qing dynasty were Manchus. The Qing dynasty was founded by Nurhaci (1559–1626). His grandson, the Shunzhi Emperor (1638–1661), was then the first of the Qing rulers to control China. Shundai describes the Qing rulers as coming from "Dattan," which normally refers to Mongols, but can also refer more broadly to various Central Asian groups. Because of Shundai's imprecise reference and his emphasis on the barbaric nature of the Qing, I deliberately use the archaic English term "Tartar," which was historically used to refer to a broad range of Turkic, Mongol, and Manchu peoples, and the use of which tended to emphasize the alien nature of these peoples to European civilization.

warrior rule. If one did not create these kinds of labels for each age, then time periods would not be distinguished and matters of past and present would become confused. For this reason, even though rulers themselves did not establish these names for the country, they came to be used by the people as a matter of course. Ever since Tokugawa Ieyasu, the Light of the East, took control of the land, he established the capital in Edo so, following the examples of the Kamakura and Muromachi, one ought to refer to the present age as the "Edo" period.[32] The standard practice among the Chinese is to refer to the present age by the name of the country for that age. In referring to the court of the present age, they call it "the court of the country," "this court," or "our court." There is no appropriate term for Japanese to use to speak of the current period, since there is no name for the country. Therefore, in this book when I speak of the time from the divine ancestor Ieyasu onward, I call it the "present age." In vulgar speech it is called "the honorable present age" or "the present honorable age." I avoid the term "honorable," though, for the reason explained above; it is not that I am forgetting to show respect.

- In ancient times, the feudal lords [*shokō*] of the Zhou dynasty were divided into the five grades of duke, marquis, count, viscount, and baron to distinguish them by the size of their country and their relative status.[33] In the regulations of the present age in Japan, those with a territory of 10,000 *koku* or greater are called daimyo; these are feudal lords.[34] They are further divided into the four grades of those with 10,000 *koku* or more, those with 50,000 *koku* or more, those with 100,000 *koku* or more, and those with 300,000 *koku* or more. Their statuses are divided into the three grades

---

32 Shundai's logic here is based on how the Kamakura and Muromachi are named after the location of the seat of the shogun's government during these periods.
33 I use the conventional English translations here for the ancient Chinese peerage ranks of *gong*, *hou*, *bo*, *zi*, and *nan*.
34 A *koku*, equivalent to approximately 180 liters, was a standard unit for measuring quantities of rice in the Tokugawa period. It was considered the amount of rice needed to feed a person for one year. Agricultural land was then measured by its estimated output in *koku*. The actual calculations involved in rating the output of land were rather complex; among other things, the output of land that produced crops other than rice had to be converted into an equivalent value of rice.

of province-holders, castle-holders, and manor-holders.[35] Their ranks are divided into the eight grades of upper counselor, middle counselor, royal advisor, middle captain, lesser captain, chamberlain, fourth rank, and fifth rank.[36] These are all ultimately feudal lords, though. In this book I refer to those with a territory of 10,000 *koku* or more as "feudal lords," without making further distinctions. I refer to all territories of 10,000 *koku* or more as "countries" [*kuni*], regardless of their size. In doing so, I take after the ancient practice of China, where a "country" is a territory possessed by a particular person; I discuss this in the main body of the book.[37]

- In the context of the court of the son of heaven, the term "officer of state" [*taifu*] refers to those of the fifth rank or higher.[38] Among these officers of state, those of the highest rank are called "nobles" [*kei*]. In the context of the subjects of a feudal lord, "officer of state" refers to those who play a key role in handling the government of the country. Among these officers of state, those exalted ones who have had rank bestowed on them by the son of heaven are called "nobles." In today's world, among those who directly serve the state, those of the fifth rank and higher are called "officers of state."[39] Among the subjects of feudal lords, those who are commonly called "house elders" are officers of state. Depending on the stature of feudal lords, there are also differences in the status of their officers of state. In China, those who are called "house elders" are the stewards of the houses of officers of state.

---

35 In Japan, a province was a geographical division that typically incorporated the territories of multiple daimyo, but a "province-holder" was a daimyo whose territory extended over the entire area of at least one province (the term also came to be used to refer to daimyo with particularly large territories, even if they did not literally possess an entire province). "Castle-holders," as the name implies, were daimyo who were lower in rank than province-holders but possessed a castle, and "manor-holders" were daimyo without a castle.
36 These are honorary court titles and ranks within the imperial system.
37 The territories of Tokugawa daimyo are more commonly referred to in English as "domains," but I use "country" as a more direct translation of *kuni* and as better suited to conveying the parallel Shundai is drawing with Chinese history.
38 In a Japanese context, this is a reference to the system of imperial court ranks. As Shundai alludes to in this section, samurai were often granted such ranks, which continued to have symbolic significance even after the samurai had displaced the political power of the imperial court.
39 By those who "directly serve the state," Shundai is referring to direct vassals of the shogun, namely *hatamono* (lit. "bannermen") and *gokenin* (lit. "housemen").

- In China in ancient times, the scions of those from the son of heaven down to feudal lords and officers of state were called "heirs apparent" or "successors." The term "accession" was also used in relation to everyone from the son of heaven down to feudal lords and officers of state. The conduct of governmental matters was referred to as "court," and the appearance of subjects before their superiors was referred to as "attending court." This was the same for everyone from the son of heaven down to feudal lords and officers of state. In later times, the scion of the son of heaven was called the "crown prince" and the scion of a feudal lord was called a "successor." The term "accession" became limited in usage to the son of heaven and feudal lords, and the term "court" too was not used in relation to officers of state. In this book when I use the term "successor," this refers to the scion of a feudal lord.
- When I speak of "executive officials" in this book, I am referring to the senior councilors of the present day.[40] "Supervisors" are junior councilors.[41] "Officials" are the various officeholders. "Functionaries" are lesser officeholders, such as police officers and clerks. "Servicemen" are foot soldiers. "Servants" are lackeys. "Court officials" are direct retainers of the shogun. "Non-officeholders" are masterless samurai.
- "Gentleman" [*kunshi*] refers to someone of scholar-official [*shi*] status or higher. "Petty man" [*shōjin*] refers to someone like a commoner or bondman. This is the ancient nomenclature. The use of "gentleman" to refer to a virtuous person and "petty man" to refer to a wicked person is an erroneous theory of Song Confucians and does not appear in the classics or the transmissions on them.[42]
- There is a passage that describes the value placed on faith in Buddhism by saying, "The Buddhist law is a great sea, and those with faith are able to enter it."[43] This means that the Buddhist law is like

---

40 Senior councilors were among the high-ranking officials within the shogun's government. There were two to five senior councilors at any given time.
41 Junior councilors were high-ranking officials subordinate to the senior councilors. There were four to seven junior councilors at any given time.
42 The terms "gentleman" (Ch. *qunzi*, Jp. *kunshi*) and "petty man" (Ch. *xiaoren*, Jp. *shōjin*) appear frequently in the *Analects* and other Confucian texts. Shundai's interpretation of these as markers of social status rather than virtue reflects his overall interpretation of Confucianism as a philosophy of government rather than a doctrine of personal moral cultivation.
43 From volume 1 of the *Dazhidu lun* (*Treatise on the Great Perfection of Wisdom*).

a great sea that is difficult to enter, but those who have a faithful heart are able to enter it. Although these are words spoken about Buddhism, they contain a peerless truth. Not only with Buddhism, but with all other matters too, one will not accomplish anything unless one has deep faith in one's heart. For this reason, Confucius too said, "I have faith in and am fond of the ancients."[44] Although in the present book I express my foolish heart in clumsy words, I make the Way of the ancient sage kings my basis, follow the teachings of Confucius, ponder the historical traces of Japan and China, and discuss the affairs of the present. Those who have faith in their hearts for the Way of the sages surely ought to grasp my meaning. Those who lack faith in the sages should not read my book. It is best to read with a receptive heart. Having a "receptive heart" means that one does not insert one's personal standpoint or refuse to let go of any ideas. A receptive heart is one that examines the various things in a book and recognizes that some are surely of value. Examining these in more detail, it grasps them more and more. However, I do not consider everything I say to be correct or demand that it all be put to use. I would be overjoyed if my readers simply considered what I have written, discovered even one good thing out of a hundred, and put it to use.

44 From *Analects* 7.1.

Volume 1

A General Discussion of Political Economy

Governing the realm and state is referred to as "political economy." This term means managing society and giving relief to the people.¹ The first character of the term "political economy" means "management," which is administration.² This is what is referred to when in the *Yi jing* [*Classic of Changes*] it says, "The gentleman uses this to carry out administration,"³ and when in the *Zhongyong* [*Doctrine of the Mean*] it says, "Administer the great management of the realm."⁴ The term "administration" originally meant to regulate a thread. The vertical threads of a cloth are called the warp and the horizontal threads are called the weft.⁵ When a craftswoman weaves a piece of silk cloth, she first sets up the warp threads. The "warp" refers to the threads that run through from top to bottom. In the language of our country, putting these in place is referred to as "assembling the cloth." The weft then follows these threads. Another meaning

---

1   Shundai's explanation here is based on breaking down the term for "political economy" (*keizai*) into its two constituent characters. The first character, *kei*, when turned into the verb form *keisu*, means "to manage." The second character, read *zai* or *sai* in its Chinese-derived pronunciation, when read in its native Japanese pronunciation as *sukuu*, means "to give relief to."
2   The equivalence Shundai establishes between these two terms relies on the fact that the character used to write "management" (*kei*) is also the first character in "administration" (*keirin*).
3   From the "Sprouting" (*zhun*) hexagram.
4   *Doctrine of the Mean* 32.1. Chapter and paragraph numbers for citations from the *Doctrine of the Mean* are taken from the James Legge translation.
5   In Japanese, "warp" (*kei*) is written with the same character as (and homophonous with) "management."

1 A General Discussion of Political Economy

of "management" is arrangement.[6] This is what is meant when in the *Shi jing* [*Classic of Poetry*] it says, "When he managed the commencement of the wondrous tower, he managed and arranged it."[7] "Manage" is glossed as "measure out," the character for which is read in Japanese as *hakaru*.[8] In the common speech of this country, this means to make an estimate. When constructing a palace, one first makes an estimate of its entire structure and makes decisions based on this; this process is called "management." The second character of the term "political economy" means "aid," which refers to salvation.[9] This character is read in Japanese as *wataru* or *watasu*, which refers to crossing a stream and reaching the opposite bank. In the *Classic of Changes*, there are the hexagrams "Already Fording" [*ji ji*] and "Not Yet Fording" [*wei ji*]. In the *Shu jing* [*Classic of Documents*], the same meaning is expressed in such phrases as "widely help him across through his difficulties"[10] and "bring peace to the people and help them across."[11] "Aid" also means to rescue.[12] The character for "aid" is read in Japanese as *sukuu*, which means to relieve a person's suffering. In addition, this same character can be glossed as "accomplishment." This refers to something being brought to completion. Although the characters that make up the term "political economy" have these various meanings, they all come down to the same thing, in that they ultimately have the meaning of regulating affairs and bringing them to completion.

Ever since Yao and Shun, when the sages and wise men of each age exerted themselves, established words, and spread teachings, this was all for the purpose of the single matter of political economy. The Way of

---

6 Following the same logic Shundai used earlier to equate the terms "management" and "administration," the character for "management" (*kei*) is the first character of "arrangement" (*keiei*).
7 From the poem "Ling tai" ("The Wondrous Tower") in the *Classic of Poetry*.
8 Shundai is citing the gloss provided in the *Maoshi zhuan* (*Transmissions on the Mao Poems*), a Han dynasty commentary on the *Classic of Poetry*: "'To manage' means 'to measure out.'" When Shundai writes of how characters are read in "Japanese," he is referring specifically to the *kun'yomi* (native Japanese reading), as opposed to either the Chinese reading or the Japanese *on'yomi* (the Japanese reading derived phonetically from the Chinese reading).
9 The character for "aid" (*sai*), which is the second character in "political economy" (where it is pronounced in the voiced form *zai*), is the first character in "salvation" (*saido*).
10 From the "Gu ming" ("Testamentary Charge") section of the *Classic of Documents*.
11 From the "Cai Zhong zhi ming" ("Charge to Zhang of Cai") section of the *Classic of Documents*.
12 The character for "aid" (*sai*) is the second character in "rescue" (*kyūsai*).

the sages has no application apart from governing the realm and state. Everyone from the seventy-two wise disciples of Confucius down to the scholars of later times studied this matter. Those who abandon this and do not study it, instead pointlessly spending their entire lives occupied with literary writings, are not true scholars. They are no different from those who practice such trivial arts as the *koto* zither, Go, calligraphy, and painting. Even if they become the most skilled of their time and achieve fame throughout the realm, it is merely for personal pleasure and the amusement of society, with little benefit for the state, so it makes of the great Way of the sages a useless diversion. It is difficult to escape blame for this. Although today's scholars were born thousands of years later and their learning and wisdom may not reach the level of the ancients, if they read the books of the sages and become conversant with their meanings, they will surely be able to use all their energy for the purpose of this single great matter and spread the techniques for regulating society and bringing peace to the people. If they achieve that, then they will not fail to deserve the label of being "the most wondrous of the myriad things" and will surely be able to repay the virtue of heaven and earth.[13]

The political economy of the sages is clearly laid out in the Six Classics. This is what is referred to in the *Doctrine of the Mean* when it says, "The government of Wen and Wu is displayed in the bamboo slips."[14] At the time when the Zhou dynasty was in decline, a ruler by the name of Duke Huan of Qi [d. 643 BC, r. 685–643 BC] employed a wise man named Guan Zhong [d. 645 BC] and performed the tasks of a hegemon.[15] Guan Zhong's government put utility [*kōri*] first, striving to enrich the country and strengthen the military. Although it did not attain the level of the government of the Two Emperors and Three Kings, his achievements of assembling the feudal lords nine times to aid him and rectifying the realm did much to improve things. For this reason, Confucius often praised his accomplishments.[16] Later Confucians' disdain for Guan

---

13 Shundai alludes to the "Tai shi shang" ("Great Proclamation, Part 1") section of the *Classic of Documents*: "Heaven and earth are the father and mother of the myriad things, and humans are the most wondrous of the myriad things."
14 *Doctrine of the Mean* 20.2. Kings Wen and Wu were identified as the first rulers of the Zhou dynasty. Wu was the first actual ruler, but Wen was posthumously recognized as the founder of the dynasty. Some early Chinese texts were written on bamboo slips.
15 Duke Huan appointed Guan Zhong as prime minister when he became Marquis of Qi in 685 BC.
16 See *Analects* 14.17 and *Analects* 14.18.

1 A General Discussion of Political Economy

Zhong for practicing the techniques of a hegemon began with Mencius.[17] Enriching the country and strengthening the military are the duties of a hegemon, but they were not originally outside the bounds of the Way of the Two Emperors and Three Kings. At the end of the Zhou dynasty, the philosophers of the Hundred Schools arose.[18] In the Warring States period, people like Shen Buhai [d. 337 BC] and Hanfeizi [c. 280–236 BC] lectured to rulers on punishments and legal techniques.[19] Although this is not the Way of the sages, it too is one aspect of political economy.

Duke Xiao of Qin [381–338 BC, r. 361–338 BC] employed Shang Yang [390–338 BC] and made his country strong.[20] When Qin Shi Huang [259–210 BC, r. 221–210 BC], the first emperor of the Qin dynasty, employed Li Si [280–208 BC], he defeated the six countries and united the realm.[21] In the end he did not enfeoff feudal lords, but instead made the realm into a single country and established districts and prefectures [*gunken*]. This was a great historical shift. The Qin dynasty disappeared after only three reigns. From the Han dynasty onward, people drew on the past and responded to the circumstances of the present when establishing institutions, but they followed the Qin dynasty with regard to the system of districts and prefectures, not making any changes to this. After more than two thousand years, all the way down to the present day, people have not returned to the government of the Two Emperors and Three Kings, but have instead upheld the methods of Shang Yang and Li Si. Because these two were exceptional, they went against the Way of the sages and came up with a different kind of political economy.

---

17 See *Mencius* 2.1.1 (section numbers for citations from *Mencius* are taken from the James Legge translation). This criticism is based on a distinction between "hegemons" (Ch. *bazhe*, Jp. *hasha*) and true "kings" (Ch. *wang*, Jp. *ō*), in which hegemons rely on pragmatic techniques of administration, as opposed to the moral force through which the true king governs.
18 The term "Hundred Schools" refers to the various philosophical movements that flourished in China at this time. "Hundred," in this case, is simply used to indicate a large number.
19 Shen Buhai and Hanfeizi both promoted varieties of Legalism, which emphasized strict laws and punishments as a means of controlling the people, in contrast to the Confucian faith in the ability of rulers to govern the people through moral suasion.
20 Shang Yang, like Shen Buhai and Hanfeizi, was a proponent of Legalism.
21 Qin Shi Huang was king of the country of Qin from 247 to 221 BC and then emperor of a unified China from 221 to 210 BC. Li Si was a powerful minister under Qin Shi Huang. He was a follower of Legalist philosophy and played an instrumental role in creating a strong central bureaucracy and suppressing intellectual dissent (such as through the burning of Confucian books). The six countries defeated by Qin to unify China were Qi, Chu, Yan, Han, Zhao, and Wei.

On Political Economy

The most important person to discuss political economy after that was Sima Qian [c. 145–86 BC] of the Han dynasty. Although there were many who discussed political economy in the Han dynasty, they often only mentioned a single aspect of it. Sima Qian, though, produced the *Shi ji* [*Records of the Grand Historian*] within which were included the Eight Treatises, consisting of the "Treatise on Ritual," "Treatise on Music," "Treatise on Pitch Pipes," "Treatise on Calendars," "Treatise on the Officers of Heaven," "Treatise on the Feng and Shan Sacrifices,"[22] "Treatise on the Yellow River and Canals," and "Treatise on Leveling."[23] These eight volumes contain the essentials of government matters. The "Treatise on Ritual" discusses ritual and the "Treatise on Music" discusses music; these are included because the Way of governing puts ritual and music first. The "Treatise on Pitch Pipes" discusses the twelve pitches. Pitch pipes are the basis for measures and standards within the realm, as described in the "Shun dian" ["Canon of Shun"] section of the *Classic of Documents* when it says, "He standardized the pitch pipes, measures of length, measures of capacity, and measures of weight."[24] The "Treatise on Calendars" discusses methods for making calendars. In the "Yao dian" ["Canon of Yao"] section of the *Classic of Documents* it says, "Yao then commanded the Xi and He families to calculate reverently in accord with the wide heavens the movements of the sun, moon, planets, and stars, and to confer respectfully the seasons on the people." Also, the words of Emperor Yao state, "Ah! Xi and He families, the circuit of the year is 366 days. Using an intercalary month establish the four seasons, and then the year will come to completion."[25] He made these statements because the clarification of the calendar is an essential task of government. The "Treatise on the Officers of Heaven" discusses astronomy. As it says in the "Canon of Shun," "Shun clarified the jade-geared rotating sphere in order to know the ordering of the seven heavenly bodies."[26] He did this because the rectification of methods for determining the calendar is based on the clarification of astronomical phenomena and the

---

22 These were sacrifices performed by the emperor; the Feng sacrifice was to heaven and the Shan sacrifice to earth.
23 These make up chapters 23 to 30 of the *Records of the Grand Historian*.
24 What Shundai is pointing to here is that the pitch pipes were used as the basis for these other units of measure.
25 From the "Canon of Yao" section of the *Classic of Documents*.
26 The exact nature of the device mentioned here is unclear, but in volume 4 of *On Political Economy*, Shundai compares it to the armillary spheres of his day (see pp. 72–73). The "seven heavenly bodies" are the sun, moon, and five planets.

1 A General Discussion of Political Economy

detailed calculation of the movements of heavenly bodies. The "Treatise on the Feng and Shan Sacrifices" discusses prayers and sacrifices. The *Zuo zhuan* [*Zuo Commentary*] states that "The great affairs of the country lie in sacrifices and arms."[27] It says this because sacrifices are an important affair of the country that the ancient kings treated with reverence. The "Treatise on the Yellow River and Canals" discusses waterways and geography, and in the *Classic of Documents* there is the chapter entitled the "Yu gong" ["Tribute of Yu"].[28] These texts were written because making productive use of waterways, demarcating geographical districts, and providing the people with places to dwell are the foundation of managing the country. The "Treatise on Leveling" discusses government policies regarding currency and grain. The "Da Yu mo" ["Counsels of the Great Yu"] section of the *Classic of Documents* speaks of three matters: the first is correct virtue, the second is utility, and the third is welfare. Regulating government policies for currency and grain is the method for achieving utility and welfare. In the *Analects*, in response to Zigong's inquiry regarding government, Confucius replies, "One must have sufficient food, a sufficient military, and the faith of the people in their ruler."[29] In addition, the *Analects* praises the government of King Wu by stating, "What he attached importance to in governing the people were food, the observation of mourning, and sacrifices."[30] Government policies regarding currency and grain are of great importance when it comes to the welfare of the people, so the Grand Historian, Sima Qian, also discussed these in particular detail. In this way the Grand Historian took great care in discussing the political economy of his time by considering things from the past down to the present. Those who produced historical works after him all followed his example and discussed the political economy of a particular period. The Grand Historian's work was truly a model for the ages.

The Grand Historian lived in the time of Emperor Wu [156–87 BC, r. 141–87 BC], though, so the things he discusses in his book do not extend to matters beyond that point. Many of the institutions of the Han dynasty were established after Emperor Wu, so even the Grand Historian's book cannot be said to include everything. Ban Gu [32–92] of the Latter Han dynasty wrote the *Qian Han shu* [*History of the Former Han*],

---

27 From the Duke Cheng, Year 13 section of the *Zuo Commentary*.
28 The "Tribute of Yu" describes how Yu regulated the flow of waterways and managed the agricultural productivity of different regions based on their types of soil.
29 *Analects* 12.7.
30 *Analects* 20.1.

which provides a detailed record of matters of the Former Han dynasty. Its format closely follows the model of the Grand Historian. Following the example of the Eight Treatises, Ban Gu created the Ten Records.[31] The only difference is that he changed the term "Treatise" to "Record." He combined the "Treatise on Pitch Pipes" and "Treatise on Calendars" into the "Record of Pitch Pipes and Calendars" and combined the "Treatise on Ritual" and "Treatise on Music" into the "Record of Ritual and Music." Following the "Treatise on Leveling," he created the "Record of Food and Goods"; following the "Treatise on the Feng and Shan Sacrifices," he created the "Record of State Sacrifices"; following the "Treatise on the Officers of Heaven," he created the "Record of Astronomy"; and following the "Treatise on the Yellow River and Canals," he created the "Record of Irrigation Channels," as well as creating a separate "Record of Geography" that provides a detailed explanation of geography. Apart from these, he created a "Record of Punishments and Laws," since punishments assist the Way of government. Since explanations of natural disasters are based on the "Hong fan" ["Great Plan"] section of the *Classic of Documents* and are useful to the Way of government, he used the theories of scholars of the five elements to create a "Record of the Five Elements."[32] He also produced a "Record of Arts and Letters," which discusses the various arts of the realm; he created this because such matters are also tools for governing the state.

Ever since then, all of the dynastic histories have followed the model set by Ban Gu. They always include "Records" that describe the creations and governmental matters of a dynasty. Because there are continuities and changes and things rise and fall, there are many differences in the tables of contents of these Records. In the phrase "continuities and changes," "continuities" refers to following the government of the previous dynasty, while "changes" refers to revising its government. There is also what is known as "subtraction and addition"; "subtraction" refers to eliminating institutions of the previous dynasty, while "addition" refers to adding new ones. The *Analects* refers to this when it says, "That which they subtracted and added can be known."[33] Subtraction and addition also take place on

---

31 These make up volumes 21 to 30 of the *History of the Former Han*.
32 The "Great Plan" includes a discussion of the five elements, and the connection between natural disasters and the five elements is discussed by Liu Xiang (77–6 BC) in *Hong fan wuxing zhuan* (*Transmission on the Five Elements in the "Great Plan"*).
33 From *Analects* 2.23: "The Master said, 'The Yin relied on the rituals of the Xia; that which they subtracted and added can be known. The Zhou relied on the rituals of the Yin; that which they subtracted and added can be known.'"

1 A General Discussion of Political Economy

the level of specific matters of government. People who read histories should understand the differences among practices of political economy over time based on the meanings of the terms that I have described above.

In discussing political economy, there are four things that one must understand. First, one must understand the times [*toki*]. Second, one must understand principle [*ri*]. Third, one must understand force [*ikioi*]. Fourth, one must understand human feelings [*ninjō*].

Looking at the first of these, understanding the times means understanding the past and present. In China, up until the Zhou dynasty the territory of an emperor was fixed at 1,000 *li* square, which was referred to as the "royal domain."[34] The remainder of the land was bestowed on feudal lords as fiefs, establishing numerous countries that these lords were each charged with governing separately. This is referred to as a "feudal" [*hōken*] system of government. Qin Shi Huang eliminated the feudal lords, abolished the names of their countries, and made the entire realm into a single country. He divided it into thirty-six districts[35] and appointed officials to govern them. The dynasties from the Han onward have followed this system without altering it. Within districts, prefectures were established. Districts in China are like Japan's sixty-six provinces, and prefectures in China are like Japan's districts. Those who govern districts in China are called "governors," and those who govern prefectures are called "magistrates." The entire land is made into a single country belonging to the son of heaven, without establishing feudal lords. Because governors and magistrates are installed and charged with governing, this is called a government of "districts and prefectures" [*gunken*]. We can see, then, that in the Zhou dynasty and earlier the realm had a feudal system, whereas in the Qin dynasty and later it had a system of districts and prefectures. This is the foremost point when it comes to discussions of political economy. The books of the Three Dynasties and earlier are not transmitted in their entirety, though, so we are not able to examine the feudal government of these times. It is only the government of the Zhou dynasty that we can grasp a basic outline of today from examining

---

34 Using the Zhou dynasty *li*, which was equal to roughly 405 meters, 1,000 *li* is a little over 400 kilometers.
35 The Chinese term used here is *jun* (Jp. *gun*). In the period in question, "commandery" or "prefecture" would be a more typical translation. In the Japanese context that Shundai goes on to discuss, a more typical translation for *gun* would be "county." I use the deliberately vague "district" to encompass the different usages in China and Japan of *jun/gun* that Shundai points out, where the term indicates a smaller territorial division in Japan than in China.

the classics and the transmissions on them. When it comes to the government of districts and prefectures, ever since the Qin and Han dynasties many detailed historical records have been passed down, so we are able to examine this form of government as it existed during these times. However, in the past two thousand years there have been many continuities and changes as well as subtractions and additions, so it is not easy to know the differences between periods.

There are no detailed records of the affairs of ancient Japan, so we are not able to know about these. What kind of laws can we suppose that Emperor Jinmu established when he acceded to the throne?[36] There were no feudal lords, nor were there districts and prefectures; it appears that several hundred years passed with things still formless and primitive. Later, when Japan came to have interactions with other countries, China already had a government of districts and prefectures, so our country followed this. In Japan they established countries and districts and then appointed provincial governors for the countries and district administrators for the districts.[37] In China, provinces and districts incorporate prefectures, so prefectures exist within these provinces and districts. Provinces and districts differ in name, but in reality they are the same; provinces can also be called districts and districts can also be called provinces. In Japan, countries incorporate districts, so districts exist within countries, meaning that the districts of Japan correspond to the prefectures of China. In Japan, "countries" and "provinces" are the same thing, whereas in China these terms have different meanings. In China, "country" is a term used in relation to the establishment of feudal lords, rather than being the name of a geographical region; "province" is used for a geographical region, whereas "country" is used to refer to the territory of the fief held by a feudal lord. For this reason, there are times when a single country incorporates several provinces, and times when a single province is divided into two or three countries. "Country" is a term used in China in the context of feudalism, so they speak of "provinces and

---

36 Jinmu is the legendary first emperor of Japan.
37 A reference to the Taika Reforms of 645, which created a centralized imperial state with provincial governors (*kokushi*) appointed by the emperor for fixed terms, as opposed to the earlier system of local control by regional elites. The term *kuni* is more commonly translated into English as "province" in this historical context, but I translate it as "country" here to reflect the contrast Shundai makes between usages in Japan, where *kuni* was a synonym for *shū* (which I translate as "province"), and China, where these terms were distinguished. Once Shundai moves past this discussion of terminology, I translate *kuni* as "province" when it refers to the divisions of Japan under the imperial government.

1 A General Discussion of Political Economy

districts" without any reference to "countries." The provincial governors of Japan correspond to the district prefects of China, and the district administrators of Japan are like the prefectural magistrates of China.

In Japan, provincial governors are the head officials of countries, and below the head officials are the assistant officials, managers, and secretaries; a country is governed with these four grades of officials.[38] It was like this from middle antiquity until the Hōgen [1156–1159] and Heiji [1159–1160] eras. After the Genpei War, though, Minamoto no Yoritomo, the major captain of the right, received a mandate from Retired Emperor Go-Shirakawa [1127–1192, r. 1155–1158] and became the general constable of all Japan. From this point on, in addition to the provincial governors, officials called "military governors" were installed.[39] They exercised governing authority, so at some point the authority of the provincial governors was seized by warriors, the court nobility gradually declined, and the people in the Kantō region known as "shogunal vassals" wielded their might everywhere.[40] This was the beginning of the rule of the land by shogunal houses and represented a great historical shift.

The age of the Kamakura shoguns is labeled the "Hōjō regency," as it was the Hōjō clan that held the reins of power.[41] Their government followed the law of the house of Yoritomo, though, and governed with the Jōei Code.[42] At the end of this period the Genkō War broke out, the

---

38 This four-grade system of officials was used to structure all varieties of official posts within the *ritsuryō* system of bureaucracy. Any official duty would be presided over by a "head official," so Shundai is explaining that in the context of governing a province (or "country," which he noted earlier was a synonym for "province" in Japan), the provincial governor filled this role.

39 In the late twelfth century, "general constables" (*sōtsuibushi*) were appointed as a kind of chief of police for each province. In 1190, Yoritomo was designated "general constable of all Japan," which gave him the authority to appoint general constables throughout the country. The position of general constable was then transformed into that of military governor (*shugo*). Military governors were appointed by the shogun to govern provinces. Although the provincial governors appointed by the emperor were not eliminated, their power was supplanted by the military governors.

40 In this period, "shogunal vassals" (*gokenin*; lit. "housemen") were high-ranking warriors who had pledged loyalty to the shogun and in exchange received the right to be appointed as military governors or land stewards (*jitō*).

41 After Yoritomo's death, his father-in-law, Hōjō Tokimasa (1138–1215), acted as regent for the two sons who succeeded him as the second and third Kamakura shoguns. This arrangement became a model for the remainder of the Kamakura shogunate, with a member of the Hōjō clan acting as regent for a figurehead shogun.

42 The Jōei Code, issued in 1232 (the first year of the Jōei era), was Japan's first code of military law. It applied only to the warrior class and was used side by side with the existing law of the imperial court.

Kamakura regime collapsed, and for a brief period power was held by the court nobles.[43] Soon, however, there was another upheaval and the realm ultimately came under the control of the Ashikaga clan.[44] Although the warrior government of this time was based on that of the previous age, many laws and institutions gradually changed in keeping with shifts in society and customs. Because the government of the shogunal house was practiced throughout the land, the court nobles declined all the more and the warriors flourished increasingly with each day. From this point on, provincial governors were no longer appointed; instead only military governors were appointed. Above these military governors were appointed people called "shogunal deputies," who ruled over numerous provinces.[45] This was another great historical shift. When the Muromachi regime declined, the shogunal deputies grew stronger and vied for power.[46] The military governors remained in their provinces, wantonly launching attacks on their neighbors. Extraordinary people rose up from among these, ultimately leading to the period of warring states.[47] The Muromachi regime had already collapsed and the realm was controlled by Oda Nobunaga, but before he succeeded in unifying the entire land, he suddenly met defeat.[48] Toyotomi Hideyoshi rose up from a lowly position and, taking the place of Nobunaga, was able to unify the land. He relied entirely on military force, though, and did not carry

---

43 The Genkō War of 1331–1333 (named after the Genkō era, which lasted from 1331 to 1334) began when Emperor Go-Daigo and his forces attacked the shogunal government in Kamakura. He initially failed and was sent into exile, but in 1333 one of his generals, Nitta Yoshisada (1301–1338), defeated the Hōjō forces in Kamakura, while another, Ashikaga Takauji (1305–1358), seized Kyoto. When Shundai writes of power being held briefly by court nobles, he is referring to the Kenmu Restoration, the period from 1333 to 1336, when Go-Daigo restored imperial rule and a civilian government of the court nobility.
44 Ashikaga Takauji was appointed shogun in 1338 after turning against his former allies.
45 Shogunal deputies (*kanrei*) were high-ranking officials who assisted and acted on behalf of the shogun. The details of the position varied over time, but during most of the Muromachi period there were two shogunal deputies, one in Kyoto and one in Kantō.
46 The Muromachi regime (named after the district of Kyoto where the shogun's palace was located) refers to the regime of the Ashikaga shoguns. After the Ōnin War of 1467–1477, the Ashikaga shoguns lost effective power to the shogunal deputies.
47 In the Japanese context, the "period of warring states" refers to the time between the outbreak of the Ōnin War in 1467 and the unification of Japan in the late sixteenth and early seventeenth centuries.
48 The final collapse of the Muromachi shogunate came in 1573. In 1582 Nobunaga was attacked and defeated by one of his own generals.

out humane government, so before two generations had passed his line disappeared.[49]

Our divine ancestor Tokugawa Ieyasu, the Light of the East, calling forth the spirit of the meritorious deeds of his predecessors of many generations, brought peace to the land and initiated a great achievement of ten thousand generations. He did so by employing the virtue of a wondrous martial talent that causes no harm[50] and by following heaven and corresponding to humans.[51] Ever since the Muromachi period, in the various provinces there have been many called "daimyo" [lit. "great names"] or "lofty houses." In addition, within the houses of people who held the office of military governor there were those who governed a province for many generations, becoming effectively its ruler, and at some point the realm became as if it had a feudal system of government.[52] When Ieyasu first took the throne,[53] he granted fiefs in important regions to noble families of the same surname as himself, as well as to meritorious retainers, thus creating bulwarks.[54] From earlier times there were already dominions of warrior leaders, and Ieyasu assured that those who had been governing these were able to continue governing them as before.[55] He

49 Hideyoshi's designated successor, his son Toyotomi Hideyori, committed suicide after being defeated in battle by Tokugawa Ieyasu.
50 This phrase is from the *Xici zhuan* (*Commentary on the Appended Phrases*) to the *Classic of Changes*: "Who could accomplish all this? Who but those ancient sages who had sagacity, wisdom, and a wondrous martial virtue that causes no harm?"
51 From the *Tuan zhuan* (*Tuan Commentary*) on the "Revolution" (*ge*) hexagram in the *Classic of Changes*: "Heaven and earth undergo transformations and the four seasons complete their course. Tang and Wu created transformations, following heaven and corresponding to humans. For a transformation to properly match the times is great indeed!" Tang overthrew the Xia dynasty to found the Shang, and Wu overthrew the Shang dynasty to found the Zhou, so Shundai is comparing the achievements of Ieyasu to the transformations effected by the sagely founders of dynasties in ancient China.
52 That is, even though military governors were officially appointed by the centralized authority of the shogun, in practice the position was often a hereditary one held by a local elite family, just as would be the case in a decentralized feudal government.
53 Although Ieyasu was the shogun and not the emperor (to whom he was officially subordinate), the term that Shundai uses here to describe Ieyasu's taking office, *tōkyoku*, is usually used to refer to the enthronement of an emperor or king.
54 The Owari, Kii, and Mito domains were all founded with one of Ieyasu's sons as daimyo. The ruling houses of these domains were together known as the "Three Houses of the Tokugawa." In addition, the Tokugawa regime transferred large amounts of land from *tozama* ("outside") daimyo (former rivals of the Tokugawa) to *fudai* daimyo (those who originally supported the Tokugawa), taking care to strategically position *fudai* daimyo where they could keep watch over *tozama* territories.
55 In the Muromachi period, *bunkoku* (translated here as "dominion") referred to the area under the official jurisdiction of a particular military governor. By Ieyasu's time, though, the term referred to the area under the de facto control of a warrior leader.

On Political Economy

established laws requiring attendance at court and payment of tribute,[56] and from this time on the realm finally became a true feudal system and thus generally resembled the Zhou dynasty of China. This was another major historical shift.

In China, then, the realm had a feudal system in ancient times, but since the Qin and Han dynasties it has had a centralized system of districts and prefectures. Japan, in contrast, had a centralized government of districts and prefectures in ancient times, but today has a feudal system. The differences between other countries and our own and between past and present are like this. If one fails to understand such things and tries to practice the ancient Way indiscriminately in the present, one will clash with the times and be unable to practice it. When one is unable to practice it, one will be wont to say that the ancient Way is ultimately of no use to governing. This is a great error. For this reason, when discussing the Way of governing it is of the utmost importance to understand the times.

The second thing one must understand when governing is principle. This principle is not the "principle" of "principles of the Way" [*dōri*], but rather the "principle" of "principles of things" [*butsuri*].[57] "Principles of things" refers to the principle that necessarily exists in each thing. Examples of this are the grain in wood and the other various patterns in things. The grain in wood is called the "principle of wood," and in such things as gems and stones, too, there is always a grain; the grain of a gem is called the "principle of the gem" and the grain of a stone is called the "principle of the stone." In the flesh of humans, as well as that of birds, beasts, fish, and turtles, there is likewise always a grain, which is called the "principle of flesh." Just as wood has a grain, in all things there is always a certain pattern, and such patterns are called the "principles of things." These can either be followed or violated; when one follows the principle of a thing it will be well managed, but when one contradicts this principle it will not. Consider, for example, what happens when planing wood. When one planes by following the grain of the wood, the blade cuts smoothly just as one wants it to, without jamming. When one planes against the grain, though, the blade always jams

---

56 A reference to the alternate attendance (*sankin kōtai*) system, established in the Buke Shohatto (Laws for Military Houses) of 1635.
57 By limiting the meaning of "principle" to certain empirical qualities of things, Shundai is rejecting the view of Zhu Xi and others of "principle" as a normative metaphysical concept.

1 A General Discussion of Political Economy

and one is unable to plane the wood. When one tries to overcome this by planing with force, the wood always splinters. Because of this, even if one uses the high-grade plane of a craftsman, one cannot plane by going contrary to the grain of wood. The same applies to such things as water and fire. Water soaks and descends, whereas fire blazes and ascends; these are examples of natural principle.[58] It is impossible to go contrary to this principle, making water ascend and fire descend. Just as all things necessarily have their respective principles, the affairs of the realm, too, have their principles. When in the conduct of government one runs contrary to these principles, one will be utterly unable to conduct either major or minor affairs. Although the common people are lowly, they will never comply with government that runs contrary to principle. No matter how fierce someone may be, he will be unable to make them comply. When one forcibly tries to make people comply with that which they refuse to comply with, it will always result in failure and is a step in the direction of rebellion. For this reason, those who practice government must seek out the principles of various affairs. Once they grasp these principles, they should act in a way that does not run contrary to them. This is what is meant by "understanding principle."

The third thing one must understand when governing is force. "Force" refers to that which lies outside the ordinary principle of things. Take, for example, water and fire. Water puts out fire, but the reason one cannot extinguish a large fire with a small amount of water is the strength of the force of the fire. To give another example, wind fans fire, but the reason the flame of a lamp is blown out by a gust of wind is because the force of the fire is not as strong as that of the wind. In a similar way, oil fuels fire, but the reason a blazing fire will always go out when doused with a large amount of oil is because of the force involved. Water flows downward, but it sometimes flows upward when dammed and guided because of force.[59] When pounding a large nail into hard wood, it is difficult to get it in by smashing it with a heavy stone, but it will go in right away when one taps it with a small hammer; this too is a matter of force.

All these kinds of things involve force and are outside of ordinary principle. The affairs of the realm have these two aspects of principle and force. When one understands principle but not force, one will not be able

---

58 From the "Great Plan" section of the *Classic of Documents*: "Water is what soaks and descends. Fire is what blazes and ascends."
59 This example of "force" appears in *Mencius* 6.1.2.3.

to conduct major affairs. When one understands force but not principle, one will not be able to enact great plans. Always clarifying both principle and force in tandem, achieving with force what cannot be achieved with principle, carrying out with principle what cannot be carried out with force, using principle to guide force, using force to assist principle, bringing principle and force to completion together, and exhausting both of their applications – these are key techniques of government.

The fourth thing one must understand when governing is human feelings. This refers to understanding the real feelings of the people of the realm. "Real feelings" refers to such things as likes and dislikes, suffering and pleasure, and sorrow and joy. "Likes" refers to preferences, "dislikes" refers to aversions, "suffering" refers to pain, "pleasure" refers to enjoyment, "sorrow" refers to lamentation, and "joy" refers to delight.[60] People are never without these feelings. Whether great men or petty men, lofty or lowly, they do not differ in the slightest in this regard. Moreover, the affectionate feelings of fathers, mothers, wives, and children do not differ between the lofty and the lowly. These feelings emerge from the genuineness of the heaven-endowed natures of all people and do not have the least bit of falsehood, so they are called "real feelings." The character for "feeling" also has the meaning of "real," so it can be read as *makoto* [true]. In addition, nobles have the feelings of nobles, commoners have the feelings of commoners, and scholar-officials have the feelings of scholar-officials. Farmers, artisans, traders, and shopkeepers have the feelings of farmers, artisans, traders, and shopkeepers. Men have the feelings of men and women have the feelings of women. People's feelings differ depending on what type of people they are, but when one speaks of "feelings," this always points to the aspect of being free of falsehood.

If one is in accord with human feelings when conducting governmental matters, then it will be easy for the people to follow. If one runs counter to human feelings, then the people will not follow. "Being in accord with human feelings" means doing what people like, take pleasure in, and are joyful about, whereas "running counter to human feelings" means doing what people dislike, suffer from, and find sorrow in. Officials usually understand rightness and have a heart that upholds the Way, so even when faced with government that is not in accord with human feelings,

---

60 In this sentence Shundai is drawing equivalences between certain Chinese-derived terms and their native Japanese equivalents, which ends up coming across in English as a list of pairs of synonyms.

they suppress and control their own feelings and follow at least for the time being. Their hearts are not fundamentally at peace, though, so it is an inevitable principle that people will also naturally emerge who break laws and violate prohibitions. The common people do not understand rightness and do not have a heart that upholds the Way, so they are unable to suppress and control their feelings. They only think about what is convenient for themselves personally, so when faced with a government that runs counter to human feelings, they will certainly not follow. It is not that they fail to understand the fearsomeness of punishments, but they are unable to endure the agony that is right before them, so they break laws and violate prohibitions. Ever since ancient times, governments that run counter to human feelings have never lasted long. The government of the ancient sages was always in accord with human feelings.

Human feelings do not differ greatly between past and present or between other countries and our own. To speak in very general terms, human feelings involve likes and dislikes. When in the *Daxue* [*Great Learning*] it says, "Liking what the people like and disliking what the people dislike – this is called being father and mother of the people," this speaks of loving the people.[61] When it comes to the things that the people like, the rulers also like these and enact them among the ruled. When it comes to the things that the people dislike, the rulers also dislike these and avoid them for the benefit of the ruled. This is the heart of a father and mother who love their child, so a ruler who acts this way is called "father and mother of the people." The love of fathers and mothers for their children is their true heaven-endowed nature, so when thinking about their children, their desire to obtain good things on top of the good things they already have comes from kindness and has no falsehood. The love of rulers for the ruled is like the love of fathers and mothers for their children, and it is called "humane government" when they understand the likes and dislikes of the people and do not run counter to their feelings. The likes and dislikes that constitute human feelings are similar to what I spoke of earlier in relation to following and contradicting the principles of things. When one goes against human feelings even slightly, people will not obey in their hearts, and when they do not obey it is impossible to force them to do so, even by mustering all the power of the realm.

---

61 The quotation is from the *Great Learning* 10.3. Chapter and paragraph numbers for citations from the *Great Learning* are taken from the James Legge translation.

Therefore, those who aim to practice political economy must strive not only, as described above, to understand the times, principle, and force, but also to understand human feelings. However, in contrast to the ease of understanding the times, principle, and force, human feelings are difficult to understand. This is because human feelings contain aspects that are outside of ordinary principle. For example, if one were to take a lowly person from among the poor, suddenly make him a scholar-official, dress him in fine clothing, seat him in the officials' hall, and feast him with delicacies, he would surely suffer greatly and find it inferior to squatting in rags in his own home while eating unpolished rice and soup of wild greens. Fine clothing and food are things that people like, but people are loath to suffer the pain of doing things they are unaccustomed to. Such human feelings are difficult to understand with ordinary principle. If one does not observe things by putting oneself in another's place, it will always be difficult to understand that person's real feelings. It is on the whole more difficult to understand human feelings than the principles of things, since the principles of things can be understood by diligently reading and studying, whereas human feelings cannot be understood with this alone. The people of the realm differ in rank, with some lofty and some lowly, and also lack uniformity in their likes and dislikes and in the things that cause them suffering and pleasure. Because of this, when one uses ordinary reasoning to make guesses about people at a distance from an outside perspective, one will get many things wrong. It is only by studying diligently, getting close to people of different ranks, intimately witnessing their affairs, putting oneself in each particular person's place, carefully observing their hidden points, paying attention to their behavior and language, and considering these things in detail that one can obtain a general idea of their feelings. If one does not do these things, then one will certainly be unable to gain familiarity with human feelings.

Those who are born into the houses of officials with hereditary stipends do not interact with common people, so even if they are intelligent, they will not be aware of the feelings of common people. This goes all the more for royalty and the nobility: residing within palaces and seated in grand halls and magnificent buildings, how could they understand the conditions of the lower orders? Because of this, the ancient kings of ancient times went on inspection tours of the realm and commanded the state historian to collect the songs of the common people from the various provinces. The king examined their words, had the master of music sing

1 A General Discussion of Political Economy

them, and listened to their sounds. This was for the purpose of understanding the customs and human feelings of the various provinces.[62] The poems collected by these state historians are called the "Guo feng" ["Airs of the States"] and are found within the *Mao shi* [*Mao Poems*].[63] This is the *Classic of Poetry* we have today. In our country, too, there are examples from ancient times of collecting songs of the common people and performing them with music at court; this is what *saibara* is.[64] The *Man'yōshū* also includes many songs of the common people, which can be compared with the "Airs of the States."[65]

On top of this, the ancient sagely emperors and wise kings always employed ministers who served as counselors. These counselors often came from lowly origins. Emperor Yao recommended Shun, who was a farmer from Lishan, and made him regent. The Great Yu, Ji, and Xie, who were illustrious ministers of Yao's time, were not of lowly origins.[66] It is not clear what were the social origins of Gao Yao, Bo Yi, Bo I, the artisan Chui, Kui, and Long, but I believe they must have come from lowly backgrounds.[67] The records of the Xia dynasty are incomplete. King Tang of the Yin dynasty promoted Yi Yin, a rustic person from Youshen, and had him serve as an exemplar.[68] Gaozong promoted Gan Pan and Fu Yue,

---

62 This process is described in the "Wang zhi" ("Kingly Regulations") chapter of the *Record of Ritual*: "The son of heaven made an inspection tour every five years ... He ordered the master of music to present the poems of each area so that he could view the customs of the common people."
63 The *Mao Poems* is the text of the *Classic of Poetry* as edited by the Mao commentarial school of the Former Han dynasty. As Shundai indicates in what follows, this became the standard text of the *Classic of Poetry*.
64 *Saibara*, which reached the height of its popularity during the first half of the Heian period, is a form of court music whose song lyrics had folk origins.
65 For example, volume 14 of the *Man'yōshū* (the earliest anthology of Japanese poetry, dating from the eighth century) consists of *Azuma uta* (Songs of the East), which are said to be the product of provincial commoners.
66 The Great Yu was Shun's minister of works, Ji his minister of agriculture, and Xie his minister of instruction. Later, the Great Yu became the founding ruler of the Xia dynasty.
67 Gao Yao was minister of crime under Shun and then became Yu's top political advisor. Bo Yi served Shun as an official responsible, with Yu, for managing flooding. Later he served Yu, becoming his top advisor after the death of Gao Yao. Bo I was appointed by Shun to the ritual post of arranger of the ancestral temple (normally his name would be romanized as "Bo Yi," but I write it as "Bo I" to distinguish him from the other "Bo Yi" in this passage). The artisan Chui was minister of works under Shun. Kui was director of music under Shun. Long was appointed by Shun as minister of communication.
68 Yi Yin first served Tang as a cook, but after showing his astuteness in political matters, he eventually rose to being an important advisor of Tang.

both of whom were of lowly origins, and had them serve as exemplars.[69] Fu Yue was hidden away in Fu Yan, mixed with prisoners, and engaged in lowly construction work, but suddenly he was raised up and made prime minister. King Wen of the Zhou dynasty promoted Lü Wang, an old fisherman from Wei Bin, and made him grand master. In the time of King Cheng, Dan, the Duke of Zhou, was an uncle of the son of heaven.[70] He acted as regent while having the status of the three excellencies.[71] At each meal he would remove food from his mouth three times, at each bath he would wring out his hair three times, and each day he would meet with seventy scholar-officials.[72] These seventy scholar-officials must have been largely people of lowly origins. After Yao and Shun, such people as Yi Yin and Fu Yue all came from low birth and poverty, so they were conversant in human feelings and governed the realm as if it were in the palm of their hand. The words of Mencius are true when he says, "Those who possess intelligent virtue and wise techniques usually come from troubled circumstances."[73] Those who have mixed with the common people for a long time, endured low status, and experienced extensive hardship are always conversant with human feelings, so as a matter of course they come to have intelligent virtue and wise techniques that are difficult to obtain simply by reading books. When one promotes such people and has them serve as exemplars, then even for one in the loftiest position of the son of heaven it will not be difficult to understand the feelings of the lower orders. This is the method that rulers use to understand human feelings. To set aside this method and employ hidden techniques to investigate the conditions of the common people is to engage in acts of petty wisdom and it is not the proper method for governing the state.

---

69 Gaozong is the temple name of the Shang dynasty king Wu Ding. Before becoming king, he spent time living among the common people. Gan Pan was his teacher when he was young, and then became a high-ranking minister of his when he took the throne. After Gan Pan died, Wu Ding replaced him with Fu Yue, whom he found working as a builder in the wilds of Fu Yan.
70 The phrase "son of heaven" refers here to King Cheng. The Duke of Zhou was a younger brother of Cheng's father, King Wu.
71 The three excellencies were the three highest-ranking ministers and served as advisors to the ruler. The positions encompassed by this term were different in different Chinese dynasties; in the Zhou, the term referred to the grand instructor, grand tutor, and grand guardian.
72 That is, the Duke of Zhou was so eager to meet with people that he would even interrupt his meals (requiring him to remove food from his mouth) and his baths (requiring him to wring out his hair).
73 *Mencius* 7.1.18.1.

1 A General Discussion of Political Economy

Since ancient times, there have never been rulers who accomplished things solely using their own knowledge, without any reliance on ministers who serve as counselors. Rulers raise up from obscurity people who have learning, are aware of the changes in society in the past and present, understand the times, principle, force, and human feelings, and discern the Way of political economy. If they make such people counselors, discuss the Way of governing, deliberate political affairs, and establish immutable standards, how could it be difficult to govern the realm? It is through this method that wise kings simply fold their arms and achieve tranquility in the world,[74] and bequeath abundance to later generations.[75] This is the foundation of governmental matters.

Political economy values learning from the past and taking the past as one's teacher. The *Classic of Documents* describes Yao and Shun as doing this when it states that "Yao and Shun learned from the past."[76] Given that even those as early as Yao and Shun learned from the past, how could it be acceptable for later people not to do so? Moreover, the words of Fu Yue state, "Study the lessons of the past, and then you will have attainments. I have never heard of anything that lasted long in the world without the past being taken as teacher."[77] When one learns from the past and regulates matters suitably in the present, affairs will be handled reasonably and improper things will not arise. When one fails to learn from the past, one will sometimes be led astray by a fixation on the advantages and disadvantages that are right before one's eyes, and as a consequence one will forget to consider what comes later. However, just because one should learn from the past and take the past as one's teacher, this does not mean that one should practice the government of the past in its entirety in the present, as there are many cases where the government of the past is difficult to practice in today's world.

Nevertheless, in government there is something called the "basic outline" [*daitai*]. When one fails to take the ancient Way as one's root, one will be unable to understand the basic outline of government. This basic out-

---

74 From the "Wu cheng" ("Completion of the War") section of the *Classic of Documents*: "He only had to fold his arms and let his robes hang down, and the realm was well governed."
75 From the "Zhonghui zhi gao" ("Announcement of Zhonghui") section of the *Classic of Documents*: "With rightness govern affairs, with ritual govern your heart, and bequeath abundance to later generations."
76 From the "Zhou guan" ("Officers of Zhou") section of the *Classic of Documents*.
77 From the "Yue ming xia" ("Charge to Yue, Part III") section of the *Classic of Documents*.

line does not differ between other countries and our own or between past and present, so one should always take the past as one's teacher. This can be compared to a doctor treating an illness. In medicine there are ancient methods.[78] Although the ancient methods are not necessarily applicable to each particular illness that people face today, when people try to seek out methods of treatment without relying on the ancient methods, this is like grasping at empty air with nothing for the hands to hold on to. Doctors have ancient methods in the same way that master carpenters have compasses and squares. Compasses are used to make circles and squares are used to make right angles. Even the artisan Chui and Lu Ban would not be able to make circles and right angles without using compasses and squares.[79] This idea can be seen in the words of Mencius.[80] The governance of the state does not differ from this in the least. To say that the ancient Way is not appropriate for the present is like doctors not believing in ancient methods, or master carpenters discarding compasses and squares. If one simply exerts oneself according to what one feels in one's heart, one will not be able to successfully accomplish things. That being said, to be mired in the past and unaware of the changes in the present is like, as the saying goes, "playing a zither with the bridge glued in place."[81]

When one practices the ancient Way in its original state in the present, there will be things that one can do, but there will also sometimes be things that one dares not do, out of fear that they would startle people or cause disruptions. This is due to a lack of discernment and ability.

---

78 In the Tokugawa period, the Kohōha (School of Ancient Methods) was a movement in Chinese medicine that emphasized the teachings of certain famous ancient doctors, as opposed to more recent medical theories based on metaphysical doctrines. This emphasis on historical teachings parallels how Shundai and others like him sought the Confucian Way in the historical reality of ancient China, rejecting efforts to define the Way through metaphysical speculation.

79 The artisan Chui was minister of works under Shun (see volume 1 n. 67 above). Lu Ban is another name for Gongshu Ban, a famous carpenter and inventor said to have lived in the country of Lu at the time of Confucius.

80 *Mencius* 4.1.1.1: "Mencius said, 'The clear vision of Li Lou and the skill of Gongshu, without making use of a compass and square, would not be able to make circles and right angles.'" Li Lou was a figure from Chinese antiquity famous for his acute vision.

81 Normally the bridge can be moved to adjust the pitch of the string, so gluing it in place forces the musician always to play in the same way. The expression comes from the biography of Lin Xiangru in chapter 81 of the *Records of the Grand Historian*. Lin Xiangru, protesting the appointment of Zhao Kuo as general, says to the King of Zhao, "For the King to appoint Zhao Kuo is like playing a zither with the bridge glued in place. He only knows how to read the texts transmitted from his father, but does not know how to meet changing situations."

1 A General Discussion of Political Economy

If one has discernment and ability, is versed in principle and familiar with human feelings, occupies a position of rank, and takes on the authority to reward and punish, then one ought to act with single-minded purpose. Why should one be driven to indecision by concern about the suspicions of ignorant people? Ever since ancient times, people praised as heroic and exceptional have all been able to do what I have described. It is in this regard that people value the determination and decisiveness of the gentleman. For this reason, one should entrust the governance of the country to people who have the virtue of the gentleman and the mettle of the hero.

In the above I have discussed the general outline of political economy. Not only are the elements of government detailed in the eight "Treatises" of the *Records of the Grand Historian*, the ten "Records" of the *History of the Former Han*, and the "Records" of the histories of other dynasties, there are also many other books that record matters relating to the management of the country. Our country does not have the kind of detailed records of ancient times that exist in China, but fragments of such records are scattered here and there in various texts and there are also things that have been passed down orally, so one can get a general picture of what existed. In affairs of government there is the root and there are the branches. When one establishes the root, the branches will be easy to govern. In the *Great Learning* it says, "It is never the case that when the root is disordered, the branches are well governed."[82] Establishing the root is the foremost task of political economy. In what follows, I now humbly put forth my own views, based on the ancient Way, to provide a point-by-point discussion of the essentials of the task of government.

---

82 *Great Learning*, "The Text of Confucius," paragraph 7.

Volume 2

Ritual and Music

Ritual consists of the etiquette and ceremonies used for various affairs; what are known as "ritual methods" and "ritual forms" are examples of this. Music consists of song, dance, and instruments. In the Way of administering the realm there is nothing that comes before ritual and music, so when the illustrious kings of the Three Dynasties took control of the realm, they always began by regulating ritual and creating music; they did this because without ritual and music it is impossible to govern the realm.

Ritual always exists together with music, and music always exists together with ritual; the two cannot be separated. Ritual is strict, whereas music is gentle. With ritual one establishes the ranks of the high and low, distinguishes the noble from the base, clarifies the distinction between men and women, and rectifies the ethical relationships [*rin*] between fathers and sons and between elder and younger brothers. With music one brings together the high and the low, puts the feelings of rulers and subjects in accord, matches the tastes of guests and hosts, and guides harmony between deities [*kami*] and humans. It is only ritual and music that, with no need for speech, allow people to transmit their feelings to others; for this reason, they are referred to as "wordless teachings."

From the end of the Zhou dynasty, ritual and music collapsed and were no longer practiced. After the Warring States period, they ultimately died out during the reign of Qin Shi Huang. When Shusun Tong [d. c. 188 BC] first created court ceremonies during the reign of Emperor Gaozu [256–195 BC, r. 202–195 BC] of the Han dynasty, Gaozu greatly rejoiced, saying that on that day he first understood what an exalted thing it is to be emperor.¹ After that the Way of ritual and music gradually came to flourish and the cultural products of that age became exemplary forms for many subsequent ages. When the kings who came after that took command of the realm, inaugurated the task of governing, and established a dynastic lineage, they never failed to create ritual and music. Although in the Han dynasty and later they did not reach the level of the ritual and music of the Three Dynasties, they never tried to do away with these in governing the realm.

In the ancient times of our own country, when the court nobles were at their height, they learned the ritual and music of the Tang court and used these at their own court. After the advent of the age of warriors, though, ritual and music collapsed and were no longer used. In the Muromachi period, the forms of behavior regulated by such houses as the Soga were used as ritual and *sarugaku* was used as music.² These have been used in court ceremonies down to the present, too. However, even though the court nobles have now suffered extreme decline, they still use the ritual and music of old, rather than vulgar ritual [*zokurei*] or vulgar music [*zokugaku*]. The reason people today, even the wretched and lowly, never fail to have their feelings aroused upon viewing the ceremonies of the court nobles is that these contain ritual and music.

Such things as the Buddhist law are teachings for beyond this world and as such exist at a remove from the formalities of humans. On the occasions when one practices the Buddhist law, though, there are always ceremonial forms proper to these occasions, which are accompanied by the playing of instruments and the chanting of Buddhist hymns. Ceremonial forms are ritual, instruments are music, and Buddhist chants are song. The reason people never fail to have their feelings aroused upon viewing the Buddhist rites performed by monks is, again, that these contain ritual and music.

Nothing arouses the human heart more vividly than ritual and music, and nothing is more immediate than ritual and music for guiding the people toward the good. Teachings expressed in language enter people

---

1   Shusun Tong was a ritual specialist at the Qin and early Former Han dynasty courts. This statement by Gaozu appears in the biographies of Shusun Tong in chapter 99 of the *Records of the Grand Historian* and volume 43 of the *History of the Former Han.*
2   The Soga and Ogasawara were both warrior clans that developed codes of etiquette. These began as codes specifically for the warrior class, but later gained broader influence. *Sarugaku* (lit. "monkey music") was a form of popular theater accompanied by music, which eventually developed into the noh theater under shogunal patronage.

on a shallow level, are effective within a narrow range, and achieve things slowly, but teachings of ritual and music enter people on a deep level, have a broad range of effectiveness, and achieve results extremely quickly. It is ritual and music that the ancient sages used to instruct the people without saying a word and to unite the hearts of the realm. There are those who say that ritual and music are the Way of ancient times, but that in the present day one should not govern with them; such people, however, do not understand the Way of governing. Although there is a difference between past and present when it comes to the times, human feelings and the principles of things are largely the same in both past and present. As long as people exist within heaven and earth, there certainly ought not be any age or country in which ritual and music are not practiced. To govern the state without ritual and music, instead using only laws and edicts, is the Way of such people as Shen Buhai, Hanfeizi, Shang Yang, and Li Si.[3] It quickly achieves results in the immediate present, so one may find it convenient, but it is not a viable plan for long-lasting tranquility. For this reason, one should find a cautionary lesson in observing that when government has been practiced without ritual and music in the past, it has led straight toward things falling apart and descending into chaos.

There are five types of rituals: auspicious, inauspicious, military, hosting, and congratulatory. Auspicious rituals are rituals for religious celebrations; they are ceremonies that celebrate heaven and earth, mountains and rivers, the deities of soil and grain, and the ancestors of rulers. Inauspicious rituals are funeral rituals; they are rituals that send off the dead. Military rituals are rituals for the army; in times of peace the ruler uses the army for hunting throughout the four seasons, but in times when conflict arises and he raises soldiers, the ceremonies used when dispatching forces, subjugating rebels, waging warfare, making announcements of victory, presenting the severed ears of slain enemies, leading troops into battle, bringing troops back in an orderly manner, toasting victory before the ancestral temple, and recognizing meritorious service are all examples of military rituals. Hosting rituals are the rituals performed by a host when receiving visitors; they include such ceremonies as those for emissaries and audiences at court. Congratulatory rituals are those for such things as coming of age, marriage, interviews, drinking, archery, banquets, and feasts. The capping ritual is the ceremony that males undergo when they come of age. The marriage ritual is the ceremony of taking a

---

3 These are all representatives of the philosophy of Legalism in ancient China.

woman as one's wife. The interviewing ritual is the ceremony with which officials meet each other. The drinking ritual is used when drinking in the country districts; it is the ceremony for giving a drink to people of these areas. The archery ritual is the ceremony for shooting with a bow. The banquet ritual is the ceremony for holding drinking parties for high officers. In the feasting ritual one entertains guests with delicacies; it is the ceremony for treating people to a meal and showing them hospitality. The myriad affairs of humans all need their respective ceremonies. This is true even of minor affairs, and it is all the more indispensable to have ceremonies when it comes to crucial affairs of the realm and state. The affairs of the realm are all contained without exception within these five types of rituals.

Ritual is something that regulates the mean [*chū*], according with human feelings and conforming to the principles of things. The ancient sages with their brilliance and wisdom were versed in human feelings and clarified the principles of things, put in place etiquette and ceremonies for all affairs, and upheld these together with the people of the realm. This is the Way of the mean, so it remains without flaws to the end of countless ages, providing a fixed and unchanging method just like a carpenter's compass, square, level, and line.[4] Because of this, it is called an unchanging and constant standard.

As for the statement about according with human feelings and conforming to the principles of things, the five types of rituals I have described above are all indispensable in the context of both human feelings and the principles of things. Nevertheless, in human feelings there are the strong and the weak as well as the profound and the shallow. The principles of things are difficult for ordinary people to know, so since long ago it has been the case that unless conventions and ceremonies are put in place, people's hearts will be as different as their faces when discussing various situations and affairs.[5] This makes it difficult to reach agreement. Even when agreement is reached, there are things in excess and things that are lacking, so it does not match the Way of the mean. For this reason, it is impossible to avoid harm when putting such a decision into practice.

4　This phrase derives from *Mencius*: "When the sages had exhausted the power of their eyes, they followed this with the compass, square, level, and line in order to make things square, round, level, and straight" (4.1.1.5).
5　From the Duke Xiang, Year 31 section of the *Zuo Commentary*: "People's hearts are different, just like their faces."

The sages established conventional methods by pondering the past, understanding the future, and gauging what would be possible to practice seamlessly for many later generations. The statement that people's hearts are different refers, for example, to how in their performance of any particular affair there are people who are fond of luxury and people who are fond of frugality. When people follow the rituals of the ancient kings, then even those who are fond of luxury will be unable to do things in a showy manner, and even those who are fond of frugality will be unable to do things with rustic simplicity. This is the Way of the mean. The statement that in human feelings there are the strong and the weak as well as the profound and the shallow refers, for example, to how there are those who when mourning a parent do not stop grieving after three years, but also those who stop grieving before three years have passed; the former is an instance of human feelings being profound and strong, and the latter one of these feelings being shallow and weak. When one follows the rituals of the ancient kings, then even those whose grief goes on will stop wearing mourning clothes after three years, and even those whose grief has run its course wait for three years before they stop wearing mourning clothes. This is the Way of the mean.

People tend to seek out what is convenient for them, so if kings had not long ago established ritual methods, then the people of the realm would all do things simply by considering what is convenient for them personally, causing the realm to go out of balance. As a matter of course, it would come to be that the wealthy neglect the poor, the lofty lord it over the lowly, and the strong tyrannize the weak. This would give rise to conflict, which would ultimately be a stage in the descent into civil unrest. Ritual has its basis in deference, so when ritual is practiced, then conflict will come to a stop. As a general rule, each affair has its proper measure; this is the mean, in which there is neither excess nor deficiency. Each person's heart is different in how it relates to this proper measure, so if people do not take the rituals of the ancient kings as their compass and square, then they will not hit the true mean. People's inborn natures [*sei*] are various, so there will always be those who exceed the proper measure as well as those who do not reach it. When people follow ritual methods, though, then those who have an inborn nature that inclines them to exceed the proper measure will hold back and stop at it, while those who have an inborn nature that inclines them not to reach the proper measure will make efforts to reach it. For this reason, the Way of the mean is not something that is established by people of the present day with their own individual hearts. Rather, one achieves the mean through the rituals of the ancient kings. Scholars of today err greatly when, relying on the theories of Song Confucians, they try to establish the mean by using their own individual hearts. They commit the great transgression of considering themselves to be sages.

Moreover, when one issues an order from above commanding that something be done in a particular way, then even though this command may be upheld temporarily, the people will go on to surreptitiously violate it if it is the least bit inconvenient to them personally. However, when one uses ritual to teach in advance that something is to be carried out in a certain way, then the people will think within their hearts that they need to do it this way, so they will perform it in accordance with this teaching without even knowing the reason behind it. In today's world, there are many baseless vulgar rituals among both officials and the common people. The reason that even ignorant women diligently uphold these is that they have been taught to do so. The same is true when it comes to authentic rituals. Even when it comes to the performance of such matters as reverence and frugality, it is difficult to get the people to follow if one merely issues strict ordinances, without setting up ritual forms. Ritual is something to be upheld by the ruler and the people together. Even if one establishes rituals, if they are not practiced by everyone from the ruler on down, then the people will fail to follow them. It is the essential meaning of ritual that it be upheld and practiced together with the people. In recent ages the ancient rituals of our country have been abandoned, and in their place such houses as the Soga and Ogasawara make use of something called "forms of behavior." These are exceedingly vulgar rituals and not something that ought to be used by people of the court.

Flourishing and decline in the world are tied to the customs of the people. When customs are exalted the country will flourish, and when customs are base the country will decline. It is ritual that preserves customs; it prevents licentiousness and proscribes excess desire. The breakdown of customs begins with licentiousness in the desires of the people. When there is ritual in a country, then the desires of people cannot run unchecked, so customs do not lose their foundation and do not descend into indecency. When customs are correct, the state will prosper; this is how ritual serves as protector of the state. How is this not to be prized?

Even though the establishment of rituals is an affair of the sages, rituals are created based on rightness [*gi*]. If one has virtue and rank and establishes rituals by pondering the past, why should this not be permissible?

Confucius said, "Ritual is the realization of rightness. If one arrives at it by bringing together various examples of rightness, then even though a ritual may not have existed among the ancient kings, it may be adopted based on its rightness."[6] If one is truly conversant in human feelings, clarifies the principles of things, thoroughly investigates the fundamentals of ritual and rightness, and understands the business of the present day, then even when faced with something that has not existed in past or present, one will be able to handle it using rightness. This is all the more true when the human affairs of the present day contain nothing that did not exist in the past.

On the level of the individual, ritual is a fortifying of the body. When one straightens one's clothing and cap, fastens one's belt, and reverently carries out a ritual with one's movements, then one's skin will tighten, one's sinews and bones will harden, and one's feelings too will become correct. Because of this, wind, cold, heat, and dampness will not be able to harm one externally and one's body will always be untroubled. When interacting with others, too, one will put reverence and deference first, so one will do nothing to arouse unlawfulness or strife and will not be disliked by others. If one abandons ritual even for a single day, then one will become sluggish and self-indulgent, one's skin will slacken, one's sinews and bones will grow soft, and one's feelings too will not be properly governed. Because of this, it will be easy to suffer external harm and one will be prone to illness. When interacting with others, one will lack reverence and deference, so one will clash with the hearts of others and always invite calamity. For this reason, ritual should be considered a talisman to protect the country and one's person. Ideas that neglect ritual and claim that there is some other technique for governing the state are all deviant theories and not the Way of the sages. One should certainly not believe them.

...

The relation between husband and wife is the beginning of human ethics [*jinrin*]. The marriage ritual is a ritual that regulates the Way of husband and wife, so the sages placed particular importance on it. In the ancient rituals of China, there were the six ceremonies of the proposal accompanied by a gift, the asking of the bride's name, the confirmation of the engagement after divination at the ancestral temple, the evidencing of the engagement through gifts to the bride's house, the request to fix a

---

6   From the "Li yun" ("Ritual Usages") chapter of the *Record of Ritual*.

2 Ritual and Music

date, and the receiving of the bride; these are called the "six rituals." The details of these can be seen in the "Shi hun li" ["Ritual of Marriage for a Scholar-Official"] chapter of the *Yi li* [*Book of Ceremonies and Rituals*].[7] The marriage rituals of Japan today are extremely vulgar, but their basis lies in the rituals of China. I think that these ceremonies should be practiced to some extent, not only of course by those of the status of scholar-officials, officers of state, and higher, but also by the common people. The marriage ritual is unique in preserving its original appellation, and on top of this people are inclined to preserve its methods, so for the time being it is surely most effective to employ these vulgar rituals. Right now I will not go into the specifics of what these are.

...

The ritual for drinking in the country districts is the ceremony for giving a drink to people of these areas. In ancient times, those who had the status of officer of state and governed over a single country district were called "officers of state of country districts."[8] They were similar to such people as the district magistrates of Japan. Once every three years they would gather together the people of their country district and hold a drinking party for them. This is referred to as "drinking in the country districts." The officer of state of the country district would act as host and treat the elders of the district as distinguished guests. Among the elders, one who had deep experience and was versed in ritual forms was designated as the guest of honor. The "guest of honor" is the highest-ranking guest. The others were designated as assembled guests. "Assembled guests" are what are commonly called "companions."

In country districts reverence is accorded to elders, so the order of seating was determined by people's ages. A person born even a single day earlier than another would be given precedence. During drinking parties, musicians would come to sing poems and perform music. Just because these were drinking parties, though, does not mean that their point was to force people to drink. From start to finish, emphasis was placed simply on bowing deferentially and comporting oneself properly, in keeping with the strict character of ceremonies. The essential meaning of this ritual

---

7 The *Book of Ceremonies and Rituals*, together with the *Record of Ritual* and *Zhou li* (*Rituals of Zhou*), was one of the three main texts on ritual in the Confucian tradition.
8 A "country district" (*xiang*) in ancient China was defined as an area containing 12,500 families.

is to clarify the proper distinction between elder and younger and to have people learn the rituals governing guest and host. When this ritual is practiced, then people will understand that they should take care of the aged and respect their elders. This leads naturally to the Way of filial piety and brotherly obedience. In teaching the people filial piety and brotherly obedience, the ancient kings did not teach by explaining things through language. Instead, they used ritual to bring about filial piety and brotherly obedience and display them. Because of this, those who witnessed these matters never failed to be moved to joy. This is an example of a "wordless teaching."

The common people are ignorant, so without the teachings provided by rulers they will not understand the Way of filial piety and brotherly obedience. When they do not understand the Way of filial piety and brotherly obedience, children and younger brothers will not listen to what their fathers and elder brothers say, nor will they follow their instructions. The lowly will commit violations against the lofty and inferiors will be contemptuous of their superiors. As a consequence, struggles for gain and other such evils arise, as well as many lawsuits. This becomes the root of civil unrest. When people understand the Way of filial piety and brotherly obedience, not only will they submit to their fathers and elder brothers within their household, they will also respect elders outside the household in the same manner as they do their own fathers and elder brothers. Harmonious calm will then prevail within the country districts and there will be no contrary behavior. This provides the foundation for the peaceful government of the state.

To explain this further, the ruler can be compared to a boat and the people to water. When the water is still, the boat will be calm; when the people are peaceful, the ruler will be at ease. When the water is made rough by wind and waves, it will always overturn the boat; when the people cause disturbances, these always become trouble for the ruler. This has been the case since ancient times. Is teaching the people filial piety and brotherly obedience, then, not a crucial task when governing a country? Mencius was correct to say that "the Way of Yao and Shun is simply filial piety and brotherly obedience."[9] When Confucius said, "Observing the country districts, I know the ease of the kingly Way,"[10] this refers to

---

9 *Mencius* 6.2.2.4.
10 From the "Xiang yin jiu yi" ("Meaning of Drinking Festivities in the Country Districts") chapter of the *Record of Ritual*.

2 Ritual and Music

him viewing the drinking ritual in the country districts and then recognizing how easily the kingly Way was practiced.

In addition, in ancient times wise and capable people were discovered among those of the country districts and presented to the ruler. This was called a "tributary offering of the country district" and was the responsibility of the officers of state of country districts. The wise and capable were discovered by putting them to the test at the archery rituals of country districts. Someone who had been put to the test and recommended to the ruler was called a "tributary scholar-official." Tributary scholar-officials were made guests of honor at drinking rituals in country districts, where their ritual comportment and demeanor would be observed further. This was done because human talent was prized. Drinking in the country districts is not a trivial matter, then, but is truly a great ritual of the country. The rituals of capping, marriage, funerals, and religious celebrations are, together with those of drinking in country districts and interviewing, called the "six rituals."[11] They are grouped together like this because they are rituals that are indispensable to the realm.

After the decline of the Zhou dynasty, the ritual of drinking in the country districts fell into disuse. In later times, those with a desire to recover the past have performed it privately from time to time. In our country this ritual never existed to begin with, so there is nothing to restore. Why would it not be possible, though, for those with a fondness for the past to create such a ritual and practice it? If this ritual carried on the idea behind the ancient ritual and resembled it even a little, it would surely be of use as a supplement to government teachings.

...

Music is by its nature something that comforts people. The glossing of "music" as "pleasure" comes from the fact that it is pleasurable to the human heart.[12] Since humans are living beings, they cannot stop being in motion, even for an instant. When their motion ceases even momentarily, a deviant heart arises and they commit wicked deeds. Whenever people successfully complete activities, they are put at ease. However, there are times when people have difficulty performing their normal activities and

---

11 This list of the "six rituals" appears in the "Kingly Regulations" chapter of the *Record of Ritual*.
12 "Music" and "pleasure" are written with the same Chinese character, although with different pronunciations.

become saddened, or when they encounter trouble with things and feel blocked. At such times, people vent their spirit by singing and releasing their voice, clear up their melancholy by playing string and wind instruments, and relieve their ennui. These are ordinary human feelings. When people gather at banquets, feasts, and the like, it is difficult for them to enjoy themselves to the fullest by passing their time simply eating and drinking, so they always use song, dance, and music to bring pleasure to guests and hosts, to cultivate intimacy, and to bind their good relations. This, too, is something necessitated by human feelings.

Music harmonizes the human heart. Ritual has its basis in strict respect, so when one upholds ritual, then the ethical relations of ruler and subject, father and son, husband and wife, elder and younger brothers, and friends will be severe and restrained and it will be easy to lose a sense of harmonious intimacy. Music has its basis in harmony, so through its use one harmonizes the relations of ruler and subject, father and son, husband and wife, elder and younger brothers, and friends. The reason that ancient ritual was always accompanied by music, then, was in order to guide people toward harmony, and the reason that music was always accompanied by ritual was in order to create a feeling of respect.

In addition, when entertaining esteemed guests in ancient times, people would sometimes perform an archery ritual and would sometimes play a drinking game called "tossing into the jar," in which people vied to toss arrows into a jar. Music was used in these cases, too, because of how it displays people's enjoyment. Music was also used to regulate rituals and formalities. When speaking of regulating rituals and formalities, "regulate" means to set the pace or rhythm. In performing major rituals, one uses music as a cue to match movement and speed to the desired tempo and to regulate the pace and rhythm of the ritual. For example, when monks carry out Buddhist rituals, they strike bells and drums as cues to advance and retreat or start and stop. For these kinds of reasons, music was always employed in major rituals.

People cannot get by without having something to comfort their hearts. There is nothing that compares to music when it comes to comforting the heart, dispelling melancholy, and exercising one's material force [*ki*]. Because of this, within all of heaven and earth, from the Middle Kingdom of China all the way to the myriad outlying countries, there is no country that lacks music. However, barbarian lands are unbalanced in their material force, so their human feelings are also distorted and the sounds of their music are often improper. In China, too, the music of the

2 Ritual and Music

countries of Zheng and Wei and the music that arises from the mulberry groves along the River Pu consist of licentious sounds.[13] It is only the refined music [*gagaku*] of the ancient kings that has sounds that emerge from the proper material force of heaven and earth and that possesses the true tones of centrality and harmony.[14]

Music is something that mysteriously moves the human heart, so when people listen to licentious music their hearts become dissipated and descend into debauchery, whereas when they listen to refined music their hearts become correct and accord with centrality and harmony; this is a mystery of nature. The *Xiao jing* [*Classic of Filial Piety*] states, "There is nothing better than music for shifting people's ways and changing their customs."[15] This shows that past and present are alike in how the practice of licentious music causes the customs of the people to deteriorate, and the practice of refined music causes the customs of the people to become correct. It is music that shifts and changes customs, so it is also music that preserves customs. For this reason, at the outset of establishing a state it is an essential task of the king to create refined music and have it practiced throughout society, and to prohibit licentious music and prevent it from being used among the people. It is with this meaning that Confucius said to "make your music the dances of Shao" and to "banish the sounds of Zheng" when explaining to Yan Yuan how to govern a country.[16]

After Confucian books were burned and Confucian scholars were executed in the Qin dynasty, the Way of ritual and music was cut off. In the

---

13 These are commonly cited in Confucian texts as examples of improper music. For example, the "Yue ji" ("Record of Music") chapter of the *Record of Ritual* states that "The tones of Zheng and Wei are tones of a chaotic age. These countries' condition is comparable to neglect. The tones that arise from the mulberry grove along the River Pu are tones of a dying country. Its government is dissipated and its people are unsettled. They slander their superiors, act selfishly, and cannot be stopped."

14 Here Shundai is using "refined music" (*gagaku*) as a descriptive term to refer to refined or proper music, which he sees as a creation of the sages, as opposed to vulgar or common music. In Japan, however, the term *gagaku* can also refer more specifically to the music developed at the imperial court from the Nara period onward. The meanings are ultimately connected, though, in that this music of the Japanese imperial court was thought to derive from the music created by the ancient Chinese sages.

15 From the "Guang yao dao" ("Amplification of the Essential Way") chapter of the *Classic of Filial Piety*.

16 Both of these quotations come from *Analects* 15.10: "Yan Yuan asked how to govern a state. The Master said, 'Act according to the seasons of Xia. Ride in the state carriage of Yin. Wear the ceremonial court caps of Zhou. Make your music the dances of Shao. Banish the sounds of Zheng, and distance yourself from clever talkers. The sounds of Zheng are licentious, and clever talkers are dangerous.'"

Han dynasty, though, an imperial edict was issued to scholars ordering them to investigate ancient books and resurrect the ancient Way.[17] From this time onward, ritual and music were revived. Although they did not attain the level of the Three Dynasties, from the Han dynasty onward rulers of each age always had ritual and music created when they presided over the realm. When there was ritual, there was always music as well. Rulers never failed to employ music when celebrating heaven and earth, the deities of soil and grain, and their ancestors. This is because in governing the realm, one cannot dispense with ritual and music. Although the music of the Han dynasty and later was not all ancient music, it was the music used at the temple of the ruler's ancestors and at court, so it was not something that can be grouped together with the licentious music of the common world.

In Japan, Prince Shōtoku [572–622] sought out the music of China, had many musicians learn it, and used it at court. Since then, it has been passed down to the present day. The reason one can say that the music that has been transmitted here in Japan is the music that existed in China from the Han to the Tang dynasty is that the *biwa* lute, *ōteki* transverse flute, *hichiriki* double-reed flute, *dōshō* end-blown flute, *shakuhachi* end-blown flute, *kakko* drum, and the like are all instruments from the Han dynasty and later.[18] However, among silk instruments there is the *kin* zither, and among gourd instruments there is the *shō* mouth organ;[19] these two are musical instruments from the most ancient times and have been passed down here in Japan. It is said that the *shitsu* zither was called the "mackerel-tail zither" in ancient times and was used in musical performances, but it has not been passed down. The *sō* zither is an instrument from the country of Qin and has been used since the Han dynasty. It is said that it derives from the *shitsu*; the *shitsu* had twenty-five strings,

---

17 Confucian learning was suppressed by Qin Shi Huang, the first emperor of the Qin dynasty. According to the traditional account in the *Records of the Grand Historian*, in 213 BC he ordered that Confucian texts be burned, and in 210 BC had more than 460 Confucian scholars buried alive. Confucianism was permitted again in the Han dynasty, and came to be promoted as the exclusive state philosophy under Emperor Wu of the Han.

18 These are all instruments used in the Japanese court music that traces its origins back to Shōtoku. For these and other instruments that have been used in both China and Japan, I use the Japanese names.

19 Chinese musical instruments were traditionally divided into eight categories based on their material of construction: silk, bamboo, wood, stone, metal, clay, gourd, and leather. "Silk" refers to the silk strings of the instruments in this category. Instruments in the "gourd" category are free-reed mouth organs with multiple bamboo pipes and a gourd wind chest.

2 Ritual and Music

which were divided in two to make the thirteen strings of the *sō*. This latter, too, is ancient. The *wagon* zither is said to be a musical instrument of our own country from the age of the gods.[20] When we look at it, though, its construction is similar to the *zhu* zither of China. China preserved the old music up until the Tang dynasty, but I have heard that from the Song dynasty its music changed greatly. The music of our country was received from people of the Tang dynasty, so it is said that, in contrast, it preserves much of the old music. The kind of music that has been passed down in our country, then, surely does not exist at all in China today. In addition, here in Japan there is the music of Koryŏ. Koryŏ is what is now Korea, but it is said that none of the music of Koryŏ survives there at all.

In China, each time the realm passes into new hands, they always establish rituals and create music. As a consequence, at some point these are transformed, with the old music dying out and new music taking its place. In our country, though, there was no such creation anew of music. In his time, Prince Shōtoku installed musicians and had them uphold music as their specialized occupation, so over the course of a thousand some years down to the present day it has not died out and has been transmitted intact. This is truly something to be prized. The playing of the *shitsu* zither can be seen portrayed in such works as the *Genji monogatari* [*Tale of Genji*]. One hears that in ancient times it was used quite widely, but at some point it stopped being played and today there are none who know it. The methods of the *biwa* lute, *sō* zither, and *wagon* zither have been passed down. The *shakuhachi* end-blown flute was beloved by Emperor Xuanzong [685–762, r. 712–756] of the Tang dynasty and in ancient times was used in refined music, but this instrument too was abandoned at some point, and the *shakuhachi* of today has now become an instrument of vulgar music. It is said that in the Hōryūji temple there is a *shakuhachi* that was played by Shōtoku.[21] Its length is 1 *shaku* and 8 *bu*, which is why it is called the *shakuhachi*, or "*shaku* and eight."[22] Today this is called the

---

20 The supposedly purely Japanese identity of this instrument is implied by its name; the *wa* of *wagon* means "Japan," and *gon* is an alternate reading of the character for *koto*, a type of zither.
21 Hōryūji is a Buddhist temple in Nara prefecture that dates from the early seventh century and is said to have been founded by Shōtoku.
22 The *shaku* and *bu* are units of measurement; the *shaku* is equivalent to roughly 30.3 cm, and the *bu* is one-hundredth of a *shaku*. The length of these instruments varies, but the traditional length given for the *shakuhachi* is actually 1 *shaku* and 8 *sun* (a *sun* is one-tenth of a *shaku*). It is unclear why Shundai gives the derivation of the name as he does, but the distinction is not relevant to his discussion.

hitoyogiri, since it is made up of one joint [*hitoyo*] of a bamboo stem.²³ The instrument played by *komusō* monks is today wrongly referred to as a *shakuhachi*.²⁴ What they play belongs to the category of the *dōshō* end-blown flute. It is made from three joints of bamboo, so it is also called the *miyogiri* [lit. "three joints"]. The *dōshō* was also originally an instrument of refined music and its methods were passed down within families of musicians. It still exists today, but there are none who play it.

Among the musical instruments of today, the *biwa* lute, *sō* zither, and *wagon* zither are called the "three string instruments"; the *shō* mouth organ, *hichiriki* double-reed flute, and *ōteki* transverse flute are called the "three wind instruments"; and the *kakko*, *taiko*, and *shōko* are called the "three drums." In ancient times, within the category of song there were *imayō* song and *rōei* chanting.²⁵ *Imayō* is a form of song from the vulgar common world; its lyrics are not rustic and crude, though, but are close to poetic refinement [*fūga*]. *Rōei* is the singing of the *Wakan rōei shū* [*Japanese and Chinese Poems to Sing*] of Major Counselor Fujiwara no Kintō [966–1041].²⁶ This was sometimes harmonized with musical instruments.

The same musical instruments were used by all, from the most exalted one down to the common people, so the common story has it that even the head courtesan of Yahagi performed these instruments.²⁷ When Taira no Shigehira [1158–1185] was taken captive and was being kept in

---

23 The term *hitoyogiri* is used today to refer to a separate type of end-blown flute distinct from both the original *shakuhachi* and the instrument known today (and in Shundai's day) as the *shakuhachi*. It dates from the Muromachi period.
24 The *komusō*, which translates as "monks of nothingness" or "monks of emptiness," were a group of mendicant monks of the Fuke sect of Zen Buddhism active during the Tokugawa period. They played a newer version of the *shakuhachi* (or at least what was called the *shakuhachi* – incorrectly, in Shundai's opinion) as part of their meditative practice and when begging for alms. They were also known for their distinctive head covering, a kind of wicker basket covering the entire head.
25 Both of these were popular among the Heian aristocracy. *Imayō*, or "modern-style" song, flourished mainly in the latter part of the Heian period, and among the forms of song and poetry of the aristocracy played the role of a kind of popular song. In *rōei*, Chinese or Japanese poems were chanted to a musical accompaniment.
26 *Japanese and Chinese Poems to Sing* is an anthology compiled by Kintō, comprising 588 poems in Chinese (by both Chinese and Japanese poets) and 216 poems in Japanese.
27 A reference to the *Jōruri monogatari* (*Tale of Jōruri*), which tells of how Jōruri, the head courtesan of Yahagi in Mikawa province, fell in love with the famous warrior Minamoto no Yoshitsune (1159–1189) when he passed through her village. In the story, he falls in love with her when he catches a glimpse of her playing music with her attendants. He then harmonizes with them on his flute. The story's authorship and exact date of composition are unclear, but the earliest mention of it appears in the late fifteenth century.

2 Ritual and Music

Kamakura, a dancing girl named Senju came and played the *sō* zither.[28] At that time, they played such pieces as "Goshōraku" ["Song of the Five Constant Virtues"], "Kaikotsu" ["Turn Abruptly"], and Ōjō.[29] There was no other kind of music then, so both lofty and lowly played this same refined music and comforted their hearts.

Only *shirabyōshi*, of which Taira no Kiyomori [1118–1181] was fond, consisted of song and dance performed by dancing girls and was a product of the common customs of our country.[30] When we examine the words of its songs, though, their meanings possess poetic refinement and they are not like the sung pieces of today. I hear that the *daigashira* dance of today derives from the ancient *shirabyōshi*, but that its sung pieces are not like those of the past.[31] From the latter part of the age of the Hōjō regents, there were such things as *sarugaku* theater and *dengaku* theater.[32] At this time they created forms of vulgar music that had not existed in ancient times. However, such things were the occupation of professional musicians; officials did not perform them. At that time, too, the only music that officials played was refined music. It is said that Nitta Yoshisada [1301–1338] played the flute, Ashikaga Takauji [1305–1358] played the *shō* mouth organ, Kusunoki Masashige [1294–1336] played the *biwa* lute, and that they all did so with great skill.[33]

---

28 Shigehira was a top commander of the Taira, one of two clans (the other was the Minamoto) involved in the Genpei War of 1180–1185. The episode referred to here is recounted in the "Senju no mae" ("Lady Senju") section of the *Heike monogatari* (*Tale of the Heike*), a literary work that tells the story of the Genpei War.
29 The titles listed here are names of *gagaku* pieces and all involve wordplay that references Shigehira's status as a condemned man. When written with different Chinese characters, "Goshōraku" ("Song of the Five Constant Virtues") can mean "happiness in the next life," "Kaikotsu" ("Turn Abruptly") can mean "circling the bones," and Ōjō (a title derived from a place name in China) can mean "passing on to the next life."
30 Kiyomori was the leader of the Taira clan at the outset of the Genpei War, a time when he served as the de facto political leader of Japan.
31 *Daigashira* was a form of recitative dance and was one school within the *kōwakamai* dance tradition (see Shundai's discussion of *kōwakamai* later in this section).
32 The "age of the Hōjō regents" is a reference to the Kamakura shogunate of 1185–1333; as noted above (vol. 1 n. 41), for much of this time the shoguns were controlled by regents from the Hōjō family. *Sarugaku* (lit. "monkey music") and *dengaku* (lit. "field music") were forms of theater accompanied by music that date from this period.
33 These three were all prominent military leaders. Ashikaga Takauji was the founder of the Ashikaga shogunate, which lasted from 1336 to 1573 (it was also known as the Muromachi shogunate, after the location of its palace).

From the end of the Muromachi shogunate, *sarugaku* theater began to flourish and was even used at banquets of the imperial court.[34] It ended up becoming the music of the military houses and has been practiced throughout the land for more than two hundred years. This *sarugaku* is the same type of thing as the jesters and variety theater of China. Its sounds are what the ancients referred to as the "rude sounds of the northern provinces" and are not the sounds of centrality and harmony.[35] Usually the human voice blends well with string and wind instruments, but the singing of *sarugaku* does not do this. The sounds of the flute in *sarugaku* do not match the proper scales, nor do they blend with string instruments. The shouts of the drummer resemble the screams of criminals. Music generally nourishes the spirit of centrality and harmony, but in *sarugaku* there are no sounds of centrality and harmony. There is only a racket like the shouting and screaming of people who are fighting and hitting each other, so those who enjoy this will surely damage their spirit of centrality and harmony without even realizing it.

There is also something called *kōwakamai* dance.[36] It is the creation of a person called Kōwaka.[37] It is not clear when it began, but it is said to be a recent development. Although it is called a "dance," it is not really a dance at all. Its performers tap their hand with a fan to keep the beat and sing stories about people of old. It is similar to the singing of *sarugaku* theater, and similarly does not conform to proper scales. It does not have the sounds of centrality and harmony, but rather consists of the "rude sounds of the northern provinces."

The tales of *biwa* priests consist of plucking the *biwa* lute and singing the *Heike monogatari* [*Tale of the Heike*].[38] It is said that it began when Yukinaga, the former governor of Shinano province, taught and sang it

---

34 *Sarugaku* gained shogunal patronage after a performance in 1374 of the troupe led by Kan'ami (1333–1384) before the shogun Ashikaga Yoshimitsu. Under shogunal patronage, it developed into what is now known as noh theater.
35 The contrast between "proper" music and the "sounds of the northern provinces" appears in the "Bian yue jie" ("Explanation of Discussions of Music") chapter of the *Kongzi jiayu* (*School Sayings of Confucius*).
36 *Kōwakamai* was a form of dance accompanied by storytelling popular among the warrior class during the Muromachi period.
37 The purported creator of *kōwakamai* (lit. "Kōwaka dance") is Momonoi Naoakira (dates unknown); his childhood name was Kōwakamaru ("-maru" is a standard suffix for male names, hence the shortening to Kōwaka).
38 *Biwa hōshi*, or "*biwa* priests," were blind traveling storytellers. The *Tale of the Heike*, which tells the story of the Genpei War of 1180–1185, came into being out of the storytelling traditions of these *biwa* priests.

2 Ritual and Music

to a blind man named Shōbutsu.[39] It is older than *sarugaku* theater. Its sounds, like those of *sarugaku*, lack the spirit of centrality and harmony, but in its gentleness it is superior to the singing of *sarugaku*.

As for *sekkyō* sermons, in ancient times among Buddhists there were those called "sermonizing priests."[40] *Sekkyō* sermons arose when they put together such things as stories about the origins of the bodhisattvas, appended them to recitations of the name of the Buddha, and sang them, and in doing so promoted the Buddhist Way among the common people. After that, they took moving and sad affairs of people of other countries and our own country in both the past and present, as well as biographies of illustrious priests, and used these to create stories that displayed the impermanence of the human world and encouraged people to achieve buddhahood. When we listen to their words today there is much that is coarse, but they possess things that are not present in the common customs of the world of today. Originally they kept the beat by playing the *shōko* drum, but today *sekkyō* has become the occupation of lowly professional musicians, who have come to harmonize the *shamisen* with it. *Sekkyō* sermons emphasize sorrow and value making people weep. Although they do not have licentious sounds, an excess of sorrowful sounds is the first step toward licentiousness.

Jōruri drama is roughly similar to *sekkyō* sermons. Its origins are not entirely clear. According to the common explanation, it arose in recent times when a woman by the name of Ono composed and sang an ancient tale in twelve parts about a girl named Jōruri, head courtesan in Yahagi in Mikawa province.[41] Subsequently, this piece was performed frequently and people came to create stories and sing songs about people of the past from other countries and our own. As for its melodies, in eastern and western Japan there were various melodies that were not uniform. It became the occupation of lowly professional musicians and blind people

---

39 This account of the origins of the *Tale of the Heike* appears in section 226 of the *Tsurezuregusa* (*Essays in Idleness*) of Yoshida Kenkō (c. 1283–c. 1352), but there is no other evidence for this theory. According to Kenkō, Yukinaga was active during the reign of Emperor Go-Toba (1180–1239, r. 1183–1198).
40 *Sekkyō* can be translated literally as "explaining sutras," and can refer simply to sermons on sutras. However, the term is also an abbreviation for *sekkyō jōruri* (or *sekkyōbushi*), a performance in which Buddhist sermons are accompanied by music. *Sekkyō jōruri* was popular in the early Tokugawa period.
41 A reference to the *Tale of Jōruri*; see vol. 2 n. 27. It was traditionally attributed to Ono Otsū (d. 1631), but because there are mentions of the story as early as the late fifteenth century, modern scholars do not accept this attribution.

On Political Economy

and was used in common society. At first, its practitioners created stories based on episodes of famous people from the past, so its words too had literary refinement [*bunga*]. Later, though, as it grew in popularity in common society, it came to include stories based on lowly people of recent times who became mired in lustful desires, committed licentious acts, and ruined their households or lost their lives.[42] Because of this, its words also came to be vulgar. Ancient *jōruri*, even while being coarse, caused little harm even when enjoyed among officials. The *jōruri* of today, though, is a pinnacle of indecency and has exceedingly licentious sounds, so it is not something that officials should amuse themselves with. When there is no prohibition on licentious sounds in a country, the common people will come up with various types of licentious music, which will lead hearts astray. Because of this, one sees in the "Wang zhi" ["Kingly Regulations"] chapter of the *Li ji* [*Record of Ritual*] that in the government of the sages, they put to death those who created licentious sounds.[43]

The sung pieces of the common world are all licentious sounds, too, but in ancient times their words were close to literary refinement. Recently, though, they have reached a pinnacle of coarseness and indecency, to the extent that they make those who hear them cover their ears. The *sō* zither was originally used only for refined music, but recently people have created a separate genre of tune that is not refined music and that accords with the ordinary songs of the common world. Because it is said that this originated among the people of Tsukushi, it is called the Tsukushi *sō*. Its origin lies in modifying the *gagaku* piece "Etenraku" ["Music from Heaven"] and now there are various sung pieces for it.[44] Although it is not refined music, it has few licentious sounds.

---

42 A reference to the genre of "love suicide" plays, the typical plot of which involves a merchant-class man who falls in love with a prostitute, and as a result is no longer able to carry out his proper obligations to his family and its business. Unable to both be with his beloved and fulfill his familial obligations, he commits a double suicide with the prostitute so that they can be together in the next life. As Shundai describes, these plays were based on actual contemporary events.

43 From the "Kingly Regulations" chapter of the *Record of Ritual*: "Those who created licentious sounds, unusual garments, strange techniques, and strange implements, thus causing doubts among the multitudes, were put to death."

44 "Etenraku" ("Music from Heaven") is a famous *gagaku* piece. As discussed above in vol. 2 n. 14, *gagaku* literally means "refined music," but can also refer more specifically to the music developed at the Japanese imperial court; when it is this latter aspect of the term that is being emphasized, I leave it in the original Japanese.

2 Ritual and Music

The *shamisen* and *kokyū* fiddle are the main instruments of vulgar music.[45] It is said that these two instruments both came over from Ryukyu during the current age. In Ryukyu they were used in refined music, but here they are only used in vulgar music. The *shamisen* is similar to the instrument in China called the *huqin* fiddle.[46] The *kokyū* is said to be of the same type as the *kugo* harp.[47] The sounds of the *kokyū* appear crude, but in fact it has aspects that are close to refinement [*ga*]. The sounds of the *shamisen* are extremely licentious. When these sounds are released, even a little, the way they quickly arouse a licentious heart in people is beyond compare with other instruments. Although its shape is similar to the *biwa* lute, the *biwa* is plucked in a drawn-out manner, whereas the *shamisen* is plucked extremely rapidly and accords with the human voice in a way that other instruments do not attain.[48] For this reason it gives people great pleasure and becomes deeply entrenched in the preferences of the common world. The *sekkyō* sermons and *jōruri* drama that I discussed above, as well as all other sung pieces of the common world, do not harmonize with the *shamisen*, so they are not able to exhaust the beauty of its sounds.[49] As a rule, vulgar and licentious music is busy, its notes many and short. This busyness reaches its extreme with the *shamisen*. Because of this, it has come to be excessive in the pleasure it gives to the ears and the joy it gives to the hearts of people of the common world. At first it was something played by blind musicians and the lowly, but now even lofty people

45 The *shamisen* is a three-stringed instrument plucked with a plectrum that resembles a banjo somewhat. The *kokyū* is similar in appearance to the *shamisen*, with a long neck extending from a sound box and (usually) three strings, but unlike the *shamisen*, the *kokyū* is played upright and with a bow.
46 The *huqin* is a family of Chinese stringed instruments that, like the *shamisen*, have a sound box and a long neck. Unlike the *shamisen*, which is plucked, the *huqin* is bowed. The type of *huqin* that is probably best known today is the *erhu*. The *kokyū* can be considered a Japanese version of the *huqin*.
47 The *kugo* harp (also known as the *kudaragoto*) is an instrument with origins in China that was used in Japan during the Nara period for certain performances of *Tōgaku* ("Tang music"), which, as the name suggests, was a type of *gagaku* explicitly modeled on the music of Tang dynasty China.
48 Although on the one hand Shundai sees musical sounds as imitating the human voice, he also sees the refined music of the sages as providing a normative structure to sound that is lacking in the spontaneous human voice. In saying that the *shamisen* accords with the human voice, then, he is portraying the *shamisen* as lacking the proper structure of the music of the sages and as descending into a chaotic state of instinct and nature.
49 *Sekkyō* and *jōruri* both used a *shamisen* accompaniment. What Shundai is saying is that these musical genres do not bring out the potential beauty of the *shamisen* (see the following paragraph for his comments about the *shamisen*, despite its licentious usage, not being in and of itself necessarily a licentious instrument).

learn it. This is to say nothing of the many among the ordinary populace who are versed in this art. Even the *shamisen* and *kokyū* fiddle would surely become refined music were one to correct their tunes and use them in *gagaku*, but because they are only used in licentious music with vulgar tunes, they have come to have completely vulgar sounds. Similarly, if one uses instruments like the *sō* zither and *shakuhachi* end-blown flute in vulgar music, they produce licentious sounds. Licentious sounds, then, are not the fault of the instrument itself, but rather of the one who plays it.

Music has its basis in the human voice. When the human voice is correct, the sounds of musical instruments will also be correct. When the human voice is licentious, the sounds of musical instruments will also be licentious. This is because music is always performed by harmonizing with song. Therefore, when it comes to prohibiting licentious music, so long as one does not prohibit licentious sounds in the songs of the common people, there will be no stop to licentious music. The songs of the common people do not speak of proper things, but only sing of lewd and obscene affairs, so both scholar-officials and the common people are accustomed to hearing these from childhood and people's hearts all grow wanton and debauched.

In addition, what in China are called "jesters" are the same as the masters of *kyōgen* comic theater in our own country.[50] What in China is called "variety theater" is the same as the mimicry performances within the kabuki drama of our own country. In China, jesters and performers of variety theater were ordered to always perform stories about such things as the people of old, filial piety, and loyal retainers, and were not permitted to perform stories about indecent and illicit matters. This is because it was feared that such things would corrupt the customs of the people. The kabuki and *kyōgen* of our country today, in seeking to conform to the vulgar conditions of the present, create things based on the lewdness and wantonness existing among the common people of today, so they teach licentiousness to all people. There is nothing that exceeds this in corrupting the customs of the people. This is all the consequence of licentious music.

The degeneration of customs is an affliction of the state, so the harm that licentious music brings to government is truly immense. In ancient times, refined music spread throughout society and even the common people took pleasure in it; this was because there was no separate vulgar

---

50 *Kyōgen* is a form of comic theater traditionally performed in the intermissions between noh plays, which were presented as a program of five plays over the course of a day.

2 Ritual and Music

music that emerged from below. In later times, various types of vulgar music emerged from below and pleased people's ears and eyes, so these people simply enjoyed that this music was close to the vulgar conditions of their own time and thus found it compelling. They came to find refined music less compelling than vulgar music, so it was cast aside.

Sarugaku theater is coarse, but it merely has rude sounds and does not conform to the proper tones of musical instruments; it does not have truly licentious sounds, so it does not arouse a licentious heart in people. Other forms of vulgar music consist entirely of licentious sounds, so they do arouse such a licentious heart. The reason they give pleasure to people's hearts is also on account of their licentious sounds. Even among vulgar music and licentious sounds, there are changes from past to present. The sung pieces of ancient times, even when speaking of licentious matters, used the refined language of our country, so they were composed with gentle language. In later times, though, styles gradually changed and grew coarse and obscene, so there were many things of the sort that would be intolerable to hear in the company of family. This is a decline in customs. This sort of thing will always happen if the state does not make use of refined music and prohibit licentious music.

The statement "hearing his music, we know the character of his virtue"[51] refers to the way that music emerges from virtue, so that in ancient times people knew the good and bad qualities of others by observing music. Vulgar music is produced among the common people, so it allows one to know the good and bad qualities of those common people who produced it. It is a mystery of nature that, just as vulgar music corrupts customs, customs will always become correct when refined music is practiced in the world. The statement "there is nothing that compares to music when it comes to shifting customs"[52] refers to the power of refined music to shift things from deviant to correct and the power of vulgar music to shift things from correct to deviant. The reason the ancient sages created music and comforted people's hearts with it was in order to preserve customs and ensure that they would never change. In putting music side by side with ritual and making these the basis of the governmental matters of the state, they truly showed deep foresight.

---

51 From *Mencius* 2.1.2.27.
52 This is a paraphrase of a passage that Shundai cited earlier from the "Amplification of the Essential Way" chapter of the *Classic of Filial Piety*: "There is nothing better than music for shifting people's ways and changing their customs."

The military methods of Sunzi and Wu Qi,[53] the non-action of Laozi and Zhuangzi,[54] the punishments of Shen Buhai and Hanfeizi, the legal techniques of Shang Yang and Li Si, and the other Ways of the various philosophers and Hundred Schools are focused on governing the realm and state, so when one uses their Ways well, then no matter which of them one uses, one will not fail to govern the realm.[55] However, because they all dispense with ritual and music, they only go as far as achieving a temporary tranquility, but are completely unable to establish a lasting transformation to peaceful government. The Way of the Two Emperors, Three Kings, and sages uses ritual and music to endlessly preserve great peace.[56] This is absent in the various philosophers and Hundred Schools. Therefore, if rulers of later ages strive to emulate the government of the ancient kings, they must necessarily promote ritual and music.

In our country of Japan, the ancient music has fortunately been passed down, so if one uses it at court and also practices it among the common people, it will surely achieve permanent results. That being said, the vulgar music that has been practiced in recent times, including such things as jesters and dancing girls, is ultimately difficult to ban, so one should set up regulations for it. *Sekkyō* sermons and *jōruri* drama should only be composed based on the filial piety, brotherly obedience, loyalty, and faithfulness of the ancients, and should not speak of lewd and obscene affairs of the present day. Kabuki and *kyōgen* theater as well should not create the kinds of things that damage the Way of human ethics. With the songs of villages and the streets, too, coarse and obscene things should be prohibited. If in this way the defenses against the licentiousness of the common people are fortified, then customs will also surely return to honest simplicity, providing a lasting foundation for the state. This is the teaching of the ancient kings on ritual and music.

---

53 Sunzi and Wu Qi were both famous military strategists.
54 Laozi and Zhuangzi were the most important philosophers of Daoism.
55 The phrase "various philosophers and Hundred Schools" refers to the philosophies that proliferated in China during the late Zhou dynasty (primarily during the time known as the Warring States period, beginning in the fifth century BC and ending with the unification of China under the Qin dynasty in 221 BC).
56 The "Way of the Two Emperors, Three Kings, and sages" is a reference to the Confucian Way. The "Two Emperors and Three Kings" are the emperors Yao and Shun and kings Yu (Shun's successor and founder of the Xia dynasty), Tang (founder of the Shang dynasty), and Wen (posthumously designated as founder of the Zhou dynasty). It is one of a number of commonly given lists of idealized rulers from ancient China.

Volume 3

Bureaucratic Offices

In governing the realm and state, priority is given to establishing the responsibilities of the hundred offices. "Offices," in the context of today's world, refers to the posts of governmental administrators. "Responsibilities" are the duties of officials; a certain office has the task of handling certain affairs, which constitute its "occupation." Officials have ranks; these are called their "status." In today's world, one speaks of having a certain "standing" or a certain "place"; this is a status ranking. Within the realm there are myriad affairs of state, so from one day to the next there are various items of governmental business to handle. The ruler cannot take care of them all by himself, so he establishes the hundred offices and has each of them handle its particular task. Although these are called the "hundred offices," their number is not necessarily a hundred; the term "hundred offices" is simply used to indicate that their number is many.

When in the *Classic of Documents* it says that "Yao and Shun, after contemplating the past, established offices that were a hundred in number,"[1] this shows that establishing officials in order to govern the realm is something that had been done since the most remote antiquity, even before Yao and Shun, which is why they established the hundred offices, reflecting on that antiquity. The age of Yao and Shun was still very early and there was little for the government to do, so they governed with a hundred offices. In the course of the Xia and Yin dynasties, the government had more and

---

[1] From the "Officers of Zhou" section of the *Classic of Documents*.

On Political Economy

more to do, so by the time of the Zhou dynasty there were 360 offices. The Duke of Zhou, acting as prime minister of King Cheng, established the positions of the three excellencies, six ministers, and the various offices beneath these, divided up their duties, and put in place methods for their functioning; this is described in the *Zhou li* [*Rituals of Zhou*].[2]

The three excellencies comprise the grand instructor, grand tutor, and grand guardian. These positions do not have fixed duties; rather, they are similar to a person's instructor or a small child's wet nurse or guardian. Morning and evening they simply attend on their lord, aiding him in virtuous action, discussing the Way of governing with him, warding off impropriety, and cautioning against debauchery. Taking these three excellencies as his instructors, the ruler hears of the proper path, clarifies virtue, and remedies transgressions. For this reason, he makes their status of the first rank and gives them an exalted position among the officials. The ruler is very particular when it comes to selecting the three excellencies, so these three positions are not always all filled. If there is no appropriate person for a position, then it is left open. The three excellencies are not chosen separately from the six ministers, but rather are promoted from among them while they retain their prior position as one of the six ministers. Next after the three excellencies are the three solitaries. These comprise the junior instructor, junior tutor, and junior guardian. The three solitaries, too, have no fixed duties, but rather accompany the three excellencies in assisting the ruler. The crown prince also always has his own three excellencies and three solitaries who aid him. However, the three excellencies of the crown prince are slightly lower in rank than those of the ruler. Both rulers and crown princes in ancient times took these three excellencies as their instructors and accorded them special respect. Every day they summoned them into their presence, sat them down, and listened to what they recounted of matters of the past and present, so as a matter of course these rulers and crown princes broadened the range of what they saw and heard and also were distanced from lewd and wanton affairs.

With the system of the six ministers, the myriad governmental matters of the realm are divided into six parts and each of these is entrusted to

---

[2] The *Rituals of Zhou*, together with the *Record of Ritual* and *Book of Ceremonies and Rituals*, is one of the three main ritual texts in the Confucian tradition. The *Rituals of Zhou* was traditionally attributed to the Duke of Zhou, although modern scholars tend to see it as dating from the end of the Zhou dynasty.

3 Bureaucratic Offices

one of six different people. Because of this, there is no affair of the realm that falls outside the purviews of these six people. These are called the "six offices" and are arranged to correspond to heaven and earth and the four seasons. The office of heaven is called the "peak councilor"; "peak" means "grand," so it is also called the "grand councilor." The office of earth is the chief of revenue. The spring office is the chief of ceremonies. The summer office is the chief of war. The autumn office is the chief of crime. The winter office is the chief of works. These six offices all have the rank of minister, so they are called the "six ministers." Among these positions of the six ministers, three are held concurrently with the positions of the three excellencies.

...

The age of Yao and Shun was a time when the world was still unsophisticated, so things were governed effectively with offices and their occupations also being simple and few. The details of the offices and occupations of the Xia and Yin dynasties are not known. Those of the Zhou dynasty are recorded in great detail, as described earlier, in the *Rituals of Zhou*. Even within the *Rituals of Zhou*, though, when it comes to the position of the winter office, who is the chief of works, the text has gaps and there is no way to know how to fill these in. In the Zhou dynasty, the countries of the feudal lords took after the system of the son of heaven. Both large and small countries set up their own offices and occupations and used these to govern; this can be seen in the *Chunqiu* [*Spring and Autumn Annals*] and various other texts.[3]

In the Qin dynasty, Qin Shi Huang unified the realm but then died only fifteen years later, so he did not have time to establish a new system of offices and occupations. As a consequence, this dynasty came to an end leaving things unchanged from the time of rule by feudal lords. In the Han dynasty, the world was peacefully governed and culture flourished, so it was a time when one would expect them to have ventured to establish the hundred offices. However, for the most part they instead carried over the system of offices from the Qin dynasty, from such high offices as the premier, the prime minister, the great military officers, the censors, and the great officers of state down to the lowest petty officials, and over

---

3   The *Spring and Autumn Annals* is a chronicle of the country of Lu that covers the period from 721 to 481 BC. It was traditionally attributed to Confucius and is one of the canonical Confucian Five Classics.

the course of the roughly four hundred years of the Han dynasty they ultimately did not establish a new system. The reason for this is that both rulers and subjects lacked a desire to pursue the ancient Way.

The Zhou dynasty and earlier was a feudal age, so the territory of the son of heaven was merely the royal domain, which extended over 1,000 *li*.[4] The area outside of that was divided up among major and minor feudal lords, so the feudal lords each governed their respective countries and were not subject to the government of the hundred officials of the son of heaven. The son of heaven was the august master of the realm, so the hundred officials of the son of heaven did not fail to know of the affairs of the realm. The area that was properly speaking the territory of the son of heaven was only the space within 1,000 *li* square, though, so these officials intervened very little.

In the Qin and Han dynasties and later there was a system of districts and prefectures, so the entire realm was a single country and all the land was the territory of the son of heaven. Because of this, the wealth of the son of heaven was more than ten times that of the rulers of the Three Dynasties and earlier. As a result, the son of heaven exceeded the rulers of ancient times in his haughtiness, and the construction of his walled city and palace too went beyond those of the past. Moreover, officials were installed in due order in the districts and prefectures of the realm, so the number of officials from the court down to the districts and prefectures was countless times that in the Zhou dynasty, and the system of offices and occupations differed greatly as well. The *History of the Former Han* says that in all the official posts, from subordinate officers up to the prime minister, there were 130,285 people. Is this not an immense number?

From the Han dynasty onward, there were changes in each successive age and the system of officials did not remain fixed. The realm continued to be governed as a system of districts and prefectures, though, so the offices and their occupations did not change much. There were times when the three excellencies were separate people from the six ministers, as well as times when they were not given separate titles but were simply included among the ranks of ministers with such titles as chief of revenue, chief of war, chief of works, and so on. There were also ages in which the positions of the six ministers were not arranged as they had been in

---

4 The royal domain was the area, centered on the capital, under the direct control of the son of heaven. The Zhou dynasty *li* was equal to roughly 405 meters, resulting in a royal domain of slightly over 400 kilometers measured from one end to the other.

3 Bureaucratic Offices

the Zhou dynasty; both their titles and their responsibilities changed in various ways and they were made into the "nine ministers." From the Tang dynasty onward, the six ministers were turned into the "six boards" with the establishment of the offices of the board of appointments, board of population, board of ritual, board of war, board of punishments, and board of works. These were created based on the six ministers of the Zhou dynasty, but the three excellencies and the prime minister were put in place above these, so the offices of the six boards were not as important as the six ministries of the Zhou. Also, from the Han dynasty onward, a prime minister was put in place above the six ministers or nine ministers and was charged with governing the realm. Although one would expect the prime minister to be a single person, there were ages in which the position was held by two people. In recent times, taking after the example of the ancient Zhou offices, presidents of the six boards were established; as with the six ministers of the Zhou, the myriad affairs were divided into six parts and given to these six people to be handled. They were granted status of the first rank and so were extremely lofty. The three excellencies were not made separate from them, but rather the grand instructor, grand tutor, and grand guardian were set up so that the three of them concurrently occupied three offices out of the six board presidencies. In the Ming dynasty, though, an office called the grand secretary was later placed above the six board presidents, and its officeholder became instructor and assistant to the son of heaven and was made responsible for handling the government of the realm. This is equivalent to the position of the prime minister. I hear that the Qing dynasty of the present day also has a system of officials that is more or less the same as that of the Ming.

China was from the beginning a country of the sages and of spirit-like brilliance. Because sages appeared there during the Three Dynasties and earlier, the offices and occupations of these times were all creations of the sages, despite the differences from dynasty to dynasty. In the Qin and Han dynasties and later, sages ceased to appear. People of later times set up offices and occupations based on their own particular inclinations and ideas, governing the world by following what was convenient at the time, so there were many things that differed from the methods of the ancient kings. However, these ultimately inherited the traces of the creations of the sages, so even in these later times there were bits here and there that preserved the form of the ancient system. Even when establishing offices and occupations in later times, then, it is difficult to do things appropriately without taking the ancient system as one's source.

On Political Economy

In the ancient times of Japan, before Empress Suiko [554–628, r. 592–628], there was no established system of offices and occupations. After Prince Shōtoku came to act as regent during the reign of Suiko, however, there arose ideas about offices and occupations.[5] After that, people in Japan gradually learned from the system of the Tang dynasty and the hundred offices were established at court.[6] In governing the various provinces, too, they emulated the system of districts and prefectures used in China at the time by not establishing feudal lords, but instead installing provincial governors and district prefects and having them carry out the government of these regions.[7]

At court, the grand minister of state, great minister of the left, and great minister of the right were called the "three excellencies." These three ministers did not have fixed duties. One among them, called the "chancellor," was in charge of the government of the realm. This corresponds to the position of prime minister in China. Below the three excellencies there were such officials as major counselors and royal advisors, who assisted the three excellencies. It is a great error that in later times royal advisors came to be called "prime ministers." The Ministry of Central Affairs, Ministry of Ceremonial, Ministry of Civil Administration, Ministry of Popular Affairs, Ministry of War, Ministry of Justice, Ministry of the Treasury, and Ministry of the Palace were called the "Eight Ministries." They were set up in the mold of the Six Ministries of China, but the rank of these ministries was lower and their systems of offices very different from the Six Ministries of China. The various other offices were also set up by emulating China, but because China and our own country are different in both their land and their customs, there were small changes in everything. It is only the division between civil and military occupations that was entirely the same as in China.

It was truly fortunate that the hundred offices were established by emulating the system of China in this way, but the court nobles made these offices hereditary and did not recruit new talent from among the

---

5 Shōtoku was Empress Suiko's nephew and was appointed by her as regent in 593.
6 Shōtoku set up a court bureaucracy along Chinese lines, including the introduction in 603 of a twelve-level system of court ranks, with ranks indicated by different types of caps.
7 The Taika Reforms of 645 established a centralized government modeled on that of China, with the provinces governed by officials appointed by the emperor.

3 Bureaucratic Offices

lower orders, which had never been the case in China.[8] The customs of our country of Japan are very harmful to government. From the time power was taken over by the house of Minamoto no Yoritomo, the major captain of the right of Kamakura, the government of the court nobles no longer extended throughout the realm, so the hundred offices of the imperial court all came to exist in name only.[9] In the age of warrior rule, both the high and the low lacked learning, so they gave no consideration to the past and had no plan for how to set up the hundred offices to govern the state; they simply muddled through without deciding on anything.

Such problems are particularly acute in the present age, which began when Tokugawa Ieyasu, the Light of the East, united the land following the disturbances of the period of warring states. Due to having experienced these events, at the time of the foundation of the country, Ieyasu did not go so far as to ponder the establishment of offices, but instead carried things out in a simplified manner by using military regulations, just as they were, for governing the country. After peace has prevailed for a long time, though, it is typical that many different affairs will arise from the court all the way down to the lowest orders, so it will be difficult to govern if at this point one does not establish and staff the hundred offices. To attempt instead to govern through military regulations, as when things were done in a simplified manner at the initial founding of the country, is like craftsmen trying to do their work skillfully without readying their tools. In carrying out even the most minor of affairs, it will be difficult to accomplish these tasks if one does not establish functionaries responsible for handling them. This goes all the more for extremely weighty matters related to the governance of the state; without the hundred offices and the officials who staff these, how can one expect to be able to manage these affairs?

...

In governing the realm, there are two systems: governing through feudalism and governing through a system of districts and prefectures. When there is not feudalism, then in both other countries and our own there are districts and prefectures. When there are not districts and prefectures,

---

8   Shundai is pointing in particular to the fact that Japan lacked the kind of examination system for the bureaucracy that existed in China.
9   A reference to the transformation of these offices into honorary titles with no actual role in government.

then there is feudalism. Since ancient times there has been no departure from these two methods. Feudalism has its own method of governing, as does a system of districts and prefectures. As long as one understands this single point, then there is nothing one cannot achieve when practicing government today by considering the past of other countries and our own. This is because human feelings and the principles of things do not differ in the least between past and present, nor do they differ between other countries and our own.

A ruler is like the head of the people, so he is called the "head in chief." If one has only a head, but no hands and feet, one will not be able to make use of one's body. The head is still, whereas the hands and feet move; the ruler can be compared to the head and his ministers to the hands and feet. In governing both large and small countries, then, it is impossible for the ruler to govern all by himself, so he always establishes the hundred offices, assigns them their respective responsibilities, and has them handle these. In establishing the hundred offices, one must always consider the past, tailor it to the circumstances of the present, and make sure that the system lacks nothing; this is the method of the sages. In the previous section when I cited the past of Japan and China in order to discuss the appropriate establishment of offices, I was not saying that today's world must necessarily be governed like the past or that the offices and responsibilities of the past of another country must be used in the present age. Rather, I cited the distant past because it is an inevitable truth that when one does not consider the past, then no matter how great one's wisdom may be, one will be unable to establish methods that serve the needs of present-day affairs.

The offices of grand judge, director of the imperial clan, and grand coachman that I mentioned earlier belong to what in the Han dynasty were the nine ministers.[10] In the Zhou dynasty there were the six ministers, but in the Han dynasty there were the nine ministers, who were placed beneath the three excellencies. Among the nine ministers, the grand judge encompassed the responsibilities of the officer of lawsuits and officer of punishments. The officer of lawsuits and officer of punishments were originally a single post, but when the affairs of the state grew numerous, it was useful to separate the two. In the *Rituals of Zhou*, there

---

10 In the preceding sections (not included in this translation), Shundai discussed the absence of these three positions in the Tokugawa regime, as well as the problems in government caused by not having them.

3 Bureaucratic Offices

are numerous offices under the purview of the autumn office, or chief of crime. Although in one sense they are a single office, they are at the same time separate offices. It is not that such a functionary is lacking in the present age, but the responsibilities of particular officials are mixed up with each other, which is ineffective for governing. The two offices of director of the imperial clan and grand coachman are among the nine ministers of the Han dynasty, but they are entirely absent in the present age, so today's system of offices is incomplete.

When warriors of the present age are appointed to the offices of major counselor, middle counselor, royal advisor, middle captain, lesser captain, and chamberlain, these are not true offices; rather, they borrow the names of offices of the court nobility and make them status markers for warriors.[11] Similarly, when warriors are called such things as "governor of Yamashiro province," "governor of Yamato province," "first assistant to the minister of the center," or "head of the housekeeping office," these are not actual positions; they simply borrow the titles of offices of the court nobility and use these as sobriquets for people of the fifth rank or higher.[12] The common belief that these are real offices is mistaken. Those of the rank of chamberlain or higher are appointed to their offices by an imperial letter. As for the others, they simply receive appointment to the fourth or fifth rank by an oral decree of the emperor. Once they have been appointed to the fifth rank, they take on such sobriquets as "governor of such-and-such," "first assistant to such-and-such," or "head of such-and-such."

When it comes to the countries of feudal lords of the present age, each has its own system and there is no uniformity among them. They are all alike, though, in failing to properly establish offices and responsibilities. In feudalism, the son of heaven governs the entire realm, while the feudal

---

11 Shundai is referring to the practice by which members of the warrior class were appointed to these offices of the imperial bureaucracy as purely honorary titles, with no expectation that they would actually carry out the duties of such offices.

12 This is in the context of the nine-rank system of the Japanese court aristocracy, consisting of one "initial rank" and eight numbered ranks (with various subdivisions within them), with a lower number indicating a higher rank. In the Tokugawa period, high-ranking members of the samurai class would be given ranks within this system, even though they were not part of the actual imperial court in Kyoto. They would then receive titles commensurate with their rank. For example, first assistant to the minister of the center was one possible position for those of junior fifth rank, upper grade, and head of the housekeeping office was a possible position for those of junior fifth rank, lower grade.

lords each govern a single country.[13] This is merely a difference between governing on a large or a small scale; the appropriate methods for governing remain the same. Because of this, when it comes to establishing the hundred offices, feudal lords should simply do as the son of heaven does, while reducing the number of officials and curtailing the affairs they handle.

Today it is customary within the countries of feudal lords to install many functionaries who are charged with the same task and to have matters directed by people who are switched out on a monthly basis.[14] There is nothing more harmful to government than this. One should always assign a single person to a single office, divide up the duties to be handled, entrust individual officeholders with their respective governmental matters, and not interfere with their work from outside. For each main functionary one should put in place two or three ancillary functionaries, depending on the extent and importance of the main functionary's role; this is based on the idea of having a chief official and assistant officials.[15] In addition, one should add many low-level functionaries beneath these; this is based on the idea of having managers and secretaries.[16] All these people should be made to assist the main functionary. As for having a single person hold two or three offices concurrently, the ancient practice has been for this to be done among the middling ranks of the court aristocracy, but not among feudal lords. However, minor feudal lords are like the middling ranks of the court aristocracy of a large country in that they have a small stipend and few people under them, so it is acceptable to appoint one such person to two posts concurrently for the sake of convenience, as long as one takes into account the nature of the posts they fill and the talents of the person in question.

---

13 Shundai is describing a general model of feudal government here, but there is some vagueness in his application of it to Tokugawa Japan, given that in a Japanese context he uses "son of heaven" to refer to the emperor (and denies this status to the shogun), but at the same time portrays the shogun as ruling over all of Japan (with the daimyo as feudal lords governing over their particular "countries" within Japan).
14 The term Shundai uses here is *tsukiban*, which refers to a system used in the Tokugawa period in which a different person would be on duty each month at a particular post.
15 In the *ritsuryō* system of bureaucracy in Japan, each office was staffed by four grades of officials: the head official (*kami*), the assistant official (*suke*), managers (*jō*), and secretaries (*sakan*).
16 These are the third- and fourth-rank levels of officials in the *ritsuryō* system (see previous note).

3 Bureaucratic Offices

Another point to consider is that feudal lords of all ranks go to Edo to attend on the shogun and remain there for a year or half a year, so they need to install functionaries both in their own country and in Edo.[17] That being said, having two people who carry out the same function brings with it the problem that the policies carried out in the feudal lord's country itself will differ from those of the country's representatives in Edo. The feudal lord's country is the root and Edo, as a temporary lodging, is the branch, so the main functionary should always be in the feudal lord's country and subordinate functionaries should be posted to Edo on an alternating basis. Minor matters should be decided by the subordinate functionary on duty in Edo, whereas major matters should be reported to the main functionary in the feudal lord's country for a decision. This is the method used in the past, and in today's world too there is surely nothing more effective than this for the governance of the countries of feudal lords. When looking at the government practiced by feudal lords in recent times, there are always separate factions of functionaries in the feudal lord's country and Edo, so all affairs are divided and a single decision is not arrived at. Even among those who carry out the same function, there are various differences of opinion and people do not achieve unity. This results in much inconvenience for the retainers and ultimately causes their lord a great deal of harm. All this happens because people are colored by prevailing customs and do not understand how to manage offices and responsibilities.

---

17 A reference to the alternate attendance (*sankin kōtai*) system, in which daimyo alternated between living in their own domain and in the shogunal seat of Edo.

Volume 4

Heavenly Patterns

In the *Records of the Grand Historian* there is the "Treatise on the Officers of Heaven"[1] and in the *History of the Former Han* there is the "Record of Astronomy";[2] these both provide accounts of matters pertaining to heavenly patterns [*tenmon*]. In the term "heavenly patterns,"[3] "patterns" [*mon/bun*] has the same meaning as in the terms "cultural brilliance" [*bunmei*; lit. "patterned brilliance"] and "cultured writing" [*bunshō*; lit. "patterned ornamentation"]. The sun, moon, planets, and stars are bright objects that form the patterned ornamentation of heaven, so they are called "heavenly patterns." In the time of Yao and Shun, the Xi and He families were in charge of matters pertaining to heavenly patterns. The second Xi brother, third Xi brother, second He brother, and third He brother were each stationed in the distant reaches of one of the four directions and made to ponder the heavenly phenomena of the four directions.[4] This was decreed by Emperor Yao when he first took over the government of the realm. When it came to the reign of Emperor Shun, he created the jade-geared rotating sphere and had people make astronomical calculations of the movements of the sun, moon, planets, and stars, all of which make up the patterns of heaven.[5] The jade-geared

---

1　Chapter 27 of the *Records of the Grand Historian*.
2　Volume 26 of the *History of the Former Han*.
3　The second character in *tenmon* (read as *mon*) is pronounced as *bun* in the other terms that Shundai discusses here.
4　This is described in the "Canon of Yao" section of the *Classic of Documents*.
5　The use of this instrument in astronomy is mentioned in the "Canon of Shun" section of the *Classic of Documents*. The translation of the instrument's name is necessarily an approximate rendering, since it is not clear what it was exactly.

4 Heavenly Patterns

rotating sphere is a device for measuring heavenly patterns, similar to the armillary spheres of today. "Astronomical calculations" refers to measurements of the movements of heaven.

Heavenly patterns are the basis for the creation of calendars. Humans are the loftiest things within heaven and earth,[6] and the Way of humans is based in heaven. From the son of heaven at the top down to the common people below, people's daily actions all ought to be performed by following heaven. Because of this, when the sages Yao and Shun governed the realm, they put particular emphasis on heavenly patterns. When the actions of humans are in keeping with the Way of heaven, then good omens will manifest themselves, and when they go against heaven, then calamities will come down on people. Even with lowly people such omens appear in keeping with their station. This is all the more so with people of the status of son of heaven or feudal lord; their actions pertain to the realm and state, so their good and bad actions will always reach heaven and a response will never fail to come in the form of good or bad fortune.

In every age from the Three Dynasties onward, importance has been placed on the Office of Heaven, which was managed by the chief historian.[7] In later times, this position was called the "imperial observer of heaven." Within the court they constructed a tall tower called the "observatory." The officials who held the posts of chief historian or imperial observer of heaven climbed this tower day and night and viewed the patterns of heaven. If a change was visible in heaven, they announced this to the ruler and respectfully urged him to cultivate virtue. Ancient rulers were extremely fearful of heaven; the sons of heaven of the Han dynasty even feared solar eclipses.[8] When these occurred, they issued decrees to the realm to seek out gentlemen who were wise, exemplary, forthright, and willing to remonstrate. They were even more fearful when it came to other types of major and minor changes in heaven.

The reason for their fear is that heaven is a living thing; it is in motion at all times. The way that living things cannot stop moving even for an instant is true not only of course of humans, but also of birds, beasts,

---

6   From the "Great Proclamation, Part 1" section of the *Classic of Documents*: "Heaven and earth are the father and mother of the myriad things, and humans are the loftiest of the myriad things."
7   As Shundai describes, the functions of this office involved not only historical recordkeeping, but also matters of astronomy and calendars.
8   Shundai's reason for presenting solar eclipses as a rather minor change of the heavens that one would not normally fear, as discussed below, p. 74, is that solar eclipses occur in predictable ways.

fish, and turtles. Heaven, however, is the father and mother of all things; its status is extremely lofty and its virtue is extremely correct, so, unlike birds, beasts, fish, turtles, and humans, its movements are not willful and arbitrary. There is regularity to day and night, each day goes by with neither excess nor deficiency, and after passing through 365 days things return to where they originally were; this is the straightforward aspect of the Way of heaven. Because of this aspect, the motions of the sun, moon, planets, and stars can all be inferred using human intelligence. The reason one can know this year of a solar eclipse that will not occur until next year is the effectiveness of astronomical calculations, but such calculations only work in the first place because of the straightforward aspect of the Way of heaven. However, because heaven is by nature a living thing, within its regularities there are also minor aspects that are deficient or in excess, which at times can become major. Because of this, the ancient sages did not consider heaven to be something that could be fathomed with human intelligence. They saw even solar eclipses as changes of heaven, as Confucius writes in the *Spring and Autumn Annals*.

In ancient times the Office of Heaven did not, as was later the case, focus on making astronomical calculations through computation. Rather, its officials simply devoted themselves to viewing the patterns of heaven day and night in order to perceive its regularities and changes. This may appear unsophisticated, but in fact it was a result of how well versed they were in heavenly patterns. In later ages, people gained great knowledge and skill and became increasingly versed in techniques of astronomical calculation, reaching the point where they could predict phenomena as far as ten years in the future. Relying on the precision of their astronomical calculations, they made no effort to understand things by viewing them with their own eyes as people had done in the past. Today they take pride in the precision of their astronomical calculations and consider the ancient Way of the Office of Heaven to have been rough and crude. This is a shameful attitude to take. People of later times fail to attain the superb skill of the ancients in many matters; this is not limited to the Office of Heaven. The ancients are the ones who created this Way, and if one were to use their expertise to become versed in their techniques, then how could one not be able to predict solar eclipses with the same accuracy that people have achieved in later ages? The ancients did not, however, predict these by computation, but rather knew about them simply by observing with their own eyes. The reason they took this approach is that heaven is ultimately a living thing, so one cannot possess perfectly exact knowledge about it at any given time.

4 Heavenly Patterns

Moreover, the intentions of heaven are difficult to fathom, so the ancients did not try to fathom them through their own cleverness. When natural calamities occurred, though, they cautioned their rulers. This is the profound wisdom of the ancient sages, and one cannot grasp the meaning of it if one does not understand their Way. The ancient sages were particularly extreme in their fear of heaven, similar to the fear that women and children of the common world have of such things as spirits [*kijin*]. From the perspective of later ages this may appear foolish, but Confucius said that "the gentleman fears three things," listing the first of these as "the destiny appointed by heaven."[9] He also said, in response to Wang Sunjia, that "when one has committed an offence against heaven, there is none to whom one can pray."[10]

Ever since the creation of the "learning of principle" among Song dynasty Confucians, the followers of the Cheng brothers and Zhu Xi have argued that heaven is identical with principle and have attempted to use principle to make conjectures about heaven. Principle is something that pertains to dead objects, which can be completely penetrated by wise people through the employment of their intellect. This can be compared to how a skilled Go player can foresee the entire game that will be played out by both himself and his opponent. The reason he can do this is that in Go there exists nothing beyond the principle of victory and the principle of defeat. The destiny appointed by heaven is not something that can be predicted in this manner, however. This can be compared to the use of dice when playing backgammon. There are those who are skilled and unskilled at backgammon, but it is impossible to know which of the numbers from one to six will come up when one throws a die. The way in which Song Confucians used principle to make conjectures about heaven is like claiming to know which number will follow which other number when throwing dice. How could such a thing be known through reasoning? When one views heaven as principle in the manner of the Song Confucians, then the destiny appointed by heaven becomes something that does not deserve fear.

Those who discuss the Office of Heaven in recent times all draw forced inferences from the learning of principle and discuss the vast and limitless heaven as if it were something held in the palm of the hand. This is

---

9 From *Analects* 16.8. The other objects of fear listed in this passage are "great men" and "the words of the sages."
10 From *Analects* 3.13.

only a knowledge of the planets and the stars, though; it is not a knowledge of heaven itself. What is recorded in the *Xing jing* [*Classic of Celestial Bodies*],[11] and what is recorded in the "Treatise on the Officers of Heaven" section of the *Records of the Grand Historian*, the "Record of Astronomy" section of the *History of the Former Han*, and the records of astronomy of other ages, is not only a clarification of the measurements of the motions of celestial bodies, but also contains many explanations of extraordinary phenomena in heaven and natural disasters. This is the teaching bequeathed by the ancient sages regarding their reverence and fear of heaven. In our country, too, during the age of the court nobles they appointed doctors of astronomy, who were put in charge of the Office of Heaven. In the age of warriors, though, rulers failed to establish this office. In the present age, there was no edict to establish such an office when the country was originally founded, but during the time of the shogun Tokugawa Tsunayoshi [1646–1709, r. 1680–1709], the Go master Yasui Santetsu [1639–1715] was selected and appointed to be in charge of the Office of Heaven. From that point on, scholars of this Way have emerged in the state. This is truly a superb undertaking that stands out in its time.

Pitch Pipes and Calendars

"Pitch pipes" are the twelve pitch pipes.[12] Here in our country they are called the "twelve notes." At the time of the Yellow Emperor, a person by the name of Ling Lun cut bamboo from the Xie Valley and used it to make the twelve pitch pipes.[13] This was the beginning of pitch pipes. Huang Zhong [Yellow Bell], Tai Cu, Gu Xian, Rui Bin, Yi Ze, and Wu Yi are considered yang notes, and Da Lü, Jia Zhong, Zhong Lü, Lin Zhong, Nan Lü, and Ying Zhong are considered yin notes.[14] The six yang pitch

---

11 A reference to the *Gan Shi xing jing* (*Classic of Celestial Bodies of Gan and Shi*), a work compiled by Ma Xian c. 579. The title of the work comes from the fact that it purports to quote from the works of Gan De and Shi Shen, both of whom were famous astronomers of the fourth century BC.
12 The "twelve pitch pipes" are the twelve notes that make up the chromatic scale of traditional Chinese music.
13 The Yellow Emperor (Huangdi) is a mythical sage ruler of ancient China. The Xie Valley was said to lie to the north of the mythical Kunlun Mountain.
14 Huang Zhong, Tai Cu, Gu Xian, Rui Bin, Yi Ze, and Wu Yi are the first, third, fifth, seventh, ninth, and eleventh notes of the twelve-note chromatic scale, and Da Lü, Jia Zhong, Zhong Lü, Lin Zhong, Nan Lü, and Ying Zhong are the second, fourth, sixth, eighth,

4 Pitch Pipes and Calendars

pipes and the six yin pitch pipes together add up to twelve. Ling Lun cut bamboo to make tubes, blew through these to determine tonal pitches, and distinguished the five tones. The five tones are Gong, Shang, Jiao, Zhi, and Yu.[15] The five tones and twelve pitch pipes were used to moderate the material force of heaven and earth, give order to the eight winds, and give birth to and nourish the myriad things. The "eight winds" are the winds of the eight directions. The sages created music, with which they gave order to the material force of heaven and earth and moderated the hearts of humans. This music had its basis in the twelve pitch pipes.

...

Pitch pipes, measures of length, measures of volume, and measures of mass are the bases that determine the systems of the realm, which is why the ancient sages placed importance on them. When the "Canon of Shun" section of the *Classic of Documents* states that "Shun created uniformity in the pitch pipes, measures of length, measures of volume, and measures of mass," this is a reference to his inspection tour of the realm, during which he collected the pitch pipes and measures of length, volume, and mass used in the countries of the four directions and examined whether they conformed to the stipulated system. These four things are implements for enacting regulations, so when there are discrepancies in them, the systems of the realm will fall into disarray. Because of this, Shun corrected these so as to make them uniform throughout the realm. When the *Doctrine of the Mean* states that "carriages have wheels of uniform gauge,"[16] this too speaks to the uniformity of the systems of the realm.

In ancient China they employed blind people as official musicians and had them correct the tonal pitches. They did so because people who cannot see are always expert at tonal pitches. In our country they did not employ blind people, but instead passed down the Way of tonal pitches

---

tenth, and twelfth notes. As Shundai describes, the odd-numbered notes were considered to belong to the yang (masculine) cosmological principle and the even-numbered notes to the yin (feminine) principle.

15 These are the names of the notes of the Chinese pentatonic scale. Whereas the twelve pitch pipes are a chromatic scale that represents the gamut of sounds in ancient Chinese music, it is the pentatonic scales derived from the twelve pitch pipes that actually functioned as the scales used in particular pieces of music. Each of the twelve pitch pipes can function as the tonic of five different pentatonic scales, resulting in a total of sixty possible pentatonic scales.

16 From chapter 28 of the *Doctrine of the Mean*.

On Political Economy

within households of hereditary court musicians; other people did not know of these matters. Refined music permeated society during the age of court nobles, so ordinary people also learned it and made it their everyday source of pleasure. Ever since the age of warriors, though, such forms of vulgar music as *sarugaku* and *dengaku* have been created and refined music has been discarded, so there are few people in the world who understand the Way of tonal pitches. In the current age the varieties of vulgar music have grown still more numerous, so refined music is increasingly discarded. In our times, discussions of the Way of tonal pitches are extremely distant from people's concerns. When one discusses it in relation to the ancient Way, then it is important as the basis for governmental matters. It is not an immediately urgent task of the present day, though, so there will be no harm in cutting short the discussion of this subject for the time being. However, one must not fail to understand that pitch pipes are the basis of all affairs.

...

Calendars are established in order to allow the people to know the days and to ensure that they do not miss the proper seasons in farming. When in the "Canon of Yao" section of the *Classic of Documents* it states that "a full year consists of 366 days, and by means of an intercalary month one fixes in place the four seasons and completes the year," these are words that Emperor Yao gave as a command to the Xi and He families.[17] From that point on, importance was placed on calendars in every age. The calendar of Japan is the same as that of China. Among the many officials of our country there were calendrical scholars who were responsible for creating calendars. From ancient times they used the calendars of China in each age, but from the third year of the Jōgan era [861] in the reign of Emperor Seiwa [850–878, r. 858–878], they began using the Xuanming calendar of the Changqing era [821–824] of the Tang dynasty.[18] It continued to be used in Japan until the Tenna era [1681–1684] of the present age, a period of over eight hundred years. During that time the calendar was changed several times in China, but here in Japan astronomical calculations were crude, so people were not aware of the discrepancies in the calendar and simply followed the old practices for eight hundred

---

17 The Xi and He families provided officials responsible for astronomical observations under Emperor Yao.
18 This calendar was used in China from 822 to 892. It began to be used in Japan in 861.

years. Because it was wide of the mark in predicting the solar eclipse that occurred in the second year of the Tenna era [1682], the shogun Tokugawa Tsunayoshi issued an edict that the calendar be revised. The Go master Yasui Santetsu created a new calendar based on the method of the Shoushi calendar of Guo Shoujing [1231–1316] of the Yuan dynasty and presented it to the shogun.[19] It was called the "Jōkyō calendar" and began to be used in the first year of the Jōkyō era [1684]. The Shoushi calendar surpassed the old calendar in the precision of its methodology. The current Jōkyō calendar too is superior to all the other calendars that have existed in Japan since ancient times. The brilliant virtue of Tsunayoshi and the achievement of Santetsu are truly something for the ages. Since today there are satisfactory calendars, what is there for me to discuss? However, the books being produced now about calendars are caught up in current trends; they are dragged along by current customs and sometimes make groundless statements. I will now present a few of these and show their errors.

...

Geography

In the term "geography" [*chiri*; lit. "principle of the earth"], "principle" [*ri*] refers to the grain of something. When the grain of wood is called its "principle," this is "principle" in the sense of a principled consistency. Within the earth, such things as mountains, rivers, and valleys all have their particular principled consistency, so one speaks of the "principle of the earth." The Chinese *Classic of Documents* has a chapter called the "Tribute of Yu," which records in detail matters of the land, mountains, and rivers of the realm.[20] This is the beginning of geography. In addition, among ancient texts there is the *Shanhai jing* [*Classic of Mountains*

---

19 As noted above, p. 76, Yasui Santetsu (also known as Shibukawa Shunkai) was the first official astronomer appointed by the Tokugawa shogunate. Guo Shuojing was a Yuan dynasty official whose responsibilities spanned astronomy, mathematics, and hydraulics. His Shoushi calendar was used in China from 1281 to 1644.
20 This chapter is in the "Xia shu" ("Books of Xia") section of the *Classic of Documents*. It describes how Yu regulated the flow of various rivers for irrigation purposes and made different regions agriculturally productive in accordance with the characteristics of their soil and their other natural endowments.

and Seas].²¹ In the Zhou dynasty, the office of the chief of works took charge of the land of the realm, and the office of the overseer of feudatories handled governmental ordinances pertaining to geography as well as tribute and duty. "Tribute" refers to goods presented to the ruler, and "duty" refers to work performed for the son of heaven. After the Three Dynasties, in the *Records of the Grand Historian* there is the "Treatise on the Yellow River and Canals,"²² in the *History of the Former Han* there are the "Record of Geography" and "Record of Irrigation Channels,"²³ and in the *Hou Han shu* [*History of the Latter Han*] there is the "Record of Districts and Provinces."²⁴ These are all books of geography. In the Han dynasty and later, each dynasty always had its own record of geography. This is because in China, whenever the dynasty changes there are changes in how geography is mapped. Apart from the records of geography of each dynasty, since ancient times there have been a great many books that record matters of geography. There are those that provide a record of the entire realm, as well as those that record the details of a particular region or district. There are hundreds of such books of geography. There are also many different types of maps of the land, varying in their scale as well as their level of detail.

Knowledge of geography is the foundation for governing the realm. However, to travel throughout the realm and understand it all by oneself, as the Great Yu did, is not something that ordinary people are capable of. For this reason, when kings of later times took control of the realm, they always established the geography of their dynasty by ordering their officials to compile books of geography. When the founder of the Ming dynasty took control of the realm, he commanded a great many Confucians and had them compile the *Da Ming yi tong zhi* [*Comprehensive Gazetteer of the Great Ming*]. Among the geographical records that have existed since ancient times, there is none more detailed than the *Comprehensive Gazetteer*. After that, many works called "local gazetteers" also appeared, which separately recorded

---

21 The *Classic of Mountains and Seas* dates in its current form to the Han dynasty scholar Liu Xiang, who compiled it from various existing texts most likely dating from the Warring States period and early Han dynasty. It consists of descriptions of different geographical regions together with mythological stories associated with these locales.
22 Chapter 29 of the *Records of the Grand Historian*.
23 Volumes 28 and 29 of the *History of the Former Han*.
24 This spans volumes 109 to 113 of the *History of the Latter Han*.

4 Geography

matters of particular regions and districts. These Ming works are comprehensive when it comes to geography.

In Japan, in the most ancient times the names of places were not settled, nor were the written characters for them clearly distinguished, but Emperor Monmu [683–707, r. 697–707] issued an edict that fixed the sixty-six provinces of the land, as well as the number of districts, and gave two-character names to these provinces and districts.[25] From this point on the geography of Japan was fixed in place and later ages did not alter this. This was truly a superb undertaking. However, unlike in China, they did not produce records of geography, so the people of the land did not understand the geography of their own country. In ancient times, it appears that officials had such things as records and maps, but because these were not circulated widely, there was no way for people to know of them. Later there were gazetteers of various provinces, but these were not spread widely either, so they were not transmitted for long.[26] In later ages they were scattered or disappeared entirely, and even with the resources of the state it is impossible to recover them. This is to say nothing of the fact that people of lower status would never be able to take a glance at such works in the first place. Is it not lamentable that several thousand years after the beginning of creation, even after writing came to be practiced in middle antiquity, not a single volume of books of geography has been passed down to the present? This is ultimately because people were unskilled at writing and neglectful in recording things. In China, the son of heaven decreed that all matters related to affairs of state be compiled in books; these were printed with woodblocks and distributed throughout the realm, allowing even the common people to see them in their entirety. In our country, though, if such books existed, they would be kept secret and not be distributed to the lower orders. This is an error that results from the failure of government to be conducted in a public manner. The reason those ancient books of our country that are useful to the state have largely been lost and not passed down is because they were all kept secret by government offices and were not widely circulated.

---

25 A reference to the system of provinces that was created as part of the Taihō Ritsuryō (Taihō Code) of 703, an administrative reorganization based largely on the system of Tang dynasty China.

26 These gazetteers were called *fudoki* (lit. "records of wind and soil") in Japanese. A comprehensive set of such gazetteers was produced over a twenty-year period beginning in 713, but, as Shundai indicates, the vast majority of these works have been lost.

On Political Economy

In the four hundred years up to the time when the realm came under the control of warriors led by the house of Minamoto no Yoritomo, the major captain of the right of Kamakura, the world followed the customs of the court nobles and the realm practiced a centralized government of districts and prefectures. In the present age, it has already been a hundred years since a feudal government was established. Major and minor feudal lords each have their respective countries and protect these territories. Accurate books of geography are not circulated now, so when landholders from feudal lords on down have disputes with neighboring countries or villages over borders, it is often difficult for the magistrate to decide them. If, as in China, imperially commissioned records of geography were circulated throughout the realm, then borders would be clear and even the common people would always know of them, so as a matter of course disputes would not arise. Even if disputes did arise, it would be easy for the authorities to settle them. Is this not evidence of the importance of records of geography as a tool for governing the realm? In Japan there were in fact maps and records of the realm at the beginning of the present age, and more recently Tsunayoshi ordered the regions of the realm to create new maps, which were then completed after several years; this is truly an example of understanding the essentials of the Way of governing. However, these maps and records are held in secret by the authorities and not circulated, so there is no way for people to know of them. The current age is a time of cultural brilliance within the realm, and the number of Confucians who are accomplished in cultured writing is also greater than before, so if one were to take advantage of this fortunate time to order Confucian retainers to create comprehensive gazetteers of their regions and then circulate these throughout the land, it would truly be a superb undertaking of its age and the people of the realm would surely treasure it.

...

Volume 5

Food and Goods

Food and goods are the Way of providing sustenance for the people of the realm, from the ruler at the top to the common people below. The "Great Plan" in the *Classic of Documents* records the Way with which the Great Yu governed the realm. Within it, the "eight objects of government" are eight essential elements in governing the country.[1] The first of the eight objects of government is food and the second is goods. These two are the most important of the eight, so they are grouped together as "food and goods." When Ban Gu wrote the *History of the Former Han*, he created a record of the Way with which sustenance was provided to the realm during the Han dynasty, discussing that government's merits and faults, advantages and disadvantages, and called this the "Record of Food and Goods."[2]

"Food" refers to things people eat, such as rice and other grains. "Goods" are worldly possessions and valuables; in Japanese the character for "goods" is read as *takara*. There are various kinds of goods. Things like cloth and cotton cover the skin and protect against the cold. Things like salt, tea, liquor, soy sauce, fish, meat, vegetables, and greens supplement the five grains and nourish the body. Things like brushwood, firewood, oil, and charcoal are used in everyday life. All the other utensils

---

[1] The "eight objects of government" are listed in the "Great Plan" as food, goods, sacrifices, the minister of works, the minister of education, the minister of crime, the entertainment of guests, and the army.
[2] See Shundai's earlier discussion in volume 1 of the ten "Records" included in the *History of the Former Han*.

that are typically used in people's houses, down to things like bamboo, wood, gravel, and stone, all have their respective uses and aid in people's lives, so these are all called "goods." There is also currency, which refers to money. There are three types of money: gold, silver, and copper. Gold money consists of things like the gold *ōban* and *koban* we have today.[3] Silver money is the silver pieces we have today, and copper money is the *zeni* we have today.[4] In ancient times, the character for "spring" was used instead of the character for "money."[5] Money circulates throughout the realm and satisfies people's needs in the same way that water gushes forth from the earth and flows everywhere, so people referred to it as a "spring," but in later times they wrote this with the character for "money." Even gold and silver nuggets are ultimately money. In China, in the most ancient times they had a form of leather currency in which they used animal skins as money. From middle antiquity, though, they came to use gold and copper money, with the use of silver coming after that. These three types of currency can stand in place of things to fulfill people's needs, so they too are called "goods."

Among the things that afflict humans, none are more pressing than starvation and cold. What relieves starvation is food and what protects against the cold is clothing. Food consists of the five grains, which grow out of the earth and come from the hands of farmers, and clothing is made from woven textiles. Cultivating mulberry and hemp is the task of farmers, while plucking mulberry leaves, raising silkworms, and making silk cloth, as well as spinning hemp and weaving cloth from it, are the work of women. The five grains, mulberry, and hemp grow out of the earth, so they can be produced anywhere. If one is provided with enough clothing and food to avoid starving and freezing, then it may seem as though one should not need anything else. However, people cannot get by with clothing and food alone; as I mentioned earlier, there are many things that are indispensable for everyday life. Moreover, even in producing clothing and food one must have the appropriate tools. On top of this, the soil of the realm is not all

3 The *ōban* and *koban* were gold coins issued throughout the Tokugawa period. Their specifications varied over time, but the *ōban* circulating at the time Shundai wrote *On Political Economy* had a weight of 44.1 *monme* (about 165.38 g) and a purity of 68.1 percent (resulting in a gold content of about 112.6 g), while the *koban* had a weight of 4.76 *monme* (about 17.85 g) and a purity of 86.8 percent (resulting in a gold content of about 15.49 g).
4 Silver coins in the Tokugawa period did not have standardized weights, so they had to be weighed at the time of a transaction. The *chōgin* was a larger silver coin, and *mame'itagin* were smaller silver coins. The *zeni* was a copper coin of the Tokugawa period.
5 In Japanese these are homophonous, both being pronounced *sen*.

the same, so there are things that grow in a particular soil and things that do not. It is because of this that the ancient sages taught the people not only agricultural cultivation, but also how to barter in order to complement each other's needs. "Bartering" refers to exchanging one thing for another. When two people exchange what they have for what they do not, they accommodate each other and both end up with what they need.

In the *Classic of Changes* it says that "the great virtue of heaven and earth is giving life."[6] The virtue of heaven and earth lies simply in giving birth to the myriad things. Once it has given birth to things, there is in addition to this a Way of nourishing these things. As long as one does not go counter to the Way of heaven and earth, then living things will never die from lack of nourishment. The teachings of the sages are the Way of heaven and earth; if people follow these teachings and devote their hearts to providing sustenance, then there will be no suffering caused by starvation or cold, nothing lacking for the needs of everyday life, and people will pass their entire lives in tranquility; this is the great virtue of heaven and earth. The provision of useful goods and securing of sustenance in the government of Yao and Shun is an example of this.[7]

People should devote their hearts to providing sustenance, but because people's hearts are various, there are those who perform their duty in this regard but also those who do not. Also, depending on the behavior of the ruler and the quality of the government, the customs of the people change in various ways, so if a wicked person gains power, then rice, grains, and goods no longer find their way to all corners of the realm, the people come to suffer, and difficulties arise for the state. Neither the lofty nor the lowly can survive a single day without clothing and food. Although ritual and rightness are the Way that people should uphold, people typically forget these when they are driven to desperation by hunger and cold. Guan Zhong said, "When granaries are full, then people know ritual decorum. When clothing and food are sufficient, then they know honor and shame."[8] This means that it is when people do not lack

---

6 From the *Commentary on the Appended Phrases* to the *Classic of Changes*.
7 From the "Counsels of the Great Yu" section of the *Classic of Documents*: "Yu said, 'Emperor, consider this. Virtue is seen in good government, and good government is the nourishing of the people. Water, fire, metal, wood, earth, and grain must be cultivated. The rectification of virtue, provision of useful goods, and securing of sustenance must be harmonized.'"
8 From "Biographies of Guan Zhong and Yan Ying," chapter 62 of the *Records of the Grand Historian*.

clothing and food and do not suffer from hunger or cold that they understand ritual and rightness. Mencius said, "Lacking a steady livelihood, they will lack a steady heart."⁹ A "steady livelihood" refers to the respective tasks with which scholar-officials, farmers, artisans, and merchants make their living. A "steady heart" refers to a heart that always upholds the Way and does not change. "When people lack a steady livelihood, they will lack a steady heart" means that when people lack an occupation that provides a living and are forced to labor day and night, their suffering from hunger and cold will cause them to lose their original heart. Focusing on surviving the day at hand, they will commit fraud and violate rightness rather than engaging in any kind of planning. When changes occur in the heart, which ought to be constant and unchanging, this is called "lacking a steady heart." Mencius said that this happens among the common people, but that scholar-officials do not lose their steady heart even when they lack a steady livelihood. However, scholar-officials too typically lose their steady heart when they lack a steady occupation and frequently fail to adhere to rightness. The popular saying that "poverty breeds theft" is true indeed.

When Guan Zhong became prime minister to Duke Huan and governed the country of Qi, he established what are called the "four moorings," which are ritual, rightness, integrity, and shame. Ritual consists of the rules for human behavior, and rightness refers to adherence to principles. Integrity means to constantly conduct oneself properly; for a scholar-official to establish the characteristics of a scholar-official is called "integrity." Shame is to have a sense for what is disgraceful and dishonorable. These are called the "four moorings" as a comparison to the function of moorings as ropes that tie a boat in place. In governing the state, one ties things together with the four elements of ritual, rightness, integrity, and shame in the same way that a boat is tied in place with four ropes, one on each corner. If one of the four ropes is cut, the boat will move a little. If two or three are cut, it will move even more. If they are all cut, it will drift away and it is impossible to know where it will go. The state is like this, too. Since ancient times there have been many instances of the four moorings being cut off and the state descending into civil unrest.

---

9 *Mencius* 1.1.7.20. As Shundai discusses in what follows, the *Mencius* passage specifically describes this as a tendency of the common people: "Mencius said, 'It is only gentlemen who, lacking a steady livelihood, can maintain a steady heart. If the common people lack a steady livelihood, then they will lack a steady heart.'"

5 Food and Goods

Ritual, rightness, integrity, and shame are upheld when the people do not lack clothing and food and when both the high and the low diligently perform their work and have no fiscal deficiencies. It stands to reason that those who lack a stable occupation will encounter difficulties getting by and that they will consistently be unable to establish a place for themselves in the world. Moreover, it is dishonorable for those of official rank, to say nothing of feudal lords who possess an entire district or province, to encounter difficulties with clothing and food and to be lacking in funds, thus putting their wives, children, and retainers in hardship. For this reason, in governing the country of Qi, Guan Zhong made enriching the country the basis of his policies. When the country is rich, then it is easy to make the military strong as well. Therefore, such an approach is called "the Way of enriching the country and strengthening the military." To label this notion of "enriching the country and strengthening the military" a technique of hegemons is a mistaken theory of worthless Confucians of later times. Beginning with Yao and Shun and extending down to the teachings of Confucius, the Way with which the sages governed the realm was nothing other than that of enriching the country and strengthening the military. Within the general concept of enriching the country and strengthening the military, it is enriching the country that forms the basis of strengthening the military. For this reason, those who govern the realm and state should concentrate on food and goods, provide for their subjects, set in place the four moorings, and consider how to avoid deficiencies in the finances of the country and the army.

In governing the realm, to value grain and disdain currency is the proper government of ancient times and the Way of the ancient kings. Grain is the food of the people and food is as heaven to the people: it is something that the people cannot get by a single day without. Currency is gold, silver, and copper. Although people think that gold and silver are superb treasures, when one is starving one cannot fill one's belly by chewing on gold and silver, while one can stave off death by eating a single bowl of gruel. When it is cold, one cannot warm up by piling gold and silver as high as a mountain and living inside it, while one can avoid becoming sick by putting on a single garment. Gold and silver, then, are not things that save people from hunger and cold.

The reason the foolish common people believe gold and silver to be treasures superior to rice and grain, though, is that they think that if one has gold and silver then it will be easy to obtain rice and grain. In a well-governed age, barter and trade flourish everywhere, so as long as one has gold and silver one can immediately obtain rice, grain, cotton, and silk. Moreover, rice and grain are bulky and heavy, so it is burdensome to carry them around, whereas gold and silver can be put in one's money pouch and carried at the waist, a single handful being sufficient to take care of many needs during a trip of 100 or 1,000 *li*. Because of this, the foolish people of common society think that there is no treasure greater than these. But if they found themselves in an age of civil unrest or, even in a well-governed age, if it were a time when rice and grain were scarce due to a bad harvest, making it difficult to obtain them with gold and silver, then what would they do? This clearly demonstrates the truth that the virtue of gold and silver is inferior to that of rice and grain.

The ancients understood this truth, so Chao Cuo [c. 200–154 BC] of the Han dynasty submitted a report to Emperor Wen in which he promoted valuing grain and disdaining currency.[10] In Japan as well, it appears that in ancient times they valued grain and did not use gold and silver in the way that later ages have. In the present age, though, the people of the realm have converged on the eastern capital of Edo and everyone lives like travelers at an inn, from feudal lords and other lofty personages down to the common people, so it has become the custom to handle everything with gold and silver, with the same practice then extending all the way out to distant provinces. As a result, the way that people disdain rice and grain and value gold and silver has become more pronounced than in ancient times. Born in a time of peace, they do not understand that food is as heaven to the people.

When one speaks of scholar-officials, farmers, artisans, and merchants as the "four types of common people," this implies that scholar-officials too are common people. However, farmers produce the five grains, artisans produce utensils, and merchants fulfill people's needs, so these three make a living through their occupations. Scholar-officials, though, serve the country and make a living from the stipend provided by their lord. For this reason, scholar-officials are sometimes

---

10 Chao Cuo was an official and political advisor who served under emperors Wen and Jing (188–141 BC, r. 157–141 BC) of the Han dynasty. Although he played an important role in reviving the *Classic of Documents*, he is known more as a Legalist than a Confucian. He was critical of the growth of merchant wealth at the expense of peasants and also played an important role in developing new military tactics, specifically with cavalry. The "Biography of Chao Cuo" in chapter 101 of the *Records of the Grand Historian* tells of how he submitted over ten reports to Emperor Wen outlining various policy suggestions. It notes that Wen did not follow any of these suggestions, but still promoted him to palace counselor because he was impressed by his ability.

5 Food and Goods

removed from this formulation, with the "four types of common people" defined as farmers, artisans, traders, and shopkeepers. "Traders" are those who travel around selling things, whereas "shopkeepers" are those who stay in their place of business selling things; both are types of merchants. In the occupations of the common people, there is the root and there are the branches. Farming is called the "root occupation" and the activities of artisans, traders, and shopkeepers are called "branch occupations."

The four types of common people are a treasure of the country, and a country cannot function if a single one of these is missing. That being said, when farmers are few, clothing and food become scarce in the country, so the government of the ancient kings particularly valued farming. Farming involves extreme hardship, though: not only must farmers toil the entire year, they also receive little profit and are not able to eat the choicest grains they produce. Because of this, they envy the fact that artisans and merchants toil little and receive great profits, leading many to abandon farming in favor of becoming artisans and merchants. Even if they do not move to castle towns, when they engage in trade in the countryside their profit is greater than they would receive from farming, so they neglect the cultivation of the land and devote their energies to trade. This is the typical situation with the common people. When this happens, it results in the decline of the country, since a reduction in the number of farmers causes rice and grain to become scarce. When artisans and merchants grow more numerous, various goods are produced and come in from all directions, so it arouses a desire for luxury in people and it becomes the custom to place great value on gold and silver. The finances of the country gradually become deficient, which brings about destitution among both the high and the low and is of great harm to the state. Because of this, in the government of the sages they corrected family registers, periodically altered the number of households and people belonging to each of the four classes, and prohibited farmers from shifting to other occupations without authorization. In the present age there are no such prohibitions, so artisans and merchants grow more numerous by the day and fill up every corner of the country. Although it may seem convenient for taking care of people's needs, it arouses in people a desire for extravagance and gold and silver currency end up entirely in the storehouses of merchants. Is this not lamentable?

To abhor hardship and be fond of ease is a natural human feeling. It is common to both past and present that the four classes all fail to perform their own occupations, envy the occupations of others, enjoy idleness, and wallow in ease. The words of Mencius state that "one must not be lax in the affairs of the common people."[11] Among the four classes it is farmers who experience particularly extreme hardship, so if they are not strictly commanded from above, but are instead simply left to their own devices, then so long as they are not immediately faced with the suffering of starvation and cold, they will be neglectful in cultivating their fields and will not be diligent in their work, causing them to go straight to destitution and poverty. For this reason, even though the Way of governing the common people is not merciless, excessive laxness is also harmful to the common people. It is appropriate, then, that those above sometimes command strictly, and that after closely examining which people diligently carry out their occupations and which people neglect them, they give these people appropriate rewards and punishments.

In China there is something called the "encouragement of farming," in which a messenger is sent from the ruler to encourage agricultural work among the common people. The ruler hears reports from an area's functionaries about people who have served their parents and elders well or exerted themselves in farming and cultivated their fields well, and these people are rewarded by the ruler for their filial piety and brotherly obedience or their work in the fields. Because of this, the common people never have thoughts of indolence or sloth and are diligent in their farming, so they never fall into poverty. When the common people are enriched, the country is also enriched. Ultimately the common people are like small children. They become either good or bad depending on the government and teachings that come to them from above.

It is land that constitutes the treasure of the son of heaven and feudal lords. When Mencius speaks of how "feudal lords have three treasures," he lists land as the first of these.[12] There are five terms for land; these are called the "five types of land." This can be seen in the *Rituals of Zhou*.[13] The first is forests, the second is rivers and marshes, the third is knolls and hills, the fourth is embankments and flats, and the fifth is meadows and paddies. In the case of mountains, earth and soil are piled up high. Forests have much bamboo and wood. Rivers are where water flows. The term "marsh" is glossed as "swamp," but it includes such things

---

11 *Mencius* 3.1.3.2.
12 *Mencius* 7.2.28. The other two things listed in the passage are the common people and the business of government.
13 This appears in the "Di guan si tu" ("Office of Earth") chapter of the *Rituals of Zhou*.

5 Food and Goods

as ponds and lakes as well. The term "knoll" is glossed as "mound"; it refers to where the earth is slightly elevated. Hills are similar, but larger. "Embankments" are the cliffs along the edges of waterways; they are what in common speech are called "bluffs." "Flats" are places where the land is low and even. "Meadows" refers to places that are high, flat, and open. "Paddies" refers to places that are low and wet.

Each of these five types of land has its use; they all sustain the people and become treasures of the state. Land is always producing things. It is land that produces valuable grains such as rice and barley, and even if it does not produce these valuable grains, it never fails to produce some kind of grain that the people can eat. In addition to food, land produces various other things that are of benefit to the country. This is how heaven and earth sustain humans. Heaven and earth do not speak, though, nor do they take people by the hand and teach them. Although there is a Way through which the five types of land all come to benefit the people and become the treasure of the country, in the absence of wise people there are none who know of this, and in the absence of heroic figures it is impossible to practice it.

In ancient China, among the subjects of the king of Wei there was one by the name of Li Kui [455–395 BC].[14] He established the Way of exhausting the power of the land, practiced this in the country of Wei, and greatly enriched the country. To "exhaust the power of the land" means to gain all the benefits that come from the land without leaving anything untapped. In later ages there were few who knew this Way, and even if they did know it, they did not have the influence to practice it within their countries, so they were unable to try out its techniques. In the mountains of the country of Chu there was a precious jade called the "Jade Disk of the Evening Light."[15] A person by the name of Bian He discovered it and presented it to the King of Chu. When the King of Chu then showed it to his jeweler, the jeweler said that it was not a

---

14 Li Kui was an influential figure in the development of what would later come to be known as Legalism. In addition to the agricultural reforms that Shundai describes, he promoted meritocracy (as opposed to hereditary privilege) to fill offices, a clearly codified legal system, and government intervention in grain markets to stabilize prices and guard against famine.
15 A reference to a famous jade disk also known as the "Jade Disk of He." The story of the discovery of this jade by a certain Mr. He is recounted in a number of texts, such as the "He shi" ("Mr. He") chapter of *Hanfeizi*. This jade is said to have eventually come into the possession of the country of Zhao, which in 283 BC was offered fifteen cities for it by King Zhaoxiang of Qin (324–251 BC, r. 306–251 BC).

precious stone, but merely an ordinary rock. Based on the charge that he tried to deceive his ruler by pretending that a mere rock was a precious stone, one of Bian He's feet was cut off. After that he presented it again. Just as before he was not believed, and his other foot was cut off. Bian He went into the mountains holding this precious stone and wailed for three days and three nights. Because of this, the King of Chu took up the stone and ordered his jeweler to polish it. When he did so, it turned out to be a beautiful jewel after all, unparalleled in the realm. When Bian He had discovered this stone and presented it as a precious jewel, but had not yet polished it, it appeared to be a mere rock, so he was labeled a deceiver and had both of his feet cut off. If he had said that there was treasure lying deep within the mountain, would people not have been even less likely to believe him?

The Way of exhausting the power of the land is also like this. People are not drawn to benefits that are not immediately seen. When one tries to set one's mind on something whose benefits will not be apparent for five or ten years, then one will never be able to find like-minded people. They will simply be skeptical because its effectiveness is not apparent and will worry about the human labor and expenditure of gold and silver involved, so there will surely be nobody willing to launch such an undertaking. In the present age, even if Li Kui were to come back to life, it would no doubt be difficult for him to practice his Way. This is to say nothing of how there are few people who resemble Li Kui to begin with.

There are surely many places within the country where the power of the land has not yet been exhausted and its potential is left unexploited. "Exhausting the power of the land" is not just limited to producing the five grains. The land is what produces all the myriad things, so whenever one understands what can be produced effectively out of the five types of land and then extracts these things, this will be of use to the people and of benefit to the country. The people of today think that land that cannot be turned into paddies is useless and consider land that does not produce the five grains to be wasteland. This is a great error. The land is what provides for the people. The five grains are what sustain the lives of the people, so they are the most valuable treasure and of course no country can get by without them. However, the land of the realm has various types of innate qualities, and there are places where it is difficult to produce the five grains. When it is difficult to produce the five grains, there is always something else that the land is able to produce. If it were the rule that the land of the realm only produced the five grains and nothing else, this would surely be inconvenient for the people. The ancient sages distinguished among the five types of land, then, because their benefits are not limited to the five grains.

There is a creator deity that produces various things out of the land and dispenses them for the use of the people, so if one is able to use human judgment to grasp the distinctions among the five types of land, does not injure the things that are produced out of these, and cultivates them well, then such benefits as exist in the land will emerge without leaving anything behind, and they will moreover not be exhausted even after being used. This is called the "inexhaustible storehouse" [*mujinzō*]. This inexhaustible storehouse exists everywhere, so if one contemplates the inexhaustible storehouse of a particular place, extracts the things of that inexhaustible storehouse, and on top of this carries out exchange with other places, bartering what one has for what one lacks, then one will not want for any necessities. This manner of governing the land is referred to as "exhausting the power of the land" and as "leaving no unexploited benefits." "Unexploited benefits" refers to when things that are of benefit to the country are left untaken and remain hidden. The Way of Li Kui teaches about such matters. This technique is something about which people of today merely have a rough worldly wisdom that they are born with, and is not something that can be achieved by people who do not have knowledge gained through learning. It is exceedingly rare for people to understand this. In recent times there are people who can be said to have exhausted the power of their land, such as an official of the feudal lord of Tsuwano named Tako, who produced writing paper and enriched his country. After that, when we observe how Tokugawa Mitsukuni [1628–1701] governed the country of Mito, it is evident that he understood how to exhaust the power of the land.[16] Apart from these, I have not heard of many cases.

From ancient times, clearing wild grasses and weeds has been considered a good governmental policy for a country. In the phrase "clearing wild grasses and weeds," the term used for "weeds" literally means "mugwort." The entire phrase refers to developing uncultivated land that has become overgrown with grasses and weeds in order to create new paddies. To have many areas of wild grasses and weeds in a country is a disgrace for

---

16 The daimyo of Mito belonged to a cadet branch of the Tokugawa family. It is not clear exactly which policies Shundai is describing here, but he may be referring to Mitsukuni's promotion of trade with the Ainu.

its ruler, and to open up lands and create new paddies is truly good government. However, the development of new paddies is a vast undertaking. If one launches into it hastily, it often damages the old paddies. There are times when it simply harms the people, and times when it brings about great harm before it can offer any benefit to the country. If a ruler takes a liking to such a policy, however, and the people responsible for handling government use it to try to gain recognition, then those below who adopt the preferences of those above in order to seek out personal profit will always raise a commotion and request such a policy. Such people do not discuss the benefits and harm to the state, nor do they consider the suffering of the common people. They only speak about schemes for the immediate moment and plot how they can launch these enterprises, so they come up with clever arguments and worm their way into the hearts of their rulers. Rulers do not have detailed knowledge of the affairs of the common people, nor are they deeply versed in geography, so they are often seduced by the arguments of those who make such requests and do not think of the harm that will follow later. When this harm eventually occurs, they put a stop to these matters at once, but the suffering that the common people have endured does not go away, nor is the harm that has been done to the country reversed. To propose such ideas is referred to as "making arguments that promote profit." "Promoting profit" means to give priority to profitable gain. Since ancient times this has been despised within the state. For this reason, even though opening up new fields is something to be celebrated, the ancients took care with it and did not undertake it hastily, since the benefits and harm that come from it are difficult to predict.

In addition, as I described above, each of the five types of land has its particular usefulness. Flat meadows and wide-open fields may seem useless when compared to paddies, but in times of peace one lets cows and horses loose in them and pastures them there, where their grazing keeps the grass trimmed and results in manure for use in paddies. For the hunting outings of rulers, too, flat meadows and wide-open fields are indispensable. In the remote chance that there is a great emergency in the country, if one does not have open spaces for the massing of several hundreds of thousands of troops, then there are times when one will end up trampling good paddies. It is beneficial to sow the five grains, but there are times when turning all pasturelands into paddies creates problems. One should think about this and take it into account.

Rivers and marshes are places where water flows and comes to a stop respectively, and they are another one of the five types of land. It is in the nature of water to flow and it ultimately ends up in the ocean, but on its way to the ocean there are places where there are hollows in the land, so the waters pool together from all directions and form ponds, bogs, and, when large, lakes. This is a result of the formations of the land and not something created by humans; it is a natural phenomenon brought about by heaven. It would be greatly mistaken to think swamplands useless just because they do not produce the five grains. Rivers have the virtue of rivers and swamps have the virtue of swamps. The character for "swamp" is glossed as "to irrigate," so it has the meaning of "abundance"; it has the virtue of giving abundance to the land. Those today who discuss promoting profit are partial to draining ponds and marshes in order to create new paddies. In draining the natural ponds and marshes created by heaven, one always opens up new waterways and creates conduits for water. In doing so, though, one demolishes many paddies and destroys villages, so the suffering of the common people is extreme and the harm to the country is great. When there are ponds and swamps, in times of drought one draws water from them to supply the paddies, and in times of long rainy spells and torrential rains, rainwater pools in these places and is kept there to irrigate the paddies later. Because of this, swamps, ponds, and lakes are things the country cannot do without. To think this a waste and to drain their water to create more paddies is to fail to understand the uses of the five types of land.

In China, when Wang Anshi [1021–1086] served as prime minister during the Song dynasty and took hold of the government of the realm, he was partial to the development of new paddies, so many people emerged from below with proposals for these and presented various arguments.[17] Among them there was one who wanted to drain a lake 500 *li* across called Lake Tai and create new paddies, so Wang Anshi was overjoyed and was ready to commence the project. On a day when he had a number of visitors, he spoke about this matter to them, asking each one for his opinion on how to drain the water out of Lake Tai. All the visitors either fawned on him or were utterly unable to judge what should be done. No answer forthcoming, a person by the name of Liu Gongfu said that the problem they had been presented was in fact quite simple to resolve. Wang Anshi then asked him to explain how it could be done. Liu Gongfu replied that

---

17 Wang Anshi was an influential politician of the Song dynasty as well as a major poet. As a politician, he attempted to carry out wide-ranging economic reforms designed to raise the standard of living of the common people.

in order to drain Lake Tai, one could excavate another lake of the same size right next to it and then drain the water of Lake Tai into this new lake. It is said that upon hearing this, Wang Anshi, being after all a man of learning, immediately understood, laughed out loud, and abandoned the project. Wang Anshi would be expected to understand this kind of thing, but even he was led astray by gain and his wisdom became clouded. What Liu Gongfu said about digging another Lake Tai took the logic of the proposal to its inevitable conclusion. When one dries out a lake created by heaven that is essential to the earth, then if one does not create another one in its place using human power, heaven will necessarily create one. However, unless one is a person who understands heaven and earth, one will not be able to grasp this principle. Since ancient times, when people filled in marshes to make level ground or drained water to create new paddies, those areas always had many problems with flooding. There are many examples of this in both other countries and our own.

Mountains, rivers, valleys, hills, mounds, and marshes are strategic points in the country and keep it secure. When building a city and erecting city walls, as a rule one relies on strategic points. In the *Classic of Changes* it says, "The strategic points of the earth are mountains, rivers, hills, and mounds. Kings and nobles establish strategic points to protect their country."[18] When one leaves marshes as marshes, then, they serve as a fortification for the country; one should not hastily eliminate them. Also, when there are trees on mountains then there is always water as well, and when there is water on a mountain, then at the base of the mountain there are marshes, which sustain the paddies of that area. When there are no trees on a mountain, there is never water. Water gives birth to trees and trees grow by receiving water, so once they have grown there is water within the trees. This is an example of being endowed with the material force of one's mother. Therefore, if one cuts down all the trees on a mountain, the material force of water on the mountain will run out and the rivers and marshes at the base of the mountain will always dry out. When rivers and marshes dry out, there will be no way to create paddies. If one has a poor understanding of what it means to exhaust the power of the land, and as a consequence completely cuts down mountain forests, this will surely invite ruin.

In addition, the production of fish from the sea truly has no limit, but in the time of Emperor Wu of the Han dynasty, the fish in the sea were

---

18 From the *Tuan Commentary* on the "Gorge" (*kan*) hexagram.

appropriated by prefectural officials, after which no more fish were produced from the sea. Later the common people were allowed to catch fish, so fish again were produced from the sea. After that, when the sea tax was raised, fish were no longer produced, but when this tax was lowered, fish were produced again. Just because something is an inexhaustible storehouse made by the creator, it does not mean that one can recklessly take everything that comes from it. For this reason, even when acting based on an understanding of the Way of exhausting the power of the land, one must consider things carefully. The term "prefectural officials" refers to governmental authorities. The "sea tax" is the yearly tribute on products of the sea. To "consider things carefully" means to give thought to what is appropriate when taking things.

There are three things that peasants offer up to their rulers: taxes, labor, and tribute. This is the method of the Tang court. "Tax" refers to tax payments; this is what in the common language of today is called the "annual payment." "Labor" refers to compulsory service. "Tribute" is glossed as "offerings of goods." It includes not only rice and grains, but also other goods that come from the land. There are many such goods, such as salt, liquor, tea, lacquer, cloth, thread, cotton, paper, charcoal, firewood, oil, wax, fruits, medicines, birds and animals, fish and turtles, feathers, and leather. These are called "products of the land." Normally one offers up one-tenth of one's output of such products; this is the ancient method and is the same in both other countries and our own.

To discuss the first of these, tax, let us set aside for a moment the method of China and the ancient method of Japan. In the present age, a field tax is taken. The standard amount is four parts in ten, so that out of 10 *koku* of rice, one offers up 4 *koku* to the ruler; this is what is commonly known today as "four pieces." Depending on the fertility of the soil and the quality of the paddies, there are cases where more than four parts is taken and cases where less than four parts is taken; the standard method of today's world is to take four as the average.[19] When viewed from the perspective of the ancient method of the well-field system, which took one part in ten, this may seem like a heavy tax burden, but in today's

---

19 The reason the actual percentage paid would vary is that the amount of tax due was based not on the actual amount that was harvested, but on the estimated yield as determined by a tax assessor. Fields that produced less than their assessed yield would have a higher actual tax rate, then, and fields that produced more would have a lower rate.

world this does not make the common people suffer.[20] To lighten the tax burden is the humane government of a king, so it is only natural that a low rate of taxation is considered good. However, the common people are like small children. As long as they have enough to survive and eat, if the government of their rulers is excessively lenient, then without realizing it they will become slothful and indolent and no longer dedicate themselves to cultivation. There are those who then end up falling into wrongdoing as they come to lack what they need for clothing and food, suffer from starvation and cold, and are pressed by their annual tax burden.

In government it is good to strike a balance between lenience and severity; this is the teaching of Confucius. However, from the past down to the present, there are a great many cases where rulers have made the common people suffer through harsh taxation and in the end lost their country. I have yet to hear, though, of cases in recent times where low taxation has reached the point of harming the common people. In the end, so long as the ruler puts a stop to extravagance and there is nothing wanting for the fiscal needs of the country, then even without taking a large amount from the common people there will be nothing lacking. To take from the common people in an unjust manner is called "harsh extraction." Harsh extraction is a form of cruel government. When one practices cruel government, this leads straight to disaster for the country. I do not have time to present all the instances of this that I have seen and heard about in recent times.

As for the second item, labor, since ancient times it has been the established corvée method that the common people are called upon and employed for military service, building projects, and hunting expeditions. However, if one employs the common people for these during seasons of agricultural work, then it brings about suffering for the common people and causes harm to the country, so the humane government of kings is to avoid doing this during seasons of agricultural work, and instead to employ people during intervals of idleness. When Confucius spoke of "employing the common people according to the seasons," this

---

20 In the well-field system of ancient China, each area of land was divided into nine equal squares in the shape of the character for "well," which resembles a hash or pound sign. The outer eight squares were cultivated by individual peasants for their own private use, while the middle square was worked communally by all the peasants for the benefit of their feudal lord. Although the precise nine-square layout of plots of land was merely a theoretical construct, the significance of the system for commentators like Shundai was its tax rate of one-ninth, not the exact layout of the fields.

is what he was referring to.[21] When in the "Kingly Regulations" chapter of the *Record of Ritual* it says, "The employment of the labor of the common people did not exceed three days in a year," this speaks of the ancient method. When it is unavoidable that the corvée imposed on the common people not be limited to three days, this is not necessarily considered unjust. It is simply that when corvée is excessive the peasants will always suffer, so it is considered humane government for the ruler to think about how to reduce it to an appropriate amount. In the present age, though, it is rare for peasants to be used for corvée. When it comes to building projects and the like, in cities people employ wage laborers. Military expeditions and conquests are not something that exist in times of peaceful government, but when people known as "border guards" go to protect places like Osaka, Kyoto, and Sunpu, these can indeed be considered military expeditions. However, even for these military personnel, the feudal lords of today do not make use of the common people of their country, but instead hire wage laborers from Edo. Wage laborers are what are commonly known today as "day workers." Whenever it comes to things that would normally be tasks for corvée, people instead pay out money to employ wage laborers, so it does not become a cause of suffering for the common people, but instead becomes a benefit for them. This is the difference in systems between past and present.

As for the third item, tribute, as I said above, the ancient method was to have one-tenth of all the products of the land presented to the ruler. For this reason, if one were to take an excess amount and be unjust in one's takings, it would lead to suffering for the common people. Such a practice is therefore considered cruel government. In the present age, it is uncommon for such things to be taken from the households of the common people. Instead, for the most part they are purchased with gold and silver from merchants. Because of this, one can say that there is no system of tribute in today's world.

...

Fluctuations in the price of rice affect the benefits and losses that come to the people. Those who govern the country must use all their energy in carefully considering this point. Among the four classes, farmers are the ones who produce grain. After paying their taxes they eat what remain, and they then sell what is still left after that and purchase things for

---

21 From *Analects* 1.5.

On Political Economy

various uses. The samurai receive a rice stipend from their lord, and with this stipend they fulfill their needs for everything from clothing and food to various other useful things. Artisans produce utensils, so by laboring with their four limbs they can exchange things for rice. Merchants sell goods and buy rice. Among the four classes, farmers and samurai sell rice, while artisans and merchants buy it. For this reason, when rice is expensive it benefits samurai and farmers and harms artisans and merchants, whereas when rice is cheap it benefits artisans and merchants and harms samurai and farmers.

From ancient times, low rice prices have been considered a sign of great peace. It is said that in the reign of Emperor Zhao [94–74 BC, r. 87–74 BC] of the Han dynasty, 1 *koku* of rice traded for 5 cash,[22] and in the reign of Emperor Taizong [598–649, r. 626–649] of the Tang dynasty, 1 *to* [= 0.1 *koku*] of rice traded for 3 or 4 cash. This is truly a benefit reaped from great peace. Although one might explain these examples away by saying that ancient measures of volume were smaller and money had more value, the fact remains that such prices as 5 cash for 1 *koku* or 3 or 4 cash for 1 *to* are extremely low. To call this a sign of great peace is to praise the fact that rice and grain were plentiful and the people did not want for food. It is true that even in those times, when the price of rice was excessively low, this disadvantaged both scholar-officials and farmers. However, from the ancient past up until recent times, people of the four classes used rice to obtain all the various things they needed, unlike the present age, when people use gold and silver. For this reason, even if the price of rice was low, rice and grain were plentiful and filled the storehouses, so neither scholar-officials nor farmers were impoverished.

Today, everyone from feudal lords down to the common people gathers together in Edo, where they live as if at an inn, so they use gold and silver to fulfill all of their needs. Because of this, when the price of rice is high

---

22 "Cash" is the standard English term for a type of low-value coin, typically made of copper alloy, used in China from the Warring States period to the end of the Qing dynasty. Even without attempting precise comparisons of coin values over time, the large price differential Shundai is pointing to between ancient China and the Japan of his own day is evident from the data he provides later, where he notes that 1,000–4,000 Yongle coins (a variety of cash coin) traded for 1 gold *ryō*, and 1 gold *ryō* purchased between 0.4 and 1.6 *koku* of rice in Japan in recent decades. The lowest rice price in recent times that can be derived from these numbers (combining the lowest rice price in *ryō* with the most optimistic cash/*ryō* exchange rate) is 250 cash for 1 *koku*, while the highest price he cites above from the Tang dynasty is equivalent to 40 cash for 1 *koku*.

5 Food and Goods

the samurai are overjoyed, and when it is low they are troubled. When the samurai accumulate large amounts of gold and silver, they spend it all on momentary pleasures and luxuries, since as warriors they are slow when it comes to matters of profit and have little inclination to save gold and silver. At these times, artisans and merchants profit and are delighted. Even though they pay high prices for rice, they only need a small amount of it to eat and they make large profits, so they do not suffer that much from rice being expensive. When the price of rice is low, the samurai lack gold and silver, so artisans and merchants too make little profit. Because of this, when the price of rice is extremely low today, the four classes all fall into poverty, even more so than in ancient times. This is something that differs between government past and present.

When the price of rice is extremely low it is harmful to scholar-officials and farmers, and when it is extremely high it is harmful to artisans and merchants, so in the reign of Emperor Xuan [91–49 BC, r. 74–49 BC] of the Han dynasty, a person named Geng Shouchang [fl. 75–49 BC] submitted a proposal for the creation of stabilization granaries [Ch. *changpingcang*, Jp. *jōheisō*], which were then constructed in various places. When the price of grain was low, the authorities would buy up grain from the people at a higher price and store it in the granaries. When the price of grain was high, they would sell what they had accumulated at a lower price. Thanks to this, the price of grain was neither too high nor too low, but always remained at an appropriate level, so the scholar-officials, farmers, artisans, and merchants all escaped harm. To store up grain is to guard in stable times against bad harvests and famine. In the remote chance of a war, this grain provides food for the army, so it is an important business of the state. These kinds of techniques are also practiced today.[23] When storing grain for long periods, as long as one stores it unhulled, insects will never infest it and it will not rot.

In the present age, from the foundation of the country down to the time of Tsunayoshi, the price of rice was very low, but the samurai did not become particularly impoverished. This is because the customs of the world were plain and simple, there was no luxury, and the prices of other things were low as well. During the time of Tsunayoshi, up until the middle of the Genroku era [1688–1704], the price of rice was still low, with

---

23 A number of domains in Tokugawa Japan, such as Aizu, Mito, Satsuma, and Tosa, had such granaries.

the price of rice in Edo being such that 1 gold *ryō* purchased between 1.2–1.3 and 1.5–1.6 *koku*. Tsunayoshi enjoyed luxury and showiness, so prices gradually increased and the samurai suffered. At that time, when samurai talked among themselves they lamented the low price of rice, saying that if 1 gold *ryō* were equivalent to 1 *koku*, then that would be enough for them to get by. However, as a consequence of the luxury of those above, a large amount of gold and silver circulated and it was also easy to borrow these, so samurai did not lack funds to fulfill their needs.

In the autumn of the twelfth year of the Genroku era, Yin Earth Rabbit year [1699], on the night of the fifteenth day of the eighth month there was a great windstorm.[24] Since the grain did not ripen, the following winter the price of warehoused grain was set at 50 gold *ryō* for 35 *koku* of rice, in other words 1 gold *ryō* for 7 *to* [0.7 *koku*] of rice. The price of rice, which had long been low, suddenly shot up, so the samurai reaped large profits and were overjoyed. Artisan and merchant commoners could barely afford two meals of gruel per day, no matter how hard they worked. The price of rice remained high like this for three years, so in the winter of the Yin Metal Snake year [1701] there were many hungry people in the capital and people dying of starvation along the roads. Tsunayoshi ordered his officials to construct small buildings in their home villages where they would boil many *koku* of rice every day into gruel and provide this to the hungry people. This went on for a hundred days, and when the spring of the following year arrived, the number of hungry people gradually decreased.

In the two subsequent years the grain ripened and the price of rice too ought to have fallen gradually, but on the evening of the twenty-second day of the eleventh month of the Yin Water Ram year [1703], there was a great earthquake in Edo. All the provinces of the Kanto region suffered calamitous harm, and both major and minor feudal lords sent many people to castle towns to work on construction repairs, causing the realm to suffer under corvée. In the following year, when the era name changed to Hōei, on the third day of the seventh month there was flooding in the region to the northeast of Edo. The grain did not grow and rice prices returned to their previous high level. In the fourth year of the Hōei era, Yin Fire Boar year [1707], during the latter part of the tenth month there was an eruption of Mount Fuji and the ash rained down over a distance of

---

24 Shundai writes "tenth year of Genroku," but from the sexagenary year and the events he describes, it is clear that this is the twelfth year of the Genroku era.

5 Food and Goods

tens of *li*. An uncountable number of fields in the provinces of the Kanto region were buried in ash and went to ruin. Because of this, rice prices rose even higher.

In the Yin Earth Ox year [1709], Tsunayoshi died and Ienobu [1662–1712, r. 1709–1712] became shogun. From the autumn of the first year of the Shōtoku era, the Yin Metal Rabbit year [1711], rice prices fell gradually. In the spring of the Yang Water Dragon year [1712], 1 gold *ryō* purchased around 9 *to* [0.9 *koku*] of rice. By this time, the shogunate had already abolished the debased currency of the Genroku era and the new currency of the Hōei era [1704–1711] was being circulated.[25] Based on a shogunal command that 2 gold *ryō* of the Hōei currency could be exchanged for 1 *ryō* of the old Keichō era [1596–1615] currency, the common people quickly discounted the Hōei currency and considered 1 *ryō* of Hōei currency to be in reality half a *ryō*. At a time when the price of rice ought to have been falling gradually, it rose again because the value of the people's money was cut in half.

In the tenth month of the Yang Water Dragon year [1712], Ienobu died and left behind an injunction declaring to the realm that the currency ought to be reformed. In the time of Ietsugu [1709–1716, r. 1713–1716], the value of Hōei currency fell gradually, and 1 gold *ryō* purchased a little over 4 *to* [0.4 *koku*] of rice. By the end of the Shōtoku era [1711–1716], there were again commoners who were suffering from hunger, but fewer than in the past. Up until the end of Ietsugu's reign, currency reform had still not yet been carried out. By now, though, there had been a return to the old Keichō currency. From the beginning of the Kyōhō era [1716–1736] up until the sixth year of Kyōhō, the price of rice again rose to its previous level. During the twenty-plus years from the Yin Earth Rabbit year [1699] to the Yin Metal Ox year [1721], the price of rice fluctuated somewhat, but even when it was at its lowest it did not go below 1 gold *ryō* for 1 *koku*. From the winter of the Yin Metal Ox year [1721], the price of rice again rose very high, and in the summer of the following year, the rice in government warehouses sold for 56 of today's gold *ryō* (112 *ryō* in Hōei currency) for a hundred sacks of rice, which is equivalent to a price of one of today's gold *ryō* for 6.25 *to* [0.625 *koku*] of rice.[26] This is

---

25 Tsunayoshi had begun a series of currency debasements in 1695. This policy was reversed with the issuance of higher-quality coinage in 1710.

26 As can be calculated from the numbers Shundai provides, each of these sacks is equivalent to 0.35 *koku*.

the most expensive that rice has been since the Genroku era. Why is it, though, that there are no starving people in the capital? It is because in the twenty-plus years since the Yin Earth Rabbit year [1699], the common people have grown accustomed to rice being expensive, they are clever when it comes to making a living, and moreover they receive much gold and silver from samurai. When one hears of times when rice was expensive in the past, one can see that there were starving people at that time despite rice not being as expensive as in recent years, in contrast to how in recent years there have been no starving people despite the extremely high price of rice, due to the difference between being accustomed to something and not being accustomed to it. Being accustomed to something means to be used to it. These kinds of matters are difficult to grasp with vulgar understanding.

It is natural principle that things change when they reach an extreme. From the autumn of the Yang Water Tiger year [1722] rice prices suddenly dropped, then increased a little, and then fell by a large amount. Over six or seven years, rice grew cheaper and cheaper, and came to be worth 40 percent of its previous high price. The common people now view rice as something as worthless as dirt. When houses of officials set aside the rice they need for gruel and sell the rest to provide for other things, it is not even enough for their pressing daily needs, and when they sell a large amount of rice to fulfill their necessities, then they do not have enough to eat. The impoverishment of the samurai is extreme. The farmers, too, are just like the samurai. They amass a large amount of grain in bountiful years, but when they sell this, it is not even enough to compensate for the labor and expenses of the people and horses that transport it, so they barely have enough to feed their households and there is no way for them to earn a profit. When the samurai are impoverished, there is little gold and silver in the world, so artisans and merchants also earn little. For this reason, commoners are now unable to eat the rice that is as cheap as dirt, and there are in fact many people who starve. This is difficult to explain with ordinary reasoning. To consider low rice prices a sign of great peace, as I described above, is a thing of the past. It is a different system from what exists today, in which extremely low rice prices cause the four classes all to become impoverished. The reason for this difference is that in ancient times they valued rice and grain, whereas today people value currency. This kind of phenomenon is called a "change in the course of things." It is difficult to practice government without understanding these changes. The ideas of Jia Yi of the Han dynasty were all of the sort that I have described.[27]

The method of stabilization granaries carried out by Geng Shouchang of the Han dynasty is also practiced today. To discuss the benefits and harm to the four classes with reference to the price of rice being high or low is only a temporary matter. When fruitful years follow one after the other, it is truly wonderful for the country that rice and grain are bountiful in the realm. The official class of today laments the low price of rice and desires that the grain not ripen, but this goes against reason. What I am arguing right now, then, is not that one should reduce the amount of rice in the realm in order to raise its price. At this time, it is desirable to carry out the method of stabilization granaries. The technique for this is to build warehouses in all the different regions of the land and to use these to store the grain of those regions, neither sending it to Edo nor selling it in its place of origin. One should keep it stored there indefinitely. If one does this, then the quantity of rice in Edo will fall somewhat and the price naturally ought to rise.

As long as there is enough rice in Edo to feed the samurai and the classes beneath them, as well as enough saved up to protect against unexpected natural disasters, then there will be no shortage. To transport the rice of the land for anything other than these two purposes should be considered pointless. Useless rice comes to Edo in large quantities, so its price falls to a very low level, causing trouble for the world. When there is little rice in Edo, its price rises. When rice in Edo is expensive, it becomes expensive all throughout the land; this is one benefit. When the price of rice is extremely low, the common people consider it as worthless as dirt. When the price of rice rises somewhat, the people all know to value grain; this is a second benefit. If one builds stabilization granaries and stores up large amounts of grain, then in the remote chance that there is a bad harvest due to things like flooding or drought, it is useful for providing relief to the common people. In the government of the ancient kings they said, "Three years of cultivation always provides enough surplus to eat for one year. Nine years of cultivation always provides enough surplus to eat for three years. After thirty years like this, even if there are disasters,

---

27 Jia Yi was a politician who pursued various institutional reforms. Among other things, he was critical of the merchant class and its pursuit of luxury and saw the peasants as the true foundation of the realm.

droughts, and floods, the common people will not be malnourished."[28] They also said, "If a country does not have stores to last for nine years, it is considered insufficient. If it does not have stores to last for six years, it is considered an emergency. If it does not have stores to last for three years, the country is considered not to exist."[29] To be "malnourished" [lit. "vegetable colored"] refers to when people are starving and eat wild greens, causing their face to take on a sickly coloring. To say that a country is "considered not to exist" means that it is destroyed and seized by others. Therefore, one should not transport grain from distant regions to Edo, but instead leave it in its place of origin and build up stores sufficient for nine or ten years, and if there is an unexpected natural disaster, one should release it and provide relief to the people. If during that time the price of rice becomes extremely high, then one should sell the stored rice at a lower price, and if it becomes extremely low, one should again buy it up and store it in the warehouses. If one does this, then the price will be neither extremely high nor extremely low and the four classes of people will be spared from harm. This is a third benefit. If grain is not transported to Edo, then there will be no shipping costs for the state. This is a fourth benefit. "Shipping" means transportation by boat. Stabilization granaries have these kinds of benefits, so if one makes use of these today, too, it will surely constitute good government. If one sets up stabilization granaries and stores up grain, one should always store unhulled rice. Hulled rice attracts insects and rots easily, but unhulled rice is good for long-term storage. In Japan as well, one can see in history books that in the reigns of former emperors they established stabilization granaries.[30]

...

In China there are what are called "public welfare granaries" [Ch. *yicang*, Jp. *gisō*]. In the reign of Emperor Wen [541–604, r. 581–604] of the Sui dynasty, a person by the name of Zhangsun Ping was the president of the Board of Equipment. The Board of Equipment was an office that handled the various fiscal needs of the state and the expenditures and intake of money and grain. During the Kaihuang era [581–600], Zhangsun Ping

---

28 From the "Kingly Regulations" chapter of the *Record of Ritual*.
29 From the "Kingly Regulations" chapter of the *Record of Ritual*.
30 A system of stabilization granaries was first established in Japan in 759, but was abandoned before the end of the Nara period. A similar system was again put in place in the Heian period.

5 Food and Goods

presented a memorial to set up public welfare granaries in all the various localities, make all the households of the common people contribute a *koku* or less of grain each year in accordance with their means, keep this in storage in the warehouse of that locality, and put the elders of the village in charge of it. In normal times it was to be left stored there, but in times of bad harvests and starvation it was to be released in order to relieve the emergency. This is what is referred to as a "public welfare granary." The label "public welfare" is applied here because the people show mercy to each other and save each other from imminent danger.[31]

Here in Japan, too, this existed in the time of Emperor Monmu, and it is also practiced today. If this is practiced not only among the common people, but also among the officials of the countries of feudal lords, then there will surely be many places where it will make up for what is lacking. In order to emulate methods from the past today, feudal lords with an income of over 10,000 *koku* should take one part in twenty out of their retainers' stipends and put it in the public welfare granary. One part in twenty means to contribute five out of a hundred sacks of rice. It goes without saying that this should be done with stipends of a hundred sacks of rice or more, but even those with small stipends of less than a hundred sacks should all be made to contribute one part in twenty. The ruler himself should also contribute one part in twenty. If his income is 10,000 *koku*, this would amount to 500 *koku*. Both the high and the low should contribute one part in twenty every year to the public welfare granary, and the grain to be stored should include both hulled and unhulled rice. Regarding any remaining surplus rice, one should wait until the price is high and then sell it in exchange for money.

From among the samurai one should select people who are honest and skilled in calculations, put them in charge of the public welfare granaries, and appoint beneath them subordinate functionaries to guard the granaries and handle receipts and disbursements. In years when there is a bad harvest or starvation and people's stipends are not enough to allow them to eat, grain should be disbursed to make up for what is lacking. If in the countries of feudal lords or their mansions in Edo there is a fire and people encounter difficulties as a result, then those in charge of the granaries

---

31 The term translated as "public welfare" is *gi* (Ch. *yi*). Elsewhere this is translated as "rightness," which is its more general meaning in Confucian discourse, but the term can also refer to what is done for the public benefit.

should disburse grain to those who have suffered damage, either giving it to them outright or lending it.

These kinds of things are troubles faced by all the people together. Sickness and mourning can also come to the household of an individual samurai, and times when they unexpectedly are driven into difficulties. Even when they are not unexpected, such things as arranging a marriage for one's daughter or taking a bride involve great cost. At such times, one ought to disburse either grain or currency and lend it to people as and when they request it. Depending on the amount, they ought to return it in the current year, within two or three years, or within four or five years. One should make them pay interest for this. This interest should be set at the level of 1 *shō* [0.01 *koku*] per month for 1 *koku* of rice. The interest on currency ought to follow this as well. The principal and interest to be returned to the public welfare granary should be deducted from the person's annual stipend.

When something unexpected occurs in the household of a samurai and he does not have enough for necessities, if he borrows from outside there are many cases where he pays out a large amount of interest, or else suddenly has the borrowed money demanded of him and is put in dire straits. On top of that, when he is urgently pressed he sells off his treasured heirlooms such as armor, weapons, and horse tack at low prices; he might even pawn off everything down to his everyday clothes, making it difficult to fulfill his duty to his lord. The way that samurai of today lack shame and lose honor arises entirely from this. There are no doubt those who have reservations about lending currency and grain from public welfare granaries and charging interest on it, but pawnbrokers and moneylenders all greedily pursue high interest when they make loans. To contribute to a public welfare granary, rather than paying out high interest to an outsider, is like putting money in one's own storehouse. One does not need to take the risk of relying on others or go to the trouble of preoccupying oneself for them, nor is there any anxiety about being pressed for one's debt at random times, so borrowing from a public welfare granary is very beneficial for samurai. In addition to establishing the kind of method described here, one should also strictly prohibit borrowing from outside and selling off such things as military equipment and clothing, issue edicts against taking on debt for anything and everything, ensure that each samurai is aware of his proper status, and practice government in a way that makes the samurai value frugality and scorn luxury.

5 Food and Goods

If a country is fortunate and goes a long time without any emergencies, then the currency and grain in the public welfare granary will grow abundant with the passage of years. If catastrophe strikes or such things as warfare arise, then if some lack prevents the satisfaction of the fiscal needs of the country or the needs of the military, both lord and subjects ought to borrow the currency and grain of the public welfare granary, take care of the emergency, and pay it back within the space of a few years after things return to normal. If a samurai dies and has no male descendants or relatives to succeed him, meaning that his house is going to be completely cut off, but there is a widow or an orphaned daughter, then one should calculate the grain that has been contributed by that samurai's paternal ancestors and give it to the widow or orphaned daughter. This, too, is an element of humane government.

The technique of public welfare granaries is roughly as I have described. In ordinary times when nothing is amiss, people ought to restrain from extravagance, be frugal with what they use, save any excess money and use it to contend with unexpected needs. However, people who show such restraint are rare and most concern themselves only with what is right before their eyes, so even if people are commanded from above, those who contend with unexpected needs with their own private means are but one in a hundred. Even in these cases people have to rely on the means of a single household, so when something unexpected arises and people have trouble with expenses, there are many who end up using up the savings of several years all at once, leaving them with empty purses and ultimately driving them to destitution.

Public welfare granaries are the savings of the country, not the savings of an individual person. There is a method for filling them and a system for disbursing from them; these are not done freely. The taking of a little bit of rice from each year's stipend is something that is fixed in place, so it does not cause the kind of suffering that arises when private households have to come up with payments out of the blue. All the countless samurai and common people have hearts that are different, and they are also different when it comes to the benefits and harm they receive from the government. All people are alike, though, in that they suffer from a lack of financial resources when they face something unexpected. Therefore, when rulers govern those beneath them, they do not concern themselves with the minor benefits and harm that come to people, but instead always think about methods for getting people

On Political Economy

through unexpected calamities and make provisions for this in ordinary times; this is considered superb government.

Things like the public welfare granaries that I have been discussing are a technique practiced in many different times and places. Today, too, I hear that in the country of Miharu in the Tōhoku region the government of the Akita clan has something similar to public welfare granaries. It is desirable for this to be practiced in the countries of other feudal lords as well. However, this kind of government should be practiced within the context of always governing a country well and ensuring that both the high and the low do not lack for salaries and necessary expenses. The feudal lords today, though, are all impoverished and retain a portion of their retainers' stipends rather than giving them the full amount.[32] It has got to the point where it would be difficult for them to pay back old debts even by using all their income from several years. Because of this, it would surely be difficult to establish public welfare granaries. People who have an ambition to practice political economy should lament this.

I do not know what kind of system of currency Japan had in ancient times, but I have heard that since middle antiquity they used gold dust. It is not completely clear when they began to use silver. As for copper coins, after the minting of Wadō coins, copper coins were seldom minted again.[33] From middle antiquity, large amounts of the Tang dynasty Kaiyuan copper coins came to this country.[34] Later, large amounts of Song dynasty copper coins came over. Because of this, it appears that even without minting copper coins here, there was no shortage of them. Many Yuan dynasty copper coins also came over, and the Ming dynasty Hongwu and Yongle copper coins, because they are from recent times, have also come over in particularly large quantities.[35] For this reason, in Japan the paddies of the Kanto region are valued in Yongle coins, and salaries too are counted in these copper coins as so many hundred thousand or so many

---

32 The pretense was that daimyo were temporarily borrowing a portion of their retainers' stipends, but given that there was no real expectation that these "loans" would be repaid, in practice it simply amounted to a reduction in the retainers' stipends.
33 Wadō coins are named after the Wadō era (708–715), when they were first produced. Wadō literally means "Japanese copper"; the era name itself was inspired by the discovery of an important copper mine, the output of which was used for the coins named after the era.
34 Kaiyuan coins were the main currency of the Tang dynasty.
35 These Ming coins were named after the reigning emperor of the time they were minted. The Hongwu emperor (1328–1398) reigned from 1368 to 1398, and the Yongle emperor (1360–1424) from 1402 to 1424.

5 Food and Goods

ten thousand coins. In this way it was common to use foreign coins, so people here did not mint any coins of their own.

In the present age, new copper coins were first minted during the Kan'ei era [1624–1643]. These are imprinted with the phrase "Kan'ei currency." They are used together with the copper coins from China that have long been used. One thousand Yongle coins are supposed to be equivalent to 1 gold *ryō*.[36] Four Kan'ei coins are then valued as equivalent to 1 Yongle coin. However, due to the production of many new coins, Yongle coins decreased in value and eventually were worth the same as Kan'ei coins. During the Kanbun era [1661–1673], new coins were minted again. The obverse had the phrase "Kan'ei currency" and the reverse had the character *bun*. These were commonly called "*bun* coins." In the Hōei era [1704–1711], more new coins were minted. They had the phrase "Kan'ei currency" on the obverse, but no *bun* character on the reverse. In the Shōtoku era [1711–1716] they were minted again, and then once more in the Kyōhō era [1716–1736]. All of these had the phrase "Kan'ei currency" on the obverse like the coins minted in the Kan'ei era, but had no *bun* character on the reverse. As the new coins that were repeatedly minted have been used, in recent times the quantity of old coins from abroad has gradually decreased.

...

During the Keichō era [1596–1615] of the present age, gold was extracted from the mountains of Sado and was used to produce gold currency. It has remained in use down to the present day. In the Genroku era [1688–1704], funds were lacking for the fiscal needs of the country, so this gold was alloyed with silver, copper, and lead to produce new gold currency, which had the character *gen* on it. In addition to the gold *ōban*, *koban*, and *bu*, gold coins were also produced in a 2 *shu* denomination.[37] These latter were worth half a gold *bu* and were small in size. All four of these denominations of gold currency lacked the true color of yellow gold and had the appearance of brass. They were called "Genroku new gold" and were used throughout the land, while the old gold of Keichō was no longer used.[38] Because this new gold was no longer pure it was

---

36 An official exchange rate of 1,000 Yongle coins to 1 *ryō* was stipulated by a shogunal edict of 1609, although actual exchange rates were determined by market forces.
37 A *bu* was equivalent to one-fourth of a *koban*.
38 The new Genroku currency was first issued in the ninth month of 1695.

On Political Economy

easy to counterfeit, so many counterfeiters emerged. When caught, they were executed by crucifixion. The people disdained this currency for not being pure gold and gradually raised the prices of goods. The nominal value of the new gold was no lower than that of the old gold, but because the prices of goods went up, this amounted in reality to a decrease in the value of gold currency. Moreover, a great quantity of counterfeit gold circulated among the people, and those who could not recognize it were victims of fraud.

Ienobu deeply lamented this situation and from the time of his accession as shogun he contemplated restoring the gold currency to what it had been before. However, he took into account the fact that Genroku gold was mixed with silver, copper, and lead in equal quantity to actual gold, so that if one were to redeem it and make it into pure gold like the old Keichō gold, then the quantity of gold currency in the realm would be cut in half.[39] Because of this, in the period leading up to the return to the old currency, as a first step he had small-denomination gold currency produced. He melted down Genroku gold *koban* and 1 *bu* coins, removed the impurities from these, and produced new currency using pure gold.[40] It was thin and small and its weight was one half that of the old currency.[41] The new gold *koban* had a weight of 2.4 *sen* and the new gold *bu* had a weight of 0.6 *sen*.[42] He did not issue a new version of the gold *ōban*. He planned to abolish the 2 *shu* coin altogether, so he did not issue a new version of this either. This new currency was used from the end of the Hōei era [1704–1711] and was used side by side with Genroku gold.[43] The new gold *koban* had the character *kan* on it, so it was labeled "*kan* gold." Ever since this currency was issued there have been no more counterfeiters, nor have people suffered from being victims of fraud, so the people considered this a beneficial change.

---

39 Shundai's numbers are approximate here. Genroku currency was in fact slightly more than half gold, with a gold content of 56.7 percent. Keichō currency was not pure gold, but rather had a gold content ranging from 84.3 percent to 86.8 percent. Reminting Genroku currency at the Keichō level of purity, then, would result not in a halving of the nominal value of gold currency, but a reduction of about one-third.
40 The actual gold content was 84.3 percent, essentially a return to the purity of Genroku currency.
41 It was actually a bit more than half (about 52.5 percent) of the weight of the old Genroku currency.
42 *Sen* is another term for the *monme*, a unit of weight equivalent to approximately 3.75 g.
43 This new currency was first issued in the fourth month of 1710.

5 Food and Goods

However, because the new coins were thin and small and their weight was half that of the previous gold coins, people tended to look down on them.[44] Because of this, they did not reduce prices by much, and sometimes even raised prices. Moreover, people were convinced that this currency would not be used forever, but was only being used provisionally to put a stop to the low-quality Genroku currency until a return to the old currency of Keichō. They realized that if there were a return to the old money of Keichō, the *kan* money would surely be halved in value.[45] Because of this, they gradually discounted the value of *kan* currency and raised prices, to avoid suffering any loss in an eventual return to the old currency. The cunning of the common people and their cleverness in matters of profiting from trade is unmatched by officials. Once things had reached this point, *kan* gold also became very troublesome. In the second year of the Shōtoku era [1712], when Ienobu was dying, he summoned his ministers and ordered that they return the gold currency to what it had been during the Keichō era. From this point on, the common people increasingly devalued *kan* gold and raised prices. It got to the point where 1 *ryō* was equivalent to only 2,600 to 2,700 *zeni*.[46]

During the reign of Ietsugu a new currency was again created, this time emulating the old Keichō currency.[47] For the time being *ōban* were not minted, just *koban* and 1 *bu* coins. These were made with pure gold, no longer had the character *kan* on them, and their size and weight were exactly the same as the old Keichō currency.[48] From the end of the Shōtoku era [1711–1716], the new currency came to be issued and used more and more. It was called "new gold." One *ryō* was equivalent to 2 *ryō* of *kan* gold and 1 *bu* to 2 *bu* of *kan* gold. One *bu* of *kan* gold, then, was equivalent to a half *bu* of Keichō currency. A half *bu* was the same as

---

44 The *kan* gold *koban* did in fact contain less gold than the Genroku *koban*, even while having a higher degree of purity. The Genroku *koban* weighed 4.76 *monme* and was 56.7 percent gold, amounting to a gold content of about 2.7 *monme* (about 10.1 g). The new *kan* *koban* weighed 2.5 *monme* and was 84.3 percent gold, amounting to a gold content of about 2.11 *monme* (about 7.9 g).

45 This is based on the logic that Keichō gold coins had the same level of purity as *kan* coins, but weighed about twice as much for a given denomination.

46 Exchange rates between *zeni* and the gold *ryō* varied considerably throughout the Tokugawa period, but the rate given here is quite low compared, for example, to the official rate of 4,000 *zeni* to 1 *ryō* at the time when the first *zeni* of the Tokugawa period were issued.

47 This currency was first issued in the fifth month of 1714.

48 Similar to previous uses of the term "pure gold," this technically refers to a gold content of 84.3 percent.

2 *shu*. It was ordered that the newer currencies be used side by side with the old Keichō currency. At this time gold currencies were many in type and complicated, making them bothersome to use. When it came to the present shogun's reign, at the beginning of the Kyōhō era [1716–1736] it was decided to stop the use of *kan* gold as well as to abolish the 2 *shu* gold coin of Genroku, and to have people use only the new gold.

After new currency was created in the Genroku era, the old Keichō currency stopped being used, so Keichō gold was no longer seen at all. However, when the new currency used today was created at the end of the Shōtoku era, this represented a return to how things had been with the Keichō currency, and the old and new currencies were used side by side. From this time onward large amounts of Keichō gold surfaced, almost matching the amount of new gold. Where could it have been hidden in the twenty-plus years since the Genroku era? It is a mystery. The edicts of the Kyōhō era ordered that all *kan* gold be exchanged for the new currency, but since the people knew that *kan* gold was pure gold, much *kan* gold must have been hidden. It is said that the old Keichō currency weighs a little less than the new currency. This is because it has been worn down with use over the course of many years. As a consequence, it came to be that people valued the new gold and disdained the old. It appears that they gradually took out the old gold that they had saved up in their storehouses and stored away their new gold. In the space of a few years, the quantity of Keichō gold gradually increased and new gold was only one part in ten of the gold in circulation. Considering how the old currency that had been abolished since the Genroku era resurfaced, it is clear that large quantities of *kan* gold are hidden away today.

Gold and silver are the currency that circulates throughout the realm, so they are not things that ought to be stored away and hidden. Such things as the low-quality gold of Genroku ought to be strictly prohibited and not used. *Kan* gold is thin and small, but it is high-quality gold. Nevertheless, so long as one prohibits it and does not use it, it will not be possible to bring out and use what has been stored away among the people. Once a certain time has passed since a changeover in currency, it is no longer possible to exchange the old currency for the new, so as a matter of course the old currency becomes the discarded waste of its age and is hidden away like a jewel buried in the ground. This is extremely regrettable and leads to hiding away the treasures of the world. It is desirable to use *kan* gold as one half the value of new gold, and to continue as before to use new and old gold side by side. If one does this, then the hidden *kan*

5 Food and Goods

gold will resurface and currency will be bountiful. This will surely be of benefit to the state and profit the people.

Since the Yin Fire Ram year [1727], the new gold ōban has been used in place of the Genroku gold ōban. With this, the revised currency that had been issued since the Genroku era was done away with and there was a complete return to the old Keichō currency. This is truly a good governmental policy to be celebrated. When the edicts of the Kyōhō era were issued, people thought that the gold currency within the land would be cut in half, and samurai and commoners alike all lamented this. After several years with the new currency in circulation, though, one does not see that kind of loss of half, and the people have forgotten the pain that came with the change. The government of the state truly ought to be practiced with resoluteness.

...

In China there are many cases where, because of a lack of copper coinage, paper bills are created and used as substitutes for coins. This is called "paper money." From ancient times such a thing had not existed in our country, but from the middle of the Genroku era, there were cases where the countries of feudal lords had insufficient funds for their fiscal needs, so they created paper money and used it only within their own countries. In the customs of the time these were called "silver bills," and their use was referred to as "presenting bills." Examining this paper money, it was about 2 or 3 *sun* in width and 1 *shaku* in length.[49] To carry it in one's pocket for even a short period one has to sandwich it between wooden boards, so it is much more troublesome than carrying things like gold *koban*. If it suffers the slightest damage from being burned by fire, soaked by water, chewed by mice, stained, wrinkled, or torn, then its value will decrease or it will become altogether worthless. Because of this, there is no limit to the harm that people suffer from it. In China, too, the use of paper money has long been considered bad government. This is because those above take all the profit from it, while those below suffer great harm. During the reign of Ienobu, a strict edict was issued prohibiting paper money in the countries of feudal lords. The paper money held by the people at that time was discarded in one fell swoop, so people suddenly lost wealth and suffered a great setback. However, they were glad to avoid long-term harm. This is good government. When there are insufficient

---

49 A *sun* is approximately 3.03 cm, and 1 *shaku* is 10 *sun* or approximately 30.3 cm.

funds for the needs of the state, ministers seeking to promote profit will always present various deluded arguments. Even among them, the idea of issuing paper money is an example of particularly bad government. One must guard against this.

In the government of the Han dynasty there was something called "leveling" [Ch. *pingzhun*, Jp. *heijun*]. A "level" is a tool that uses water to even something out. Today it is customarily called a "water level." "Leveling" refers to ensuring that the prices of various goods remain in balance, becoming neither too high nor too low. The *Records of the Grand Historian* discusses this in a chapter called the "Treatise on Leveling."[50] The common people are clever when it comes to profit. This is what Confucius refers to in the *Analects* when he says that "petty men are acquainted with profit."[51] Day and night they contemplate nothing but profit, so they are extraordinarily resourceful when it comes to such matters.

The various goods are produced by the common people. When the prices of goods are high, it is to the advantage of the common people and the disadvantage of the samurai. When prices are low, it is to the advantage of the samurai and the disadvantage of the common people. The goods that are produced by the common people and purchased by the samurai are things that serve needs, though, so even when prices are high, there is no choice but to buy clothing, food, drink, and other things necessary for a household. Artisans and merchants know this and always make prices high. Although from time to time there are edicts from above that prohibit the raising of prices, people will neither sell for low prices nor buy for high prices, so samurai do not take care of their needs. This eventually leads them to end up buying even while realizing that prices are high. The greedy pursuit of profit through trade can be understood through a comparison to the way that sake is produced from rice and water, so that high rice prices lead to high sake prices and low rice prices ought to likewise lead to low sake prices. When the price of rice rises, then the price of sake suddenly rises as well, but when the price of rice falls, sake producers say that their sake was produced when the price of rice was high, and so do not immediately lower the price they charge for sake. All things are like this. Sellers raise prices on various pretexts, and once they have been raised they do not lower them at all.

---

50 The "Treatise on Leveling" is chapter 30 of the *Records of the Grand Historian*.
51 *Analects* 4.16.

5 Food and Goods

On top of this, there are specialists for each type of goods. Specialists are what are today called "wholesalers." Specialists always have cartels. "Cartels" are associates. Beginning with Edo, Kyoto, and Osaka, and extending to all the other regions, specialists form cartels and thus create syndicates. Whenever a disruption occurs in the state that would be expected to lead to an increase in prices, they dispatch post-horse messengers to announce it to their cartel. Taking advantage of the emergency of the country, they immediately raise prices. Other times, powerful specialists take over the goods of those who have become destitute. In the end, then, there is a jump in prices. Although the land is broad, they can act at will within this land as if they held it in the palm of their hand because of the formation of cartels and the convenience provided by post-horse messengers. At this point, even though the authorities may issue strict edicts and threaten punishment, there is nothing that can be done. There are also cases where trading ships stop at sea on the way to Edo, pretend that goods are scarce, and raise prices. The state does not know of this, and when it orders officials to patrol the seas and pursue those who are stopped, these officials are bribed and asked for a moment's mercy.

The cunning of the common people and their cleverness in matters of profit is difficult for other people to attain, no matter how wise they might be. This is because it pertains to their interests and privileges. "Interests and privileges" [*riken*] refers to the right to freely pursue profit in things. Those who practice government well hold on to interests and privileges at the top and do not allow the common people to possess them. This technique is not something that most people are able to achieve. When it comes to scholars, neither students of the classics who follow Zhu Xi nor those occupied with literary writing understand it in the least. Unless one is accomplished in the political economy of both past and present, one will surely not be able to practice this.

In the Han dynasty, such people as Dongguo Xianyang, Sang Hongyang, and Bu Shi were all originally merchants, but they were summoned by the son of heaven and rose to important positions, entered the ranks of palace officials, and were allowed to hold rights and privileges within the realm. This is because they were able to understand and practice things that ordinary officials do not understand or achieve. Because of this, they did various things that profited the state, but since they were originally merchants, they were only intelligent when it came to the Way of profit and did not understand the techniques of the Way of the sages. Because they did not clarify the great methods of governing the country, they all later did many things that ended up damaging the state. However, the method of leveling that they practiced was good for government and is practiced today as well. In this method, the authorities install officials and functionaries in the places where various goods are originally produced, and these people gauge the quantities of things and their price levels and send them to the capital. When they are inexpensive they buy them up for the authorities, and when they are expensive they sell them on behalf of the authorities. When one does this, then wealthy traders and large-scale shopkeepers will not be able to greedily take large profits. This is called "leveling." The meaning of "leveling" is to smooth out the high and the low.

When those above are fond of profit and compete for it with the common people, their profit will always be taken by the common people, which will be damaging to the country. The cleverness of the common people in matters of profit is something not attained with the wisdom of gentlemen, so if these gentlemen try to compete over profit, they will always lose out. Unless the authorities are indifferent to profit and do not think about gain and loss, they will not be able to take back interests and privileges from the common people. Even so-called "leveling" involves a small amount of loss for the authorities. To attempt to avoid any loss at all for the authorities and suppress the profit of the common people is an attitude taken by those who lack learning and proper techniques. When one tries this, one will straight away have one's profits taken by cunning common people. Among the four classes of common people, there are none more clever regarding profit than traders and shopkeepers. For this reason, in both well-governed ages and ages of unrest, and in both bountiful years and years of famine, wealthy traders and large-scale shopkeepers always profit, even while the other classes of common people sometimes gain and sometimes lose. Those who govern the country, then, ought to ponder this carefully, discern the conditions of traders and shopkeepers, practice the method of leveling, and maintain control over privileges so that profits are not all taken by wealthy traders and large-scale shopkeepers.

...

Volume 6

Celebrations

"Celebrations" refers to celebrating deities and celebrating one's ancestors; all such matters are called "celebrations." In the *Zuo Commentary* it says, "The great affairs of the country lie in sacrifices and arms."[1] "Sacrifices" are celebrations and "arms" are the military; the passage describes these two as great affairs of the country. The son of heaven celebrates heaven and earth, the prominent mountains and great rivers of the realm, and the deities of soil and grain. The feudal lords celebrate the deities of soil and grain, as well as the prominent mountains and great rivers situated within their own countries. Officials celebrate the five forms of household worship. "Deities of the soil" are deities of the local soil and "deities of grain" are deities of the five grains. The "five forms of household worship" are the worship of the deity of the entrance door, the deity of the hearth, the deity of the gate, the deity of the pathway, and the deity of the inner eaves. The "pathway" refers to travel and the "inner eaves" refers to the courtyard in the middle of the house. One must carry out celebrations personally, even if one is the son of heaven. This of course goes all the more for feudal lords and those of lower rank.

All things within heaven and earth that are not performed by humans are acts of deities [*kami*]. Moreover, even the activities of humans have aspects that go beyond what can be achieved with human power alone; when it comes to these, it is the assistance of deities that makes the difference between success and failure. This can be compared to when a farmer

---

[1] From the Duke Cheng, Year 13 section.

works diligently at cultivating his fields, never slacks off, and expends all his energy, and yet there are times when the grain ripens and times when it does not, as well as bountiful years and famine years; this depends on heaven and there is nothing one can do about it. Because of this, the ancient kings placed importance on celebrating deities, performed various celebrations throughout the course of the year, revered deities and repaid virtue, prayed for the annual crops and carried out purification rites to ward off disasters, and prayed that the state be at peace and the people at ease.

The people of Japan call our country the "divine country" [*shinkoku*], but its ceremonial rituals are extremely crude. To begin with, in Japan people do not construct temples to the deities of soil and grain. In China, the temple which the son of heaven constructs for the deity of the soil is called the "great temple of the deity of the soil," and the temples the feudal lords construct for the deity of the soil are called "provincial temples of the deity of the soil." Both the son of heaven and the feudal lords always perform the celebrations at these temples personally. Wherever there is a hamlet with twenty-five households of commoners, the villagers construct a temple to the local deity of the soil and celebrate this deity on the appropriate days of mid-spring and mid-autumn. The days for these celebrations are the days belonging to the dog sign of the zodiac that are closest to the vernal and autumnal equinoxes, either before or after them.

The earth gives birth to the myriad things, nourishes humans, and is where we find repose in the present day. Among the five elements, it is earth that has the greatest virtue. Because of this, one celebrates the deity of the soil with the intention of repaying this virtue. In Japan, though, people do not perform celebrations for the deity of the soil; this is a defect of the state. In addition, when people in China travel, upon their departure they perform what is called the "celebration for the guardian deity of the road." The "guardian deity of the road" is the deity of travel. When dispatching soldiers, they celebrate the deity of the army and the deity of horses. The deity of the army is Chiyou.[2] The deity of horses is the group of stars known as the Heavenly Four-Horse Chariot.[3] These kinds of celebrations pertain to important human affairs. There are various

---

2   In Chinese mytho-history, Chiyou is a tribal leader who fought against the Yellow Emperor. Although eventually subjugated by the emperor, he was renowned for his fighting prowess.

3   This is a group of four stars within what in the European system of constellations is known as Scorpius.

6 Celebrations

celebrations for other minor matters as well. In China they exceed our country in their reverence for deities and performance of celebrations for them. Moreover, in Japan the son of heaven and the feudal lords do not personally perform celebrations. Instead, they leave these for priests to perform and do not even bother to purify themselves. This is extremely crude. Whenever there are prayers to be performed, they depend on monks, priests, ascetics, and the like for these, and never personally involve themselves with them at all. When it comes to celebrations of deities, the deities will not be receptive to these celebrations unless those performing them purify themselves, perform ablutions, change their clothes, eliminate impurities, and exhaust their sincerity and reverence. This is called "revering as if present." "As if present" refers to the reverence that comes from acting as if the deities were in fact there.

...

In China, from ancient times down to the present day they have not done away with the rituals of the state ancestral temples. Since middle antiquity the Buddhist law has flourished and among sons of heaven, kings, and the nobility there are those who revere and have faith in it. However, for funerals and celebrations they always use the Way of the sages, not the Buddhist Way. The same is true of officials. Even when there is a believer in Buddhism who calls for a Buddhist priest and has him perform a service, the believer's involvement in the service does not go beyond providing a monetary contribution to the priest. Moreover, just because they have such a service performed, it does not mean that they do away with the celebration within their own household.

In our own country, since ancient times there have been no ancestral temples, not even with the son of heaven. It is difficult to know the specifics of how people had celebrations performed. The national histories do not provide details about this during the primitive period before the introduction of Buddhism, so there is no way to investigate the facts. Ever since Buddhism came to be practiced, it appears that celebrations were only carried out using Buddhism. In ancient funerals they buried people in distant places, rather than within temple precincts; this was true of sons of heaven as well as those of lower rank. Since middle antiquity, though, even sons of heaven have come to be buried within temple precincts. Things only got worse during the age of warrior rule. There were none who studied the Way of the Chinese sages, nor were there any who looked into the ancient times of our own country. They simply went along with what was convenient, following the teachings of Buddhists, discarding funeral rites, and performing nothing but Buddhist services. In the present age, the realm has reached a time of cultural brilliance. Confucian learning is pursued among officials and there are many who read books, study cultured writings, and inquire into the Way of filial piety, brotherly obedience, humaneness, and rightness. This is truly because the divine brilliance of Ieyasu, the Light of the East, surpasses earlier ages in how it brightly illuminates Japan, the Dragonfly Island.[4] At such a time, ceremonial rituals in ancestral temples should be regulated so that nothing is left unperformed. Lamentably, though, ever since the foundation of the country, people who hold office merely conduct a vacillating government and there are none who discuss ancestral temples. The problem is not only one of prevailing customs. The laws of the country in the present age contain extremely strict prohibitions against Christianity. People throughout the land, regardless of status, are commanded to serve the tenets of the Buddhist law, so they are convinced that without Buddhism there would be no way of performing funerals. This leads them to shun the Chinese Way of the sages in the same way as Christianity and not practice it at all, sticking to what has been done since times of old by leaving things to Buddhism. This is an error in customs. The prohibition against Christianity is truly a superb idea for the state, but why should the Way of the sages be treated the same as Christianity?

As I stated earlier, sending off the dead with Buddhist services is something to leave to people's own preferences. Especially in the present age, when it is the law of the state that people be assigned to a temple of a particular sect, there is no harm in them being made to carry out their various Buddhist services within these temples.[5] It can be convenient for impoverished commoners to leave ceremonies to Buddhist monks and have nothing but Buddhist services performed. However, those of the official class and higher who have stipends, to say nothing of people like the rulers of countries, ought to set up an ancestral temple or hall in

---

4 Akitsushima (Dragonfly Island) is an ancient poetic name for Japan.
5 Shundai is making a reference here to the *danka* system, in which each household was affiliated with a particular temple. This system had existed since the Heian period as a form of voluntary association, but became mandatory in the Tokugawa period. One aspect of the transformation of the system in the Tokugawa period was its use in enforcing the ban against Christianity (for example, people were required each year to obtain a document called a *terauke* that certified they were not Christian), but the system functioned more broadly as a governmental tool for registering and monitoring the populace.

their country or village and perform the celebrations of the four seasons there. It should be considered a violation of filial piety for them to leave it to monks to perform Buddhist services the way common people do, not carry out purification rites themselves, not abstain from liquor and meat, and not conduct even minor celebrations within their own houses. No matter what kind of grand Buddhist services one may put on, one's ancestors will surely not accept it if one does not personally perform celebrations as a filial son and filial descendant. While one's parents are still alive, one cannot fail to nourish them even for a day. When they are deceased, there is no need to prepare food and drink on a daily basis in order to nourish them; one simply celebrates them once in each of the four seasons. This is not particularly difficult, so one who neglects even this cannot be considered a filial son.

...

Educational Systems

"Educational systems" refers to government ordinances regarding learning. In governing the realm and state, priority is placed on obtaining human talent. Human talent emerges from learning, so a government that makes the people of the realm engage in learning so that human talent emerges is called a "government of learning." People's inborn qualities include the wise and the foolish and the superior and the inferior. There are those who are intelligent even without learning and those who still lack intelligence even with learning. However, those who have good inborn qualities, but lack learning, only know what they see with their own eyes and hear with their own ears in the present moment. They do not know of matters of the distant past or of the wider world. For this reason, their experience is narrow and their knowledge is scant. Even in just cultivating their individual person and managing a small household, there are times when they become confused about right and wrong and are at a loss for what to do. Even more so when governing the realm and state, they have a narrowness of knowledge that is like looking at the heavens through a tube. How could they possibly practice government on a large scale? Those who have read books and studied know of matters of other countries while remaining in their own country, and know of matters of the distant past of thousands of years ago despite being born in today's world. They uphold the teachings of sages and worthies, ponder the good government and unrest throughout history and the merits

On Political Economy

and faults of governmental matters, and conform to the circumstances of today. This is the benefit of learning.

When Emperor Taizu [927–976, r. 960–976] of the Song dynasty said that for a prime minister one should employ a person who is versed in books, these were the words of a true sovereign. For this reason, in the reigns of the ancient kings they established schools not only of course in the capital cities of the son of heaven and of the countries of feudal lords, but also in all the rural districts and villages, and thus promoted learning among the gentry and the common people.

...

The Qin dynasty eradicated learning, so there is nothing to be said about it. In the Han dynasty down to the periods of the Northern and Southern Courts and the Six Dynasties, the Way of learning flourished, but because the realm had become a system of districts and prefectures, the system of learning was not the same as in the Three Dynasties and earlier. Both the drinking ritual and the archery ritual had died out, and scholars were simply recommended for promotion from their local regions without making use of these rituals. However, from the Han dynasty to the Sui dynasty, they still retained the ways of the past in that they did not test people with literary writing. From the Tang dynasty onward, they started having people compose poetry and prose to test their talents. This is one change that occurred in later times. Poetry and prose are a special ability and have no connection to whether people are intelligent or foolish, or superior or inferior. Poetry and prose belong among the arts. Those who are accomplished in them are a tool for the state, but they are not an essential matter for the government of the realm. To test people's talents only with poetry and prose is a departure from the ancient Way. However, people's intelligence is a product of reading books and studying, so there are many people whose wisdom emerges out of learning poetry and prose. Why should we abolish these? Generally speaking, the custom of China from ancient times down to the present has been to promote people based on their learning and talents. Even children of the common people can receive status and salaries and go on to become wealthy, so people compete with each other and put effort into learning.

In China, human talent is not sought out through Confucian learning alone. Military learning and soldierly tactics, as well as the various

6 Educational Systems

other arts, each have their respective methods of testing people. People who succeed at these tests are summoned and given positions in the state school. To succeed at such a test and be summoned is called "passing the test." Because of this system, people of the realm strive to pass the test related to their own preferred area of learning.

In the age of the court nobles Japan too made use of learning, so there was a method of passing tests and there were many scholars.[6] With the advent of the age of warriors, though, learning was discarded and people all thought that only Buddhist monks ought to engage in learning. Is this not lamentable? In the present age, owing to the brilliant virtue of Ieyasu, the Light of the East, officials engage in learning and it has become the custom among all from the court nobles and rulers of countries down to the common people to esteem and have faith in Confucian learning. Tsunayoshi revered Confucian learning, there are many who were promoted from lowly status based on their Confucian learning, and the houses of officials with hereditary stipends also devote themselves to reading books. In the five hundred years since the inception of warrior rule, there has yet to be a time that flourished as much as today. However, Tsunayoshi unfortunately passed away at a time when a government that promoted learning had yet to be established, and Ienobu and Ietsugu only ruled the country for a short time. There was no way for them to promote Confucian learning and there was a momentary pause in the transformation of the land through cultural brilliance. In the Kyōhō era [1716–1736], the state is once again showing an appreciation of scholarly techniques, and there are many cases of people being promoted to official positions based on their talents and accomplishments in civil and military matters.[7] At this time, the transformation of the land through cultural brilliance is on the verge of surpassing all previous ages. My own private wish is that institutions of learning be established by both pondering the past and conforming to the times. If this were to be done, then there would surely

---

6 A civil service examination system modeled on that of China was used in Japan in the early Heian period, but its role was limited to staffing the lower ranks of officialdom.

7 The shogun Tokugawa Yoshimune (1684–1751, r. 1716–1745) instituted a system in 1723 called *tashidaka* (supplementary stipends), a reference to extra payments, limited to the period that an official held office, paid to those who were promoted to positions higher than would normally be permitted by their hereditary status. By tying these payments to specific service, without making a change to the person's permanent stipend as determined by hereditary status, this policy was designed to promote and reward people of ability without upending the overall hereditary status system.

be no limit to the ever-increasing spread of knowledge of the basis of good and bad government and the production of human talent.

Ever since the Genroku era [1688–1704], there have been a great many cases of members of the samurai class who are learned in Confucianism being pulled out of poverty, given stipends, and allowed to associate with officials. However, these people do not go beyond serving in the role of scholars and scribes and are not involved with affairs of government. Those who gain official posts and are involved with affairs of government are all from houses of officials with hereditary stipends. In the "Bi ming" ["Charge to the Duke of Bi"] in the *Classic of Documents* it says, "Those from households with hereditary stipends seldom observe ritual." Those in houses with hereditary stipends have full bellies and warm clothes, do not know the techniques of learning, are not conversant in the reality of things, and when it comes to the successes and failures of government are as dumbfounded as a drunk. This is like a doctor who does not read medical books or study ancient methods, but who attempts to cure people's illnesses using his own individual intelligence. Of course there will be many errors.

If the ruler were to try to make learning flourish today, there would be nothing better than to encourage learning among officials with hereditary stipends. The encouragement of learning that currently exists consists of nothing more than issuing commands to people that they engage in learning, but this is not something that truly encourages people. Whether commands are issued or not, if among the officials there are those who enjoy learning, are virtuous in their actions, and have talents and accomplishments, then one ought to reward them generously. These rewards should consist of such things as conferring rank, paying money, increasing stipends, providing land for a house, relieving them of alternating guard duty, or shifting their post. There ought to be something appropriate in keeping with the qualities of the person in question. It is a natural human feeling to want to put in effort when one sees the potential for profit. Upon seeing that the ruler rewards learning, even those who do not achieve such learning are envious of it. There will surely be those who, even though they themselves may not have learning, will encourage their children and grandchildren to devote themselves to it. It does not necessarily have to be like ancient times, when they established schools where people were made to study. So long as people who have learning are rewarded, those below will always make efforts to learn. This is one element of educational systems.

6 Educational Systems

In addition, it is a natural human feeling to experience joy at becoming an official and being employed by the ruler; this is true not only of course for those of the official class, but even for feudal lords who possess countries of over 10,000 *koku*. Because of this, if one always selects people with learning and appoints them to major and minor posts, then people can be expected to lean toward learning even without being ordered to do so; this is an inevitable principle. The reward mentioned earlier of relieving someone of alternating guard duty means to remove him from the group of those who serve as guards. To shift someone's post is to change his occupation. From ancient times, the common practice has been to grant promotions in rank to those who have virtue and to increase the salary of those who have accomplishments. To have a fondness for learning today is a type of virtue, so as a rule one ought to reward it with a promotion in rank. A "promotion in rank" refers to such things as raising someone from sixth to fifth rank or from fifth to fourth rank.

When it comes to the varieties of learning, Confucian learning of course occupies the foremost place. Next after that is military learning. "Military learning" refers to Sunzi's Way of soldierly methods and warfare. Beside these two, there are many types of civil and military arts. The civil arts include such things as Chinese poetry and literary prose, astronomy, calendar making, medicine, divination, calligraphy, painting, arithmetic, music, *waka* poetry, and the investigation of our country's ancient practices and usages. The military arts include such things as archery, horsemanship, swordsmanship, hunting birds with firearms, the use of the spear, boxing, swimming, horse medicine, and falconry. In addition to these, when people are accomplished in various crafts, expert at cooking and serving food, take pleasure in tea, practice flower arrangement, raise birds and animals, or practice various minor skills and arts, their achievement of supreme excellence in their chosen endeavors never fails to be of use to the state. These kinds of arts should not be limited to hereditary houses of practitioners. Rather, one should use a process of selection and testing of officials and, in keeping with the extent and level of their qualities, not only pick out people from among the courtiers, but also summon people from among the commoners and employ them. One should bestow on them a stipend that will take care of them for life, but their children should be returned to their original status if they are not capable of carrying on the work of their father. This is how it is done in China. In Japan, the scholars of various Ways and the followers of arts tend to pass down their specialty within their house and serve the state with this, also receiving a hereditary stipend. As a consequence, the arts gradually deteriorate and it is rare for people with mastery to emerge. In addition, there can be cases where an occupation loses status and samurai no longer study it at all. This is the problem with having specialized hereditary occupations.

...

Volume 7

Regulated Dress

"Regulation" refers to cultured regulation. In Japanese this is glossed as *aya* [patterning]. "Dress" refers to apparel. In Japanese this is glossed as *kimono* [clothing]. This does not refer only to what is worn on the body; everything from a cap worn on the head to shoes worn on the feet is called "dress." When the capping ceremony is referred to as "dressing the foundation," "foundation" means the head, so the term means that the head is dressed.[1]

When we look at the myriad things, we see that birds have feathers, animals have fur, fish have scales, and turtles have shells. Feather, fur, scales, and shells are means for birds, animals, fish, and turtles to protect against cold and heat. Humans are naked, though. Without clothing they have nothing to cover their skin, nor any way to endure cold and heat. Because of this, the ancient sages created garments to allow people to protect themselves against cold and heat. However, the feathers, fur, scales, and shells of birds, animals, fish, and turtles each have their respective ornamentation; a pheasant looks like a pheasant and a tiger like a tiger. This is the regulated dress of nature. Humans are originally naked and are not born with any ornamentation on their bodies, so if they remain naked and do not put on clothing, then there will be no difference between the son of heaven and a commoner. The sages recognized this and in dressing people with clothing in order to cover their skin and protect them against cold and heat, they created various institutions governing this clothing

---

[1] The capping ceremony (*genpuku*; lit. "dressing the foundation") was a coming-of-age ceremony for boys.

as well as different types of ornamentation. By doing so, they established distinctions between the noble and the base, the high and the low. This is the origin of regulated dress. One should realize, then, that humans cannot get by without regulated dress.

...

Ever since the advent of the age of warriors, the people of the land have come to value the martial. In all matters, they observe what warriors do and imitate it. Even the court nobles have gradually forgotten the cultured refinement of the old imperial court and closely imitate warriors. Although the court nobles of today wear court caps and robes, their palanquin-bearers copy the appearance of warriors and race about competing with them. In doing so they have forgotten their roots. In the past even warriors wore court caps and robes and had proper deportment, but now they lack court caps and robes, so their deportment does not equal that of the past. Why is it, though, that court nobles and monks find this desirable and strive to learn from it? The vulgarity of their hearts is beyond laughable. In this way warriors have come to be held up as a standard for the people of the land, so it is necessary to regulate court caps and robes and put customs in order.

...

Ceremonial Guards and State Processions

In the term "ceremonial guards," "ceremonial" is the same as in "ceremonial majesty," "ceremonial rules," and "ceremonial forms." "Guards" refers to military guards. "Ceremonial guards" refers to the large numbers of armed soldiers who stand in rows and guard against disturbances in order to provide protection for the court. In addition, when the son of heaven and the feudal lords go out, the many armed soldiers who attend on them are likewise called "ceremonial guards." These are also called "state processions."

The ceremonial guards of China have been regulated by particular systems in each dynasty, as can be seen in the histories of those dynasties. In our own country, the ceremonial guards of the age of the court nobles are described in such things as legal texts, but today there are none who know of these systems in detail. The court nobles of today have already declined, so naturally they have lost many of the old systems. Even if

7 Ceremonial Guards and State Processions

the old systems still exist, it is in less than one case out of ten. Nor do warriors have detailed knowledge of the systems of the Kamakura and Muromachi periods.

The present age uses practices left over from the period of warring states and has not established its own system for ceremonial guards. The ceremonial guards today wield bows, arrows, bird-hunting guns, spears, poles, and scimitars. Among these, they are only allowed to carry bows, arrows, and bird-hunting guns when stationed in guardhouses at gates and when journeying to battles in distant places. On outings within the capital, even the highest rulers are not permitted to carry bows, arrows, and bird-hunting guns. Feudal lords and those lower in rank are only allowed to carry spears. Even feudal lords are not allowed to carry scimitars unless they have been granted special dispensation. Regarding spears, normally they are only allowed to carry a single one. To be permitted to carry two or three one must have a special dispensation. "Special dispensation" refers to what is permitted only to a particular person or particular house. These are the laws and systems of the present age.

In China, ceremonial guards carry raised banners; there are various systems regulating different types of banners, and they have different names. In imperial processions, they perform music en route; this music is called "rousing with drumming and blowing." Nobles and officials, too, raise banners when traveling to ceremonies and make use of this "rousing with drumming and blowing." The ceremonial guards that accompany embassies from Korea and Ryukyu are of course different from those of China, but they still all have remnants of Chinese ways.[2] In China, envoys of the son of heaven and of feudal lords carry something called a "jointed tail tassel." They take the tail of a yak, tie it up like the joints of a stalk of bamboo, and carry it attached to a pole. This is so that en route they can make it known, even when seen from afar, that they are envoys of the son of heaven or of feudal lords. It is these people who are referred to as "envoys." The reason they are called "jointed section envoys" is because they carry a jointed tail tassel. Because in China people are furnished with cultured objects in this way, one can know people's status while on the road, even when seeing them from a distance, and perform the appropriate courtesies. The decoration of palanquins also contains gradations in accordance with people's various ranks, from the son of heaven on

---

2 Ryukyu is today part of Japan, as Okinawa prefecture, but in the Tokugawa period it was an independent kingdom and so sent diplomatic envoys to Japan.

down. This is so that when people see a palanquin, they can know the status of the person to whom it belongs.

Here in Japan these kinds of cultured objects do not exist, so on the road there is no way to distinguish the status grades of feudal lords and those beneath them. By looking at the sheath of someone's spear one can know that it is so-and-so, but it is difficult to recognize all the spear sheaths of several hundreds or thousands of people. Even if one knew their names, one would still not know their rank or what office they held. Because of this, people make a point of having a large number of attendants so that others will know their wealth and status. These attendants are numerous enough to clog up wide roads and give no thought to the obstruction they cause. They hike up their skirts and expose their buttocks, flail their arms and stamp their feet, and put on an appearance like an angry praying mantis, considering this all quite splendid. One cannot think that such a thing could have existed in the past, even in this country. This goes without saying for the age of court nobles, but the same is also true for the age of warriors, in which they wore court headgear and court dress up until the end of the Muromachi period. Although people say that the current situation is a leftover practice from the period of warring states, if there were proper institutions in the state, such a custom surely would not arise. However, due to the lack of institutions and cultured objects, even kings, nobles, and officials admire the behavior of crude and lowly people, finding enjoyment in things that belong neither to the civil nor to the military. This is a despicable custom. If one were to try to reform this custom and return to the past, it would surely be difficult to do so without setting up a system of ceremonial guards and state processions and producing cultured objects.

...

Military Preparations

"Military preparations" refers to vigilance in military matters. The character "preparations" is as in "cautionary preparations"; it has the meaning of being vigilant about things at times when nothing is amiss. The character "preparations" is glossed as "provisions." It refers to putting something in mind or at hand in advance, before it occurs, so that when one encounters it one is not affected by it and does not suffer a reversal.

7 Military Preparations

This can be compared to the preparations one makes by storing up water every day for the purpose of extinguishing fires.

It is said that the ancient kings held the civil in their right hand and the military in their left. The civil and the military are like the two wheels of a cart; one cannot one-sidedly discard them. To "one-sidedly discard" means to use one while throwing out the other. When the realm is at peace, it is considered wise not to forget the military. The *Zuo Commentary* explains the character for "military" by saying, "stopping arms makes for 'military.'"[3] It says this because when the two characters for "stopping" and "arms" are combined, they form the single character for "military." "Stopping arms" means to put a stop to warfare. Such things as employing soldiers, fighting with others, destroying others' armies, attacking others' castles, and seizing others' land are not what is meant by the "military." The true meaning of "military" is considered to be governing one's own country well, guarding against intrusions by hostile neighbors, dispatching troops to quell any disturbances that arise in neighboring countries, displaying one's military might to one's neighbors on all sides, avoiding being spied on by hostile neighbors, and calculating to instill awe in others.

In times of warring states and unrest, people grow accustomed to military matters and, even without being taught or studying, they are aware of the Way of such matters and become accomplished in their methods. Although there are emergencies day and night, people are agile in responding to changes. When there has been peace for a long time and the land is tranquil, though, people consider it splendid to leave their swords in their cases and wrap their bows in their bags. Both high and low live in ease, indulge themselves with drink and sex, and take pleasure in hunting expeditions. At some point it then becomes the custom to forget the martial. This is the same in both past and present. Sima Qian makes a superb argument when he writes, "Although a country may be large, if it loves war it will always perish. Although the realm may be at peace, if it forgets war it will always be in danger."[4]

In China, during the Three Dynasties the realm was governed by a state established by sage kings, but every one or two reigns there would be someone who violated royal commands and launched a rebellion. There were

---

3   From the Duke Xuan, Year 12 section.
4   From "Biographies of the Marquis of Pingjin and Zhufu," chapter 112 of the *Records of the Grand Historian*.

also cases when after violence erupted in borderland countries, the son of heaven dispatched generals, sent out armies, and subjugated these areas. Viewed from the perspective of later ages this may appear to be the result of having half-baked laws, but that is not the case. On the contrary, it actually shows the profound foresight of the sages. People face external troubles and internal troubles. "Troubles" are difficulties. To be in tranquility with no difficulties within or without is something attained only by sages. For those of lower status who are not sages, when they do not have external troubles they always have internal troubles. This is because there is nothing they fear. Fearing external troubles makes people exercise caution and govern the internal, so internal troubles are avoided. An explanation of this can be seen in the *Zuo Commentary*.[5] This can be compared to how people who very rarely become ill are not careful about their health, so there are cases where they contract a major illness and die a premature death, whereas people who occasionally become ill are cautious and take care of their bodies, so they do not come down with major illnesses and live a long life. The sages took this into consideration, left minor external troubles here and there, and made rulers and ministers of later times realize that they should not forget about unrest and should maintain military preparations. One should realize, then, that when the realm is pacified to the point that it is like a vast sea without a single ripple, it in fact is on the verge of unrest. For this reason, those who govern the state ought not to forget military preparations even for a single day.

...

It is difficult to know what warriors were like in Japan in the most ancient times. Since middle antiquity, those with the status of warriors were all farmers; they were like the so-called "country samurai" of today.[6] They normally lived in country villages and were occupied with farming. Those who were prosperous strove to learn archery, horsemanship, and the martial arts. They enjoyed themselves in the fields and mountains pursuing game, and going to rivers and marshes they caught fish and turtles. Sometimes they rode galloping horses, and sometimes they

---

5 From the Duke Cheng, Year 16 section: "It is only sages who are able to be without either external or internal troubles. I am not a sage myself, so when I am externally at ease, I always have internal distress."

6 In the Tokugawa period, "country samurai" (*gōshi*) were people of samurai status who did not live in castle towns (where most samurai lived), but instead lived in rural villages and engaged in farming.

7 Military Preparations

went swimming or crossed steep terrain. They accustomed themselves to hardship, their sinews and bones grew tough, and their gait was energetic. Those who were poor spent their days toiling in the fields. They labored while persevering through heat and cold, so they were able to endure any kind of hardship. Such were the customs of the age. Being a warrior was originally a lowly occupation, so they prized being strong in their sinews and bones and vigorous in their actions, even if their hands and feet grew calloused and their skin chapped.

The warriors of today, though, have for several generations all received hereditary stipends and lived together in cities, so at some point they forgot the original character of warriors and their hearts, bodies, and customs became like those of court nobles and palace ladies. Only one out of several dozen appear as if they could be of use in military matters. This is due not only to the long-lasting peace, but also to the fact that they live in cities. According to a certain person, within the country of Satsuma there are forty-eight external fortresses,[7] and in each of these there are, on the low end, two or three hundred soldiers and, on the high end, seven or eight hundred, with an average of about five hundred each. Multiplying this by the forty-eight external fortresses, this amounts to over twenty thousand warriors. It is said that they are all country samurai and ordinarily make farming their occupation. In the country of Tosa as well, three hundred remaining members of the Chōsokabe clan all live there today as country samurai.[8] These are popularly called "those who suffice with a single suit of armor." It is these kinds of people who must surely retain the customs of the warriors of old. In the present age, it is only the thousand-man constable of Hachiōji who ordinarily live in the countryside and are occupied with farming, and when called to military duty hoist their long spears and set out.[9] This is similar to the method in ancient times of having soldiers reside temporarily in farming areas. Although members of the thousand-man group only receive a meager annual stipend, they live in the countryside and are occupied with farming, so their productive output is considerable and they are able to provide amply for

---

7 "External fortresses" refers to fortifications outside the main castle.
8 The Chōsokabe were a warrior clan that ruled over Tosa. They fought on the losing side of the battles of Sekigahara in 1600 and Osaka in 1615. After Sekigahara they lost their position as daimyo of Tosa, and after Osaka the leader of the clan, Chōsokabe Morichika (1575–1615), was executed together with his sons.
9 The "thousand-man constable of Hachiōji" was a group of *bakufu* retainers who lived in Hachiōji and were responsible for keeping the peace in the area.

their fathers, mothers, wives, and children. Their counterparts living in the capital, though, engage in no productive activity to supplement their annual stipends. Living in a prosperous place, they make it their practice to indulge in extravagance in their clothing, food, and daily life and to be lazy and pass their time in idleness, so there are many who suffer from dire poverty and are unable to provide for their fathers, mothers, wives, and children. These types of people are soft in their limbs and unable to withstand hardship. They have lost the true essence of the warrior and cannot be expected to be of any use in military matters.

In order to manage the state and protect it with the military in today's world, if we made bannermen[10] and those below them in rank live in the countryside within an area of 20 *li*, and put palace guards and sentinels on duty in the eastern capital for a fixed annual period of thirty or fifty days or so, spending the rest of their time in the place of their birth occupied with farming, practicing archery, horsemanship, and the martial arts, enjoying themselves with hunting and fishing, and learning the ways of country samurai, then within the space of three to five years they would surely become tough in their sinews and bones and energetic in their gait, lose the effeminate manners of court nobles, and become true warriors. If that happened, then even though they may be haphazard in their military training, there would surely be aspects in which they would surpass those warriors of today who devote themselves fully to the martial arts. This is the technique for restoring the Way of the warrior to how it was in ancient times. Moreover, there is surely no better method than this for rescuing today's warriors from their dire poverty.

...

In response to Zigong's question about government, Confucius replied, "There must be sufficient food and a sufficient military."[11] A country is protected through the military, so it is of course a crucial point of government not to be lacking when it comes to arms. However, arms cannot be developed without food, so food is the basis of arms. Therefore, enriching the country by cultivating a government that provides for food and goods is the first task in military preparations and the most important matter of political economy.

---

10 Bannermen (*hatamoto*) were samurai who directly served the shogunate.
11 *Analects* 12.7.

Volume 8

Laws and Edicts

Laws and edicts are the regulations and decrees of a country. Regulations establish fixed methods for the myriad affairs; these are what today are called "rules." Whenever a particular affair arises, decrees order that it be handled in a certain way. There are two types of decrees: commands and prohibitions. Commands are dictates and mandates; they command that something be done in a certain way. Prohibitions are bans and proscriptions; they prohibit a certain thing from being done. Commands consider it valuable that something be performed without hindrance, whereas prohibitions consider it valuable that something be quickly stopped. Taken together, their practice is called "commanding and performing, prohibiting and stopping."[1]

Laws are rooted in faithfulness [*shin*]. "Faithfulness" refers to not deceiving the people. To "deceive" is to trick. Once a law is established or a command is issued, to keep these forever unchanged is called "faithfulness." When laws are faithfully maintained, the lower orders too will have faith in them and not dare to violate them, so the realm will be well governed. When laws are frequently changed, then the people will not have faith in them. Even though a command may be issued, they will not follow it. The people think in their hearts that this law too will surely soon change, so they cling to the laws that existed before and are not minded to uphold the new commands. When those above deceive those below, those below will deceive those above, too. When the high and the low deceive

---

[1] This phrase appears in a number of texts in the Confucian tradition, the locus classicus being *Xunzi*, where it appears three times.

each other, it is not possible to establish laws. Even though there may be commands, they will not be carried out, and even though there may be prohibitions, they will not put a stop to things. When this happens, the state will not be well governed. The common saying today about "three-day regulations" refers to a lack of faith in laws leading them to be readily violated.

The technique for establishing fidelity in laws is to use rewards and punishments. When something ought to be done a certain way, one issues a command that people who do it this way will be rewarded. Any who diligently follow this command then ought to be rewarded quickly. Likewise, when something ought not to be done a certain way, one establishes a prohibition that punishes people who do it like this. Any who dare to violate this prohibition should be punished without delay. To reward what ought to be rewarded, punish what ought to be punished, and have both rewards and punishments in keeping with what is promised, is referred to as "faithful rewards and certain punishments."

In the past, when Lord Shang first practiced government during the time of Duke Xiao of Qin, he set up a tree 3 $jō$[2] tall at the south gate of the market in the capital. He issued a command that if there were a person who moved this tree to the north gate, he would reward that person with ten gold pieces. The people did not know his true intentions, though. They were suspicious and there was nobody who dared to move it, so he again issued an order, this time proclaiming that he would give fifty gold pieces to the person who was able to move it. At that time there was one among the people who, although not knowing how it would turn out, was attracted by the idea of receiving fifty gold pieces, so he moved the tree to the north gate. Lord Shang then gave him fifty gold pieces in accordance with his promise, making clear that his initial command had been no deception. From this point on, he carried out everything in this way by using the method of faithful rewards and certain punishments. It is said that because of this, within the space of ten years he produced for his ruler the successful results of "commanding and performing, prohibiting and stopping," so the people greatly rejoiced and the country of Qin was well governed and strong.

The Way of Lord Shang is a Way that uses laws to govern the country, so it is referred to as "legal techniques." Although it is not in accordance with the Way of the sages, it has aspects that are convenient when

---

2 A $jō$ is equal to 10 *shaku* or approximately 3.03 m.

practicing government in later times. To explain this further, in the age of the ancient kings they obtained wise men and installed them in the hundred offices, so these officials practiced governmental matters using loyalty [*chū*] and considerateness [*jo*]. "Loyalty" refers to thinking of the affairs of both the high and the low as one's own affairs and making diligent efforts. "Considerateness" refers to surmising the private feelings of others and then handling matters by carefully considering these feelings. One establishes a great law for the state and divides this law into a small number of articles, and when faced with additional things not specified in these articles, one exercises discretion upon careful consideration of the circumstances. In doing so, one handles things so that there is no great harm to either the high or the low. Because of this, one does not need to go so far as to establish detailed laws in the manner of people like Lord Shang, nor does one insist on relying on the law alone. This is the government of the humane.

As a consequence of such methods, obtaining human talent is considered the foremost task in practicing government. The government of the ancient kings relied on and entrusted things to people, not laws, so the legal techniques of people like Lord Shang are considered to go against the Way of the sages. However, it is extremely difficult to obtain human talent within the state. If one does not find humane and wise people, but instead appoints people without the requisite abilities and just has them act in accordance with what is expedient, then in most cases it will cause harm and become a source of unrest. In the *Classic of Changes* it says, "If they are not the appropriate people, the Way cannot be carried out."[3] The Way of the ancient kings cannot be practiced if one does not obtain appropriate people. Employing the Way of people like Lord Shang and governing by entrusting things to laws is something that even ordinary people can do. Therefore, a government in which regulations are clarified and rewards and punishments are faithfully fulfilled, and what is commanded is carried out and what is prohibited comes to a stop, uses as a shortcut the legal techniques of people like Shen Buhai, Shang Yang, and Hanfeizi.

A government that entrusts things to laws can easily become cruel, though, so even though it may achieve momentary success, before long it breaks down and becomes a source of unrest in the state. The government of the ancient kings bases itself on humaneness and considerateness and

---

3 From the *Commentary on the Appended Phrases* to the *Classic of Changes*.

does not commit cruel acts, so even though it may be somewhat slow in achieving success, through its good government the state is put at peace and taken out of danger. This is the difference between entrusting things to people and entrusting things to laws. Even the government of the sages does not discard laws and punishments, but in making use of laws and punishments it bases itself on humaneness and considerateness, something not done in the techniques of people like Shang Yang.

...

 In establishing laws, it is good that they be concise and strict and bad that they be complicated and neglectful. "Concise" means that their articles are simply worded and few, whereas "complicated" means that their articles are minutely worded and many. In affairs of the state, there are differences of scale and importance. When establishing laws, one should concern oneself with affairs that are large in scale and important, establish laws in relation to them, have both high and low strictly uphold these laws, and punish those who violate them in accordance with their offenses, without showing any mercy. One should not bother to establish laws for affairs that are minor and of little importance. Laws should be kept brief. When laws have few articles, they are easy to remember and also not difficult to carefully uphold. In addition, it is easy to tell when someone has violated them. When laws have many articles, they are difficult to remember, so there are people who violate them simply because they have forgotten them. If one does not punish those who commit a violation, the law will not take hold. However, if one tries to mete out punishment every time there is a violation, there will come to be many criminals and the common people will not value their own lives. This is the source of the failure of laws.

 Particularly trifling laws are difficult to uphold one by one. This is called being "troublesome." Troublesome laws are called "oppressive laws" or "oppressive government." When the *Record of Ritual* says, "Oppressive government is more fierce than a tiger," these are the words of Confucius.[4] In ancient times, the realm of the Qin dynasty collapsed due to oppressive laws. The term "oppressive government" is glossed in Japanese as "strict rule," so it is wrong to interpret it as government that is actually cruel and brutal. The character for "oppressive" is used in such terms as "bothersome" and "exacting"; it simply refers to when

---

4 From the "Tan Gong xia" ("Tan Gong, Part II") chapter.

governmental decrees are complicated and intrusive. When trifling laws are established they are difficult to uphold, and because they are difficult to uphold there are many who violate them. Because there are many who violate them, those who carry out punishments will be driven to haste and it will be difficult to investigate each individual case, so even without any intentional lenience there will naturally be times when things slip through the cracks. Seeing that the laws have come to be neglected without anyone realizing it, those below who violate them will gradually increase in number. This is the beginning of the downfall of laws. When Emperor Gaozu of the Han dynasty got rid of the oppressive laws of the Qin, then, and abbreviated the laws to three sections, this was truly the beginning of the foundation of a great enterprise of four hundred years.[5]

...

In today's world, feudal lords and those beneath them of course strongly uphold the statutes of the ruler of each age, as well as the orders issued by the ruler at different times and in different situations. Everything else, though, has been created by those below and has then become customary. The things that everyone does have ended up transforming into customs as a matter of course, even though they have not been written down in the statutes created after the foundation of the country, nor are they special ordinances issued by the ruler outside of ordinary statutes, nor are they something ordered by those who handle governmental matters, nor is it clear when they were created or by whom. Everyone is pulled along by these conventions, convinced that what they dictate is an ordinance issued by the ruler and a ritual form of the state, making it unacceptable to do otherwise. There are cases where not only ordinary feudal lords and officials, but even those who administer the government of the entire land, are convinced that things that have merely come to be conventions are in fact fixed regulations of the state. This is a great confusion. In the end there is not a single fixed law in the state, nor are there institutions for the myriad affairs. People simply make use of what has been created by feudal lords and the officials and commoners who are beneath them, taking these things just as they are and considering them to be the ritual forms of the world. When they are used at court as well, they become solidified as if they were the fixed regulations of the state. Such

---

5   A reference to the length of the Han dynasty, which lasted, with a brief interruption, from 206 BC to AD 220.

a situation is extremely common in today's world, but eight or nine of these conventions out of ten are not beneficial. Due to there having been peaceful government for a long time, affairs have grown numerous with the passing of the years, so this kind of thing too has gradually increased.

For this reason, if today there were a heroic and extraordinary person among the feudal lords and the officials beneath them, he would surely depart from these conventions and, unlike other people, would act in accordance with what he personally believed. If there were governmental officials who were suspicious of what he did and criticized him for it, then in response he would say that the existing conventions are not something written down in the statutes of the successive ages of the state, nor are they in edicts issued by rulers in response to particular times and situations, nor are they in the fixed regulations of the state. They are rather, he would say, merely things created by those below that have at some point become customary, which people follow because they consider it best to go along with whatever others think is appropriate. He would go on to say that if in the future these matters were institutionalized through the establishment of a law or the issuance of a decree, then these should be dutifully upheld. So long as this does not happen, though, he would say that he cannot be blamed for his actions. Even if his critic were an official of such a rank as to force others to do things that go against reason, he could not but submit to this logic. If such an extraordinary person existed and carried out affairs in this way, then surely this would help somewhat to reform bad customs and people would be pleased.

However, unless one is a heroic and extraordinary person, one will not be able to do such a thing. Among the countless millions of people who have existed since ancient times, it is rare to find even a single such heroic and extraordinary person. Today, when martial spirit has atrophied and there are many flatterers, how could one possibly expect to find such a person? Just like the water in a river, it is inevitable that the customs of the world gradually flow downward to a place of filth and do not return to their source. During this process there are sometimes ordinances issued by the ruler, but since these do not rely on the laws of the ruler's ancestors, but rather are new laws established for that one age, it is like when a dwelling that has been lived in by generations of one's ancestors is changed bit by bit in every generation according to what is convenient for each individual. Before long a new, separate law emerges and the old law dies out, so the lower orders treat the new law lightly and do not comply with it. This is how the term "three-day regulation" came about. Is this not lamentable? When the laws of the state are not fixed and unchanging, they cannot be called laws. When the high and the low alike do not uphold them, laws are not put into practice. Without faithfulness, the law will not become established. Laws are considered good when they are strict and their statutes are few in number. These are the essential points when it comes to laws.

...

Punishments and Penalties

Punishments are the methods for chastising people who disturb government and harm good order. Penalties are the methods for admonishing and disciplining people who commit errors. This is what in today's customs is called "suppressing lapses." Punishments and penalties are tools that aid in government. When one issues ordinances and establishes prohibitions, and the people carefully uphold them and do not violate them, then one does not need to go so far as to use punishments and penalties. However, because people's inborn natures are various, among the many people there will always be some who go against ordinances and violate prohibitions. If one is lax and lets these go unpunished, then it will be the beginning of the downfall of government and will bring about the collapse of the state. Because of this, from the time of Yao, Shun, and the Three Dynasties, they never failed to make use of punishments to aid in governing. This can be compared to how in nourishing the human body one primarily uses the five grains, and if there is an insufficiency, it is normal to do such things as supplement a person's vital force with ginseng and atractylodes and nourish a person's blood with angelica root and rehmannia root. However, if at that time there is a stoppage, one causes diarrhea with croton-oil beans and sodium sulfate, induces vomiting with gourd calyces and fermented black beans, cools fever with rhubarb and gypsum, spurs on cold with aconite and dry ginger, pierces sick parts of the body with acupuncture needles, and drives away the bad with moxibustion.[6] None of these can be dispensed with. The employment of punishments in the governance of a country is the method for clearing up stoppages and getting rid of wrongs. Punishments are not something

---

6 Moxibustion is a traditional Chinese medical practice in which dried mugwort is burned on or above the skin at particular points on the body.

that sages and gentlemen like to make use of, but it is difficult to attain the Way of good governing if one discards them, so these have been employed from the time of Yao and Shun.

...

In Japan, ever since Fujiwara no Fuhito [659–720] created the Code of Japan based on the Tang Code, the world of the court nobles has made use of it and carried out punishments.[7] Legal scholars were appointed and made to study this code. This scholarship was transmitted by the Sakanoue clan, who were called "legal officials." In the age of the court nobles, even when handling a single transgression or carrying out a single punishment, they always had a legal scholar consider the relevant code and submit a document called an "investigative report," which was used as the basis for carrying out punishments; this is what an "investigative report of a legal official" refers to. The five punishments of the Code of Japan are the same as those of the Tang Code, namely, as mentioned earlier, whipping, beating, penal servitude, banishment, and death. In carrying out these punishments, too, they largely followed the system of the Tang dynasty. In later ages, though, this code gradually waned and was no longer practiced.

With the advent of the age of warriors the institutions of the realm were changed, so they used the code of the court nobles less and less. In the Kamakura period, in the first year of the Jōei era [1232–1233] the Hōjō clan created the Formulary of Adjudications and fixed it in place as the law of the military houses.[8] During the period of the Hōjō regents, they governed by using this code. Later, in the Muromachi period, the institutions of military houses underwent a change and they no longer used the Kamakura code, instead creating a different legal code for that age. From the end of the Muromachi period, the land entered a time of warring states. There were many years of unrest and methods of punishment were not established.

There is nothing in particular to mention about the ages of Oda Nobunaga and Toyotomi Hideyoshi, but with the advent of the present age, the

---

7 The "Code of Japan" is a reference to the *ritsuryō* legal code that was introduced at this time. Fuhito was involved in producing two versions of the *ritsuryō* code: the Taihō Code, enacted in 703, and the Yōrō Ritsuryō (Yōrō Code), compiled in 718 and enacted much later, in 757.

8 The Goseibai Shikimoku (Formulary of Adjudications), promulgated by the regent Hōjō Yasutoki (1183–1242), served as the legal code of the Kamakura shogunate.

8 Punishments and Penalties

land was unified and the state came to be at peace to a degree surpassing all past ages. However, a lingering remnant of the period of warring states is that there are frequently no institutions for various affairs, which has led government to be carried out using provisional systems. As a consequence, methods of punishment have not been fixed in place. Not only are the methods of the ancient kings of China not used, the codes of the court nobles have also been eliminated. The transgressions of the samurai and commoners are dealt with simply using a vaguely defined method of punishment. Only the statutes relating to such things as rebellion and conspiracy are still used today, while the remainder have all been discarded.

It is the custom today to regard samurai as people who do not deceive or steal and for whom it is a great shame to be gossiped about maliciously, beaten, kicked, and bound; this is how it is with the warriors of our country. Depending on the situation, such a custom can have harmful effects, but for the purpose of governing it is best not to change it and to instead promote such warrior customs and cultivate a sense of shame. Therefore, in enforcing punishments as well, one should strive not to endanger this custom. To this end, one ought to make the statutes relating to punishments few, handle the most extreme transgressions with the death penalty, and for light transgressions simply arouse shame in people's hearts and caution them against repeating these offenses. The laws of the present age are for the most part like this. This in fact approaches the customs of the ancient kings and is superior to the Qin and Han dynasties and later, when their use of laws eroded officials' sense of shame. This is to say nothing of the feudal system of the current age, in which feudal lords govern by setting up their own regulations in each of their separate countries, making it useless to try to pass down judgments for the entire land using a single fixed law as they did in the age of the court nobles. What surely works best today is simply to establish a rough set of methods for punishments and practice these methods strictly; with other matters use ritual, rightness, and a sense of shame to push officials to act; and with an emphasis on humaneness and considerateness, attempt to extend benevolent favor. This is the meaning of the saying that "punishments do not reach as high as grand officials."[9] There is surely no better way to handle the transgressions of those of the scholar-official class and higher.

---

9 From the "Qu li shang" ("Summary of Rituals, Part I") chapter of the *Record of Ritual*.

Punishments are the Way of governing the common people. In enforcing punishments, strictness is prized. If one keeps the statutes relating to punishments few and is strict in enforcing them, then the common people will fear transgressions and not violate the law. This is the benefit of having punishments. When methods of punishments are not faithfully upheld and are established in name only, so that when offenders emerge they are not punished in the manner prescribed by law, then the people will not fear the law. When one simply establishes laws and issues threats, but does not actually enforce punishments, then it is the same as if there were no laws at all.

...

Volume 9

Institutions

In governing the realm and state, the foremost task is to establish institutions [*seido*] pertaining to the myriad affairs. "Institutions" refers to the regulative methods put in place for these affairs. When we divide the term "institutions" into its two constituent characters, the first character, "regulation" [*sei*], is glossed as "making" and is used in the term "creation." It refers to when everything in the realm has its own way of being done and made. The second character, "measure" [*do*], is glossed as "rule." Taken in the sense of "method" it is used in the term "ordinance," and taken in the sense of "restriction" it is used in the term "moderation." It originally referred to a measuring rod, what is commonly called a "yardstick." With a measuring rod one measures the size and length of things, so it is called a "measure." The standards of size or length that exist for all things in the realm are called their "measure." When one speaks of "institutions" on the level of a particular thing, then, "regulation" refers to the regulative methods for creating it, and "measure" refers to the prescribed dimensions for its size or length.

In administering the realm and state, at the outset one ought to establish institutions for the myriad affairs, bequeath them for a long posterity, leave them unchanged, and have high and low together strictly uphold them. In promulgating laws and carrying out punishments as well, if there are originally no fixed institutions of the state, then there will be no expectations for the myriad affairs and people will not know their parameters, so it will be difficult both to enforce laws and to carry out punishments. In the distant past when the ancient kings governed the realm, they considered the creation of ritual and music and the establishment of offices and responsibilities to be forms of government through institutions, and thus created institutions for all the myriad affairs. In the Qin and Han dynasties and later, the realm was governed as a system of districts and prefectures and there were many aspects that were different from the age of the ancient kings, but there was never a failure to establish institutions.

In Japan as well, in the age of the court nobles there were institutions for the myriad affairs, and such things as books of laws and ceremonials containing descriptions of institutions. With the advent of the age of warriors, the institutions of the court nobles fell into disuse. That being said, the warriors did not establish separate institutions, but simply went along with the natural tendencies of things and let them run their course. Things produced from below were used in the state and people considered these to be the institutions of the time. It was like this from the Kamakura period to the Muromachi period and then all the way down to the age of Oda Nobunaga and Toyotomi Hideyoshi. The peace that reigns in the realm in the present age surpasses previous ages, so institutions certainly ought to be established, but as a lingering attitude from the period of warring states it is considered useful for government to be vacillating and transitory. Because of this, neither high nor low pay attention to institutions, instead always just acting by following the course of things and gauging the circumstances. This has led to a situation where in the affairs of everyday life of everyone from feudal lords to officials to the common people, what people believe to be institutions of the state are in fact mostly things that originated from below. Generally speaking, there is nothing in the state today that can truly be called institutions. However, with the accession of successive shoguns a series of what are called "Laws for Military Houses" have been issued which each consist of seventeen articles.[1] These are displayed to the land of Japan under the label of "itemized laws" and people stringently uphold them. Apart from these, one cannot see institutions or regulations in anything, which is a

---

[1] The Laws for Military Houses consisted of edicts issued by the shogunate that governed the conduct of the daimyo and other samurai. The first version of these edicts was issued in 1615, and new versions continued to be issued by successive shoguns until Yoshimune, whose version was issued in 1717. It is unclear why Shundai describes them as having seventeen articles; this was the number of articles in the 1710 version issued by Ienobu, but the earliest version had thirteen, and the version in effect at the time Shundai was writing (that of Yoshimune) had fifteen.

serious deficiency of the state. In what follows I will now put forth several important matters of state where, in my humble opinion, it is unacceptable not to have institutions.

When the ancient kings governed the realm, they made filial piety their foundation. An essential point of filial piety is the regulation of mourning clothes, and in our country, too, there were mourning clothes in ancient times. People wore a type of clothing called a "plain garment" and remained confined indoors for a hundred days or even up to a year. At some point mourning clothes were done away with, though, and today they survive in name only. To be more specific, the range of deceased relatives for whom one wears mourning clothes extends no further than, in older generations, one's father's brothers, in younger generations, nieces and nephews, and in the same generation, sons of one's father's brothers who are older than oneself. One does not wear mourning clothes for one's father's cousins or their wives, grandnieces and grandnephews, second cousins, and those more distantly related to oneself. Because of this, people today think of people like second cousins as if they were outsiders to their family. Human ethics [jinrin] and feelings of obligation have never been weaker than in today's world. I would like to inspire a discussion of mourning clothes and establish an institution that is suitable for the customs of the present, even if it may not be the ancient system of China or Japan. In doing so I would like to teach the people of our land the Way of filial piety and strengthen their ethical feelings of obligation. If this were accomplished, it would surely be a great blessing. The remainder of my discussion of these matters can be seen in the chapter on ritual and music.[2]

Humans place importance on the clan. A "clan" is what today is called a "surname." A clan name distinguishes people by their origin and is passed down from one's ancestors, so descendants ought to uphold it eternally and never change it under any circumstances. To give one's own surname to another or to discard one's own surname and assume that of another both amount to discarding one's ancestors and are extremely unfilial.

In China such a practice originally did not exist, but Emperor Gaozu of the Han dynasty bestowed the surname of Liu on a lowly person by the name of Lü Jing, after which this person came to be called Liu Jing.[3]

---

2   Shundai discusses this in a section of vol. 2 that is not included in this translation.
3   See the "Biography of Liu Jing" in chapter 99 of the *Records of the Grand Historian*. Liu Jing was a trusted political advisor of Gaozu.

From this time, there were many cases of rulers of later times bestowing the surname of the country on their subjects. Such things as Emperor Taizong of the Tang dynasty bestowing the surname of Li on Xu Shiji [594–669] is an example of the same kind of thing as Liu Jing of the Han dynasty.[4] A "surname of the country" is the surname of the ruler.[5] In Japan, from the time of the court nobles to the time when government passed into the hands of warriors, there was no bestowal of surnames of the country, but Toyotomi Hideyoshi bestowed the surname of Hashiba on a number of generals.[6] This was the first instance in Japan of the practice of bestowing the surname of the country on subjects. Following this precedent, in the present age there are many cases of the surname Matsudaira being bestowed on feudal lords and meritorious retainers.[7] The feudal lord of Kaga is of the Maeda clan, the feudal lord of Satsuma is of the Shimazu clan, the feudal lord of Sendai is of the Date clan, the feudal lord of Chikuzen is of the Kuroda clan, the feudal lord of Aki is of the Asano clan, the feudal lord of Saga is of the Nabeshima clan, the feudal lord of Nagato is of the Mōri clan, the feudal lords of Bizen and Inaba are both of the Ikeda clan, the feudal lord of Awa is of the Hachisukashi clan, and the feudal lord of Tosa is of the Yamanouchi clan, but the surname Matsudaira was bestowed on all of these. The feudal lords listed above are not hereditary vassals of the Matsudaira house. They are people who in the previous age were subjugated by heroic and powerful men, so the shogun ordered that they be given the same surname as himself in an effort to become close to them and have them be considered unified with him.[8] The feudal lord of southern Matsuyama was of the Hisamatsu clan, but because he was a younger half-brother sharing the same mother with Ieyasu, the Light of the East, Ieyasu showed him deep favor and made him equal to a full-fledged brother by bestowing on him the surname Matsudaira. The feudal lords of Matsumoto today are styled the hereditary governors of Tanba province. Their original surname was Toda and it is not clear why the surname Matsudaira was bestowed on them in the past. It was wrong for Tsunayoshi to bestow the surname of the country

---

4 Xu Shiji (later Li Shiji) was one of Taizong's top generals.
5 In the two examples given above, Gaozu of Han's personal name was Liu Bang and Taizong's personal name was Li Shimin.
6 Hashiba was Hideyoshi's surname before he changed it to Toyotomi.
7 Matsudaira was the original surname of Tokugawa Ieyasu.
8 The daimyo listed above were so-called *tozama*, or "outside," daimyo, meaning that they only pledged loyalty to the Tokugawa after the Battle of Sekigahara in 1600.

9 *Institutions*

on Yanagisawa Yoshiyasu [1658–1714] to show him favor, and to bestow the surname of the country on Honjō Munesuke [1629–1699] on account of him being a relative on his mother's side.[9]

The way in which surnames of the country are bestowed in such large numbers in the current age is something unheard of in either China or Japan. As this custom works its way downward, there are many cases of feudal lords bestowing their surnames on vassals and heads of artistic houses giving their surnames to pupils. The disordering of clans begins with this and it leads to the bad customs of thinking of one's blood relatives as outsiders and thinking of outsiders as one's blood relatives. As a consequence, people of today discard the surname of their own house more easily than they throw away worn-out sandals. Although one might consider this a typical custom of barbarians, in ancient times it did not exist. It has taken hold in the world of today, though, so people make no distinction between those of the same surname and those of different surnames or between relatives and outsiders. Sometimes people take the surname of their mother for no reason, and sometimes when a child is born to them in middle age they do not raise it themselves, but instead have it become the child of an outsider and take on that person's surname. These kinds of bad customs are all the result of failing to treat surnames properly. It would be desirable to reform this and have clan names made correct not only among feudal lords, as goes without saying, but also among officials and commoners. This is one method for putting a stop to the wickedness that occurs among the lower orders.

To take in a child of a different surname, adopt it, and make it one's heir is something that exists in barbarian customs, but did not exist at all in the country of the sages. However, at the end of the Zhou dynasty there was no heir to the ruler of the country of Kuai. The ruler of the country of Ju was the son-in-law of the ruler of Kuai, so the son of the ruler of Ju, as an external grandchild of the ruler of Kuai, succeeded him as ruler of Kuai. In the *Spring and Autumn Annals*, though, Confucius writes that "the person from Ju extinguished Kuai."[10] An "external grandchild" is a child born to a daughter who has married into a different family. Because the ruler of Kuai made this external grandchild his heir, the bloodline of

---

9   Yanagisawa Yoshiyasu was Tsunayoshi's chamberlain and was Ogyū Sorai's patron early in the latter's career. Honjō Munesuke was daimyo first of Ashikaga domain and later of Kasama domain.
10 From the Duke Xiang, Year 6 section.

the country of Kuai was cut off. The ruler of Ju sent his son to inherit the country of his wife's father, so he committed the transgression of extinguishing the country of Kuai. When Confucius writes that "the person from Ju extinguished Kuai," he does so with the intention of strongly censuring the ruler of Ju and his high ministers. From this one incident we can understand the warning provided by the sages.

To take a child of a different surname, make it one's own, and have it inherit a state always amounts to cutting off the bloodline of one's ancestors. The kind of thing seen in the country of Kuai was rare in ancient times, and after it one does not see similar incidents. When Empress Dowager Lü [241–180 BC] of the Han dynasty lamented that Emperor Hui [210–188 BC, r. 195–188 BC] did not have children, secretly took the children of another, and pretended that they were the children of Hui, this was different from adoption.[11] From the end of the Han dynasty onward it occurred very occasionally that people raised the child of another and made it their own, but when this happened it was due to the reach of barbarian customs. In later ages this kind of thing grew more and more frequent, but only among the common people; it remained extremely rare among scholar-officials, officers of state, and those of higher rank. In the Ming dynasty this practice was prohibited and the statutes prescribed a punishment for it. This is because they heeded the warnings of the sages and emphasized human ethics. In Japan, too, this kind of thing did not exist in ancient times, but from middle antiquity it began to occur occasionally. Nevertheless, until recent times it was still rare. In the present age, though, it has become extremely common.

There is nothing that destroys ethics and damages the country more than this practice of adoption. Relatives of the same surname, even if they no longer have contact with each other, and no matter how distantly related they may be, are all descendants of the same ancestor and retain a blood relationship. Because of this, when one lacks a child in the present and takes another of the same surname to be one's heir, then both one's

---

[11] Empress Dowager Lü was the empress consort of Gaozu, the founding emperor of the Han dynasty. She acted as regent during the entire reign of Emperor Hui. In the episode that Shundai is discussing, the issue was not actually that Hui lacked children altogether, but rather that he lacked children with his wife, Empress Zhang Yan (d. 163 BC). Lü arranged for two of Hui's sons by concubines to be adopted by Zhang Yan, but pretended to the world (and the sons themselves) that Zhang Yan was their mother. Lü then had the concubines who were their biological mothers put to death. The adopted sons went on to reign as the third and fourth emperors of the Han dynasty.

9 Institutions

ancestors and oneself can enjoy this child's celebrations of ancestral worship. In the *Zuo Commentary* it says, "Spirits do not accept the sacrifices of those not of their own kind. The people do not sacrifice to those not of their own clan."[12] No matter how much one displays the utmost sincere reverence and offers up delicious foods, spirits do not enjoy the celebrations of those of a different bloodline. Because they do not enjoy these celebrations, the spirits do not receive the food that is offered and so go hungry. When Mencius said that to lack an heir is first among the three types of unfiliality, this is what he was talking about.[13] For this reason, if there is no child or grandchild who is able to be the successor to one's house, one should look among relatives of the same surname, choose an appropriate person to make one's adopted child, and have him carry on the legacy of one's ancestors. This is authentic adoption. If there is not a single relative of the same surname to be found, the fact that there is nobody able to carry on the house means that it is being extinguished by heaven. When a house is extinguished by heaven, there is nobody against whom one can direct one's resentment, and one ought to peacefully accept the command of heaven. One certainly ought not adopt an outsider.

If such improper adoptions are not strictly prohibited from above, there will surely be no end to them. In the world today, though, there are no prohibitions against them, so people who have many children set aside the eldest son to be their heir and then hand over their remaining sons to be taken in by the houses of outsiders. People who are completely lacking in sons toss aside relatives with the same surname and make a child of a different surname their heir, sometimes seeking out those with power and sometimes aiming for financial gain. Even when it comes to people with many children, if they give all of them to outsiders save their eldest son, and the eldest son then suffers misfortune and dies, they end up taking in an outsider to be their heir just like the other people I described. Such situations are not uncommon among feudal lords and those of lower rank. It is the pinnacle of foolish confusion and the ultimate in unfiliality. Particularly notable is that the military houses of today suffer from poverty and so always demand payment when raising the child of another family. Because of this, people who are of lowly rank but prosperous take

---

12 From the Duke Xi, Year 10 section.
13 *Mencius* 4.1.26.1: "Mencius said, 'There are three things that are unfilial, and having no heir is the greatest of them.'"

this opportunity to pay to have their children raised by families of officials, and for a few hundred gold pieces they take over the house of a stipendiary official. One loses count of the hundreds or thousands of cases in which a house that was given a hereditary stipend at the time of the foundation of the country based on its military merit or loyal service has ended up in the hands of lowly people lacking in lineage. It goes without saying that lowly people will grasp for profit, but why is it that people with the status of officials commit this evil and deceive those above them? This happens because there is no prohibition against adopting a child with a different surname. It is indeed lamentable.

Human ethics begins with the relation between husband and wife. The Way of husband and wife emerges out of the marriage ritual. The ancient sages placed importance on the initiation of marriage, regulated the marriage ritual, clarified the distinction between men and women, and corrected human ethics. The significance of this is presented in detail in the Six Classics. Although the rituals for marriage differ greatly between past and present and between other countries and our own, the essential meaning of the ritual of marriage lies in selecting a match. A "match" is a partner; it refers to a spouse and in Japanese is glossed as "lining up side by side." A husband and wife are people who ought to be lined up side by side with each other and exist in relation to each other, so they are called a "match." When a husband and wife are not well matched, the house will not be well governed. When the house is not well governed, there will be no harmony among relatives. Everyone down to retainers, servants, and menials will take their master lightly and trouble will ensue.

"Selecting a match" involves investigating and seeking out a partner who is appropriate for oneself. The first point to consider in the appropriateness of a partner is virtue. "Virtue" refers to a person's inborn nature and everyday actions. People's dispositions are various, so their daily actions too are various in accordance with their dispositions. A husband and wife are companions for an entire lifetime, so one ought to seek out a person whose disposition is commensurate with one's own and who is thus a good fit. To be "commensurate" means to be suitable. If people's dispositions are not commensurate, then there will be disharmony within the house and antagonism will come about between husband and wife. "Antagonism" refers to viewing people with hostility.

The second point to consider is age. A husband and wife of course ought to be matched in age, with the husband older and the wife younger. However, it is not good for the husband to be very much older or the

9 Institutions

wife to be very much younger, as this often gives rise to strife within a marriage. This is what is meant when the *Classic of Changes* speaks of "an old husband having a young wife."[14] When the wife is older than the husband, this is contrary to what is ordinary and, viewed from outside, looks bad. Moreover, it becomes the occasion of disharmony within the house. This is what is meant when the *Classic of Changes* speaks of "an old wife having a young husband."[15] Both of these situations arise from not selecting someone who is appropriately matched in age.

The third point to consider is that a husband and wife should be selected whose houses' positions as well as their stipends and official ranks are matched. "Position" refers to the status of one's lineage and background. This is referred to as one's "position" or "rank." Officials have a lineage as well as a stipend and official rank. A husband and wife should be sought whose positions as well as stipends and official ranks are matched. Feudal lords take possession of a country and pass it on from generation to generation, so their lineage is clear. However, there are large and small countries and high and low ranks. If one is to contract a marriage, those of large countries should seek out those of large countries, those of small countries should seek out those of small countries, those of high rank should seek out those of high rank, and those of low rank should seek out those of low rank. Officials' lineages are various, so it is crucial to properly select these. Next, one should distinguish between great and small stipends and high and low rank, seeking out a person who is matched with oneself. In short, those from families of scholar-officials ought to contract marriage with those from families of scholar-officials, and those from families of high officers ought to contract marriage with those from families of high officers. However, high officers are promoted from the ranks of scholar-officials, so even though a person may be a scholar-official today, this does not preclude him from becoming a high official in the future. Depending on the situation, then, there are cases where there is no harm in someone from a family of high officials contracting marriage with someone from a family of scholar-officials.

When feudal lords and those beneath them forget about this process of selection and contract a marriage with a person who is not matched with them, various types of harm result. When the house of the husband is superior and that of the wife is inferior, it will be easy for the husband

---

14 From the section on the "Great Exceeding" (*da guo*) hexagram.
15 From the section on the "Great Exceeding" (*da guo*) hexagram.

to feel contempt for his wife, and when the house of the wife is superior and that of the husband is inferior, it will be easy for the wife to take her husband lightly. In either case, this leads to disharmony within the household. Particularly of note is that when the wife's house is wealthy and the husband's is impoverished, then the husband will take every available opportunity to curry favor with his wife's family and bow down before them and will sometimes be fearful of his wife. This amounts to a loss of manly honor and is something wretched and lamentable. In ancient times, a person named Hu [d. 695 BC], ducal son of Zheng, was the son of the ruler of the country of Zheng. He performed meritorious action for the country of Qi, so the ruler of Qi was overjoyed and wanted to marry his daughter to him. Hu declined the offer, though, on the grounds that Zheng was a small country and Qi was a large country, meaning that she was not an appropriate match for him. This is recounted in the *Zuo Commentary*.[16] Because of this, Hu was considered a wise man in his own age as well.

The three methods of selection listed above are the great Way of contracting marriage. To be lustful and greedy is the Way of the petty man, not something for officials. In gathering courtesans and taking mistresses, it is acceptable to choose them based on their beauty. When taking a wife, though, one should not choose her based on her beauty. To take as one's wife a woman from a wealthy family who does not match one's own status, simply because one covets riches, is not consistent with the principles of officials. When Wang Tong [584–618] said, "To speak of wealth when taking a wife is the Way of barbarians," these were wise words.[17] To "speak of wealth" means to make assessments of the quantity of someone's wealth. "Barbarians" are savages. The "Way of barbarians" refers to what goes against the Way of gentlemen of China.

For the marriages of the common people, as well as for those of official rank and higher, the need to choose an appropriate match is a crucial matter, so the authorities should firmly establish institutions and place high importance on making people select proper matches. On top of this, when officials and those of higher rank take a wife or daughter-in-law, they should be required to announce the planned marriage to the authorities and receive permission, and the authorities should investigate the

---

16 This episode appears in the Duke Huan, Year 6 section.
17 Wang Tong (also known as Wenzhongzi) was a Confucian scholar. The quoted passage appears in volume 3 of his *Zhongshuo* (*Explanation of the Mean*).

9 Institutions

suitability of the marriage partners. Those who make false statements and deceive the authorities during this process should be severely punished. This is the Way of making human ethics correct. In the world today there is no such institution, so among officials there are those who are lustful and marry entertainers or women of pleasure. There are also those who are greedy and marry women from families of farmers, artisans, traders, shopkeepers, and other types of lowly people, receiving a great deal of money as a result. Particularly of note is that officials today suffer from impoverishment and are in a pitiful position, so by marrying such women they receive several tens or hundreds of gold *ryō* and are rescued from their immediate emergency. When that money runs out, though, they tyrannize their wives. There are cases where the wife cannot bear it and begs to leave, upon which the husband happily sends her back while not returning the money, and then again takes a bride from another wealthy family and repeats the whole process several times over. There is nothing more lacking humaneness, rightness, ritual, and proper measure. Among feudal lords, too, there are those of small countries who marry into the families of feudal lords of large countries, receive their stipends, and bow and scrape before their wives' families. There are also a great many feudal lords of small countries who suffer from impoverishment and always demand payment when taking a bride. There is nothing worse than this for causing a breakdown in the sense of shame. All these things occur because no institutions have been established for selecting spouses.

. . .

The Way of governing the people has its basis in attachment to the land. "Attachment to the land" means that the people of the realm all reside on the land. This is also called "attachment to the soil." In China this happens as a matter of course. In our country, too, in ancient times the people were all attached to the land. In the present age, it is only farmers who are attached to the land, while the rest are all separated from the land and are like guests at an inn. Because of this, the number of people who abscond has grown large and there is no end to people who commit wicked deeds. The realm cannot do without a census, as I described in an earlier chapter. With the establishment of a census, there is no way to carry the survey out unless one first attaches all the people of the country to the land. This is a fundamental policy for governing a country.

. . .

On Political Economy

The people of the realm are all common people under the authority of the king, so it is the Way of the common people to pay land tax and be used for corvée. However, ever since Buddhism has been practiced in this country, among the common people there are many who take religious orders and become monks. Once they have taken religious orders, they are removed from their family register and become separate from the four classes of common people. As a result, they neither pay land tax nor are they used for corvée, and they become people who live without working. Because of this, in China they did not permit people to be removed from their family registry and become monks of their own accord. People who wanted to become monks were allowed to take religious orders only based on having received a monk certificate. If they did not have a monk certificate, they were not able to take religious orders and shave their head. If they violated this law and shaved their head of their own accord, then they would be punished along with their master and disciples. This law has remained unchanged from ancient times down to the present.

In Japan, too, during the age of the court nobles people were allowed to take religious orders based on monk certificates issued by the Bureau of Buddhism and Aliens. A "monk certificate" is a document that gives someone permission to take religious orders. Even with the advent of the age of warriors, up until the Kamakura period people were permitted to take religious orders only after having received a monk certificate from the Bureau of Buddhism and Aliens. In an old temple in Mutsu province I once saw a monk certificate from the Bureau of Buddhism and Aliens that had been granted to a disciple of the Kenchōji temple of Kamakura. This law disappeared at some point in recent times and so it came to be that both samurai and common people took religious orders of their own accord. This is why there are so many monks in the world today, and why there are so many degenerate and wicked monks. For this reason, in the future it will be desirable to return to the ancient system and require that people who take religious orders receive a monk certificate. When people take religious orders, they are put outside the four categories of common people, making them exempt from taxation and corvée. Because of this, when they request a monk certificate they should have to pay a release fee. The authorities ought to bestow a monk certificate only after collecting such a fee. This is not a form of cruel government and ought to be carried out decisively. Moreover, the people in Japan called *yamabushi* resemble the Daoist masters of

China.[18] In China, a monk certificate is also required to become a Daoist master. This should apply all the more to the *yamabushi* of Japan; they practice the Way of the Buddha, so monk certificates ought to be bestowed on them.

...

In the *Zuo Commentary* it says, "Hereditary lords are not something ancient."[19] "Hereditary lords" refers to when the people who handle the government of the country as officials pass on their position to generation after generation of descendants. The passage states that this is not the ancient method. In Japan, both court nobles and warriors have hereditary offices. Without regard for whether they are wise or foolish, descendants inherit the office of their ancestral line from one generation to the next. This does great harm to government. It is extremely rare for people's descendants to be wise generation after generation. Offices and their responsibilities are a tool for governing the country and so ought to be entrusted to people chosen for their wisdom and talent. It goes against the Way for someone who lacks the requisite ability to be appointed to a position simply because it is the office of his ancestor. If a person's descendants are wise and have talent and intelligence that matches their ancestor, then they should be allowed to carry on their ancestor's office. If that is not the case, then one ought to select someone else.

...

What in China are called "bondmen" are in Japan called "hereditary servants." What are called "workers" in China are what we call "employees." They are employed for a day, for ten or twenty days, or for one or two months. In Japan these are called "daily employees" or "monthly employees." The kind of temporary employees that are used in people's houses today do not exist in China; the people called "workers" in China resemble these but are not the same. The temporary employees of today are, to be more specific, annual employees. Temporary employees change their master each year, so their employers have little inclination

---

18 The *yamabushi* were mountain ascetics who followed a syncretic religion that drew heavily on Shingon Buddhism.
19 This passage does not actually appear in the *Zuo Commentary*. However, the *Gongyong zhuan* (*Gongyong Commentary*), which, like the *Zuo Commentary*, is a commentary on the *Spring and Autumn Annals*, twice contains the phrase "hereditary lords are not proper ritual" (in the Duke Yin, Year 3 and Duke Xuan, Year 10 sections).

to dispense kindness, nor do the employees themselves have much inclination to exercise loyalty toward their master. Particularly in Edo, many degenerates who have absconded from rural areas come from all directions and make a living as temporary employees, so there are a great many people who run away. The city-dwellers who maintain them are degenerates, too, so they cannot be relied on. It is impossible to know how many people lose money and treasure each year from using temporary employees. Among officials, those who own estates use people they summon from the lands they possess, but those with no estates will not have anyone they can use unless they make use of temporary employees from the city.

This type of temporary employment is something that did not exist in ancient times, even in Japan. It began in the present age and causes great trouble to both the samurai and the common people of today. It is ultimately caused by the lack of family registers among the common people and the fact that people do not make use of hereditary servants. In a world that is peacefully governed it ought to be possible to muddle through with such a system, but in the remote chance that there is an emergency in the state, what use will these temporary employees be when dispatched on military duty to quell disturbances? If they are included in a military force and head out on a campaign, they will certainly abscond along the way. Because of this, temporary employees cause great harm to the government of the state. I would propose to reform this and, as was done in the past, have menials be employed in one place for a long period. When we think of someone as a person who ought to be employed on a long-term basis, then the master will forgive minor errors and treat the person with kindness, and the servants will think that if they leave their current house there will be nowhere for them to go, so they will not be resentful about small grievances and will be inclined to be loyal to their master's house. These are all natural human feelings. When people who are neither relatives nor enemies enter into relations of ruler and subject, friends, or colleagues and pass many years like this, then a heart of compassion and fidelity will arise out of this familiarity. This is the Way of humaneness. The humaneness of the gentleman is something that always emerges from familiarity. With temporary employees there is neither humaneness nor rightness, and there is nothing worse than this when it comes to the breakdown of the Way of humans.

...

9 Institutions

The common people who perform the proper occupations of farmers, artisans, traders, and shopkeepers are called "upright people." Others are called "miscellaneous groups." This can be seen in what I wrote earlier. However, there are people who in their inborn natures have a fondness for proper occupations as well as those who dislike proper occupations and are fond of the improper occupations of miscellaneous groups. Those who have a fondness for improper occupations are all degenerates. To transform these degenerates through education and make them into upright people is something that not even Yao and Shun could achieve. For this reason, in imperial capitals and royal cities various miscellaneous groups are established to carry out the occupations of degenerates. Such things as theaters, houses of entertainer girls, brothels, and unlicensed prostitutes are all examples of this. The number of such places varies, depending on the size of a city and its population.

Today the major cities of Japan are Edo, Kyoto, and Osaka. Osaka is smaller than Edo and Kyoto is smaller than Osaka, but the number of theaters and brothels in Kyoto is several times the number in Edo. Edo is the largest city of the land and there are countless people there of the official class and below. However, there are no theaters or brothels apart from the brothels of Yoshiwara and the theaters of Sakaimachi.[20] Up until recent times they had existed in various places in the city, but in the Shōtoku [1711–1716] and Kyōhō [1716–1736] eras they were all eliminated. Nobody can know how many thousands of degenerates who until then had made their living in improper occupations instantly lost those occupations and ended up starving and freezing. They originally had a lazy and degenerate inborn nature, making it impossible for them to learn a proper occupation and become upstanding people. There was no appropriate way for them to support themselves while remaining in a state of indolence, so as a matter of course they became gamblers. In the end they suffered destitution and became outlaws who committed theft and arson. This is natural principle and the inevitable course of things.

Because such things occur, one aspect of the Way of governing is that in imperial capitals and kingly cities one ought to establish large numbers of places of entertainment such as theaters and brothels. There are three benefits to this. The first is that due to this entertainment the city will be bustling, which is a sign of great peace. Without such entertainment

---

20 Yoshiwara was the licensed prostitution district of Edo, and Sakaimachi was the main theater district.

the city will be quiet, which is a harbinger of decline. The second benefit is that people whose heaven-endowed inborn nature is degenerate can make a living through these establishments and so will not commit such wicked deeds as theft and arson. People of course do not enjoy committing wicked deeds when they know that they will certainly be punished for them; such deeds arise from people being destitute and having no choice. The third benefit is that it is good for the money of the world to circulate and not stagnate. When there are many places of entertainment, the money of the rich will be distributed and circulate in the world. If there are no such places of entertainment, there will be nowhere for the rich to spend their money and it will be put away in storehouses for long periods, causing the amount of currency circulating in the world to shrink. All three of these benefits pertain to the advantages or disadvantages to the state. To indiscriminately set up prohibitions without investigating these advantages and disadvantages is the policy of officials who do not understand the Way of governing.

There are two things that ought to be prohibited among the people. First of all, monks ought to preach the Buddhist law only within temples, but in cities today there are those who preach the Buddhist law by gathering together ignorant people or by taking on the persona of a layman. This is something that goes against both the law of the Buddha and the law of the country. Second, no such Way as Shinto existed in Japan in ancient times. What is called "Shinto" today was created by Urabe Kanetomo [1435–1511] and is a Way for priests to serve spirits.[21] It is not a Way for governing the country or cultivating the self. There is no benefit in ordinary people studying this and for them to do so in fact causes harm. If one is going to lecture on this Way, one ought to just gather priests in the house of another priest; ordinary people should not be allowed to listen to this. Today, though, there are those who are not priests and yet study this Way, gather ignorant people in the city and lecture to them, and even lecture to passing travelers. The two things I have described cause great harm to government and I hope they can be strictly prohibited. The failure to prohibit things that ought to be prohibited in the state, and the prohibition of things that ought not be prohibited, are due to officials not understanding the general tenets of government.

...

---

21 Urabe Kanetomo (also known as Yoshida Kanetomo) was the founder of what was called "Yoshida Shinto."

9 Institutions

The government of the state has its basis in the samurai and common people being attached to the land, as I discussed earlier. For this reason, once a feudal lord has established a country, by permanently residing there without leaving, he creates the solidity of a boulder. When the authorities move feudal lords around and frequently change their territories, though, this causes the deterioration of the state. In times of peace such houses fall into destitution, and in chaotic times they lack care in military preparations and are easily defeated. Therefore, in governing the realm it is considered a desirable policy not to move feudal lords. In the current age there is something called "changing places," in which feudal lords who are hereditary vassals of the shogun and on particularly close terms with him are frequently moved to different fiefs.[22] There are cases where several such changes occur within the lifetime of a single feudal lord. This leads to suffering for the feudal lords, wearies the samurai and common people, goes against humane government, and causes laxity in military preparations. It is desirable that this practice of changing places be abolished and that feudal lords be made to possess their countries permanently. If that is done, it will surely lead to peace within the land and be in keeping with the government of the sages.

---

22 The term translated as "hereditary vassals" is *fudai*, which in this context refers to daimyo who had already pledged loyalty to the Tokugawa at the time of the decisive Battle of Sekigahara in 1600. One purpose of the movements that Shundai describes was to put close allies of the shogun in strategic locations.

Volume 10

Non-Action

When a country is first founded, the Way of political economy requires that a perspicacious ruler and his wise counselors establish the hundred offices, put in place institutions, make statutes strict, and practice a government that will remain unchanged for a hundred generations; this is the highest form of political economy. The next best form is when, the middle of an era having been reached, heroic rulers emerge who employ wise ministers to reform long-standing errors, correct customs, promote and demote officials, make rewards and punishments credible, and cultivate the government of the ancient kings. Similar to how one repairs an old house or provides medical care to heal a sick person, they invigorate a state that has declined and extend a favorable state of affairs. This is called a "revival." The two methods described above will not achieve success if both rulers and ministers do not attain the Way of governing, consider the past, and act according to an understanding of the times. Ever since ancient times it has been hard to find perspicacious rulers and wise aides, and it has also been extremely rare for rulers and ministers to act in unison, so in both other countries and our own it has been exceedingly difficult to achieve success in political economy.

To reform existing government without carrying out true political economy, instead merely considering temporary expediency and looking at the minor advantages and disadvantages that are right before one's eyes, brings unrest to the people and is of great harm to the state. Rulers of later times often modify the government of their predecessors bit by bit in each age in conformity with their own individual preferences.

10 Non-Action

To compare this to living in a house, it is like when a son finds it inconvenient to live in the house built by his father, so he modifies this and that to conform to his own preferences and considers the result to be superior to his father's dwelling. The grandson in turn finds it inconvenient to live in and modifies it again. In this way, the dwelling changes with each generation, so that even though a person in a particular generation considers it convenient and superior to his father's dwelling, from the perspective of an outside observer it always involves gaining one thing at the expense of losing another, with no overall advantage or disadvantage. Moreover, because it is a house that one has not constructed oneself, improving it here will cause damage over there, and improving it over there will damage it in some other place. In the end, it will not be a satisfactory dwelling. As the dwelling changes with every generation, each time people modify it they cut out pillars and remove beams, open holes in the roof here and close up windows there, and wreak havoc on the house in various ways. In the end, then, this weakens the house, and the form of the house constructed by one's ancestors is entirely lost, leaving it looking like nothing more than an old broken-down shack that has been mangled all over.

When it comes to the Way of governing the country, to change the government of previous rulers according to the individual preferences of the rulers of each generation is not true governing, but is merely a Way of staving off unrest. When there are heroic rulers and extraordinary ministers, it will not be impossible to practice true political economy even in a later age. However, in a time when government has been practiced merely through stopgap measures from the very start, with no proper institutions, no strict statutes, and no consideration of the past, and when, after the passage of several decades or a century, gentlemen receive hereditary stipends and live in luxury and profligacy while the common people discard their fundamental task and occupy themselves with peripheral gain,[1] with customs broken down and both the high and the low driven to destitution, then it will be completely impossible to change the existing government just by changing things here and there without having true political economy. In these kinds of times, there is nothing better than to give up on governing the country and simply practice the Way of non-action [*mui*].

"Non-action" refers to not doing anything. There are two types of non-action: the non-action of the sages and the non-action of Laozi. In

---

1 That is, ignoring agriculture and pursuing commercial gain instead.

the *Analects*, Confucius says, "Did Shun not govern with non-action?"[2] This is the non-action of the sages. When Shun governed the realm, he established offices and responsibilities and employed such sagely and wise people as the Great Yu, Ji, Xie, Gao Yao, Bo Yi, Kui, Long, and Bo I, making them into various types of officials.[3] He entrusted all governmental matters to the various ministers, with the ruler simply being at the top doing nothing. Like the sun and the moon illuminating the land, he merely observed whether the ministers below were hardworking and loyal, whether the realm was well governed, and whether the common people were at peace. In the *Classic of Documents* it says, "He let his robes fall down and folded his hands and the realm was well governed."[4] In the *Doctrine of the Mean* it says, "He is sincere and respectful and the realm is at peace."[5] These all refer to non-action. The non-action of the sages does not refer to those above and below not doing anything at all. Rather, it refers to the hundred officials fulfilling their respective talents, the ruler being at ease above and entrusting the affairs of government to these officials, the common people being at ease below, and all throughout the land there being none who fail to attain their appropriate place.

The non-action of Laozi, in contrast, means that both those above and those below do not do anything at all; instead, they entrust things to the natural course of heaven and earth without laying a hand on the affairs of the realm, leaving things alone to run their course just as they are. Although from the perspective of Confucians this seems to lack humaneness, in reality it does not; rather, this Way is appropriate for a decadent age. Laozi lived in a time when the Zhou dynasty was in decline. Observing the government of the realm at that time, he saw that although people spoke of the Way of the ancient kings, for the most part it had lost its roots. Both rulers and those who served them nevertheless attempted to govern the state, so the kind of government they practiced always became a malady of the people and a harm to the state, leading day by day toward unrest. Laozi lamented this and wrote a book to explain the natural Way of non-action. Although his "non-action" shares a name with the

---

2 *Analects* 15.4.
3 Shun appointed Kui as director of music, and Long as minister of communication (described in the "Canon of Shun" section of the *Classic of Documents*). See vol. 1 n. 67 above for discussion of the other figures listed here.
4 From the "Completion of the War" section of the *Classic of Documents*.
5 *Doctrine of the Mean* 33.5.

"non-action" of the sages, its meaning is different. Laozi's non-action is entirely a Way for governing a decadent age.

Laozi made a superb argument when he wrote that "governing a large country is like cooking a small fish."[6] In this metaphor, a "small fish" refers to a small fresh fish. "Fresh" means that it is unsalted. The meat of unsalted fish is fragile, and on top of this the fish he describes is particularly prone to falling apart because it is small. When cooking a small unsalted fish, from the time one puts it in the pot until the time it is finished, one does not touch it or move it. One simply waits for it to be done and then takes it out and eats it. When one pokes it about with a spoon and chopsticks while it is still in the pot to check whether it is done, the bones and meat fall apart and the body of the fish disintegrates. Governing a large country is the same. When one attempts to govern by issuing various decrees, the people will be poked about by these decrees and will not be at ease, and there will be many who are left destitute or set adrift. In this case, governing causes more harm than not governing. The human heart finds rest in doing what it is accustomed to, so when one simply leaves things alone as they have been up to now, there will be no disturbances and things will be well governed. In this case, not governing amounts, rather, to governing. This is referred to as the "government of not governing" and is what is meant by Laozi's "non-action." There is nothing that surpasses this when it comes to the Way for managing a decadent age.

This can be compared to a person who is ill. Past the age of fifty, his illness has various symptoms, including symptoms of heat, symptoms of cold, symptoms of emptiness, and symptoms of substance.[7] Phlegm, bad blood, tissue accumulations, and colic exist inside his body. With various illnesses together in the body of a single person, the suffering is extreme. When a doctor tries to cure the patient by using a supplementary medicine to compensate for symptoms of emptiness, the body will refuse it and not take it in. When he uses purging medicines to induce vomiting and diarrhea, it damages the patient's vital force. If he provides medicines of heat when faced with symptoms of cold, it brings on a fever. If he employs cooling agents when faced with symptoms of heat, it causes symptoms of cold again. When he uses moxa it causes burning, and when he uses acupuncture it causes constipation. Various illnesses combined together

---

6   From chapter 60 of the *Dao de jing* (*Classic of the Way and Its Virtue*).
7   These are classifications of types of symptoms in Chinese medicine.

like this are difficult to cure, and the doctor, not knowing their origin, treats the signs of illness in accordance with how symptoms manifest themselves externally. Methods of treatment and medicines are mixed together and there is no evidence of improvement. When one illness goes away, another flares up, and as the patient goes back and forth between these over the years, his vital force gradually declines, his intake of food and drink diminishes, and his body wastes away. He does not die, though, but just lies in bed as long as there is still breath in his body.

Dozens of doctors exhaust their techniques, fold their arms idly, and walk away, but for all these there is a single good doctor who cures the patient. His method of curing is to stop using medicines, give the patient things to eat that are pleasing to the mouth and stomach, give him clothing appropriate to the temperature, have him avoid the external irritants of wind, cold, heat, and humidity, have him lightly exercise his four limbs, change things in accordance with the seasons, gradually put his spleen and stomach in order with food, and nurture his vital force. After doing this for half a year or a year, the patient's vital force slowly recovers and he makes some progress in his food and drink, so his mood gradually becomes cheerful and his body regains health bit by bit. The illness he had up to that time is not so painful either, and as the years and months drag on like the branch of a willow, out of ten symptoms five or six get better, and although the patient's condition is not the same as before he became ill, he suffers from no great pain and his life extends for five or ten more years before he dies. Even when in their prime, people contract illnesses that are difficult to cure and pass years suffering from these. When doctors dispense various medicinal preparations in their efforts to cure these illnesses, the illnesses still do not go away, and the more they try to cure them the worse they get. In medical books this is referred to as "exacerbating the symptoms" or "exacerbating the illness." "Exacerbating the illness" refers to creating complications in an illness. When the symptoms of an illness are made worse in this way, this does not bring about a cure, but rather hastens death. Especially when it comes to people who are middle-aged or older, their original vital force has declined, so there are many things in their body that are not at full strength. At such times, when one tries to cure an illness that is difficult to cure, inevitably this does not cure the illness, but rather damages the spleen and stomach, breaks down the patient's vital force, and hastens death. The medical treatment provided by a good doctor could be called, as the saying goes today, a "treatment of not treating."[8] That is to say, by not treating the illness, it in fact treats it. This is namely the Way of non-action of Laozi.

The Way of governing the state is the same. When one attempts to govern and improve in one fell swoop a state that has grown worse through complications, while not improving its foundations and simply allowing it to follow along with the changes in the world, this is like an average doctor treating a difficult illness. The more one issues government decrees, the more one goes against the sentiments of the people. This does not lead to effective government, but rather invites unrest. At such times, a person who understands the Way of non-action does not lay a hand on things and does not govern, but simply nurtures the vital force of the people and aims somehow or other to extend the fortunes of the country for a bit. This is considered good government and is called the "government of not governing." When the fortunes of the country are called the "pulse of the country," then, this is because of their similarity with the pulse that indicates life in a person.

In ancient times, when Emperor Gaozu of the Han dynasty first took control of the realm, he made Xiao He [d. 193 BC] prime minister and had him govern.[9] At that time, Cao Shen [d. 190 BC] was prime minister of the country of Qi and was living in Qi.[10] He took the Daoist adept Gai Gong as his teacher and studied the techniques of Huang and Lao. "Huang and Lao" refers to Huangdi and Laozi, and the "techniques of Huang and Lao" refers to the Way of non-action. Cao Shen used this Way in governing the country of Qi and the country was well governed. Later, Xiao He died and Cao Shen took his place as prime minister of the Han.[11] He would gather people at his house and drink liquor day and night. Because he would attend court in the morning drunk, he did not

---

8 In the original Japanese, the comparison with government is even more explicit, as the words that Shundai uses for "to provide medical treatment" (*jisu*) and "to govern" (*osamu*) use the same character. In addition, he uses the identical expression, *fuji no ji*, to mean both "the governing of not governing" and "the treatment of not treating."
9 Gaozu was the founding emperor of the Han dynasty. Xiao He was appointed prime minister upon the establishment of the Han and held the post until his death.
10 Cao Shen was a military leader who played a key role in the conquests made by Liu Bang (the future Emperor Gaozu) that resulted in the establishment of the Han dynasty. Qi was one of the countries conquered by Liu Bang's forces. After it was conquered, Cao Shen was sent there to govern it.
11 Cao Shen served as prime minister from Xiao He's death in 193 BC until his own death in 190 BC.

listen to affairs of government there. After withdrawing from court, he would drink again. When those officials who had public affairs to discuss went to Cao Shen's house with the intention of reporting on these to the prime minister, he would be in the midst of a drinking party. He would summon these officials to sit with him but would not let them say anything, instead first making them drink. Because it was a command of the prime minister, they could not refuse. When after drinking they requested to take their leave and tried to say something, Cao Shen would observe their expression and simply order them to drink, thus forcing them to drink more. The officials would in the end get completely drunk and lose any desire to discuss public affairs, instead enjoying themselves to the utmost, and then leave. An account of this can be seen in the *History of the Former Han*.[12] This is the government of non-action of Cao Shen. When Cao Shen governed the realm like this to the end of his days, the realm was exceedingly well governed.

After that, when Emperor Wen and Emperor Jing [188–141 BC, r. 157–141 BC] both used the techniques of Huang and Lao to govern the realm with non-action, the state was prosperous and the people were at ease. Emperor Wu revered Confucian techniques and did not make use of Huang and Lao. However, it was his heaven-endowed inborn nature to enjoy luxury, and when he did such things as commission construction projects, seek out wizards, attack barbarians, take pleasure in hunting, and give himself over to music and women, the land deteriorated and the peasants became destitute. From this point on, the realm of the Han dynasty went into decline. This is like when a middle-aged person suffers from a severe illness and even after being cured his vital force declines. It does not return to the level of his prime, and after that it gradually progresses toward the weakness of old age. Although it is a good thing that Emperor Wu did not prefer Huang and Lao, but instead promoted Confucian learning, he did not attain the Way of the ancient kings. He merely borrowed its name while pursuing his own personal whims, so this in fact became harmful to the realm and was no match for how Emperor Wen and Emperor Jing governed by using the Way of non-action of Huang and Lao. This is not the fault of Confucian learning itself; it is because he did not follow the Way of the ancient kings. When even Emperor Wu, who was truly an uncommon ruler, ruled poorly, there was no proper government. When an average ruler who does not attain the level of Emperor

---

12 The biography of Cao Shen is included in volume 39 of the *History of the Former Han*.

Wu practices half-baked government, this will cause even greater harm to the people and destroy the state. In this situation there is nothing better than simply to practice the Way of non-action and carry out the government of not governing.

Confucians of later ages have not been well versed in scholarship and so have not been clear about what kind of Way the Way of Laozi is. They have been ignorant in making it out to be an unconditionally heretical doctrine and casting it aside. The Way of the sages can be compared to the five grains. The five grains are what people ordinarily eat to nourish their bodies and extend their lives, but when one eats something bad or eats too much, it damages one's spleen and stomach and brings on the illnesses of abdominal swelling, stomachache, and diarrhea. When practiced poorly, the Way of the sages brings disorder to the realm and state just as one can suffer from indigestion and food poisoning after eating the five grains. The Ways of Laozi and the various other philosophers can be compared to medicines. Medicines cure illness, so when even the five grains bring on an illness by becoming stopped up in a person's stomach, one cannot get by without curing this with medicine. Medicines are typically lopsided in their qualities. Rhubarb and gypsum have an extremely cold quality, whereas aconite and dry ginger have an extremely hot quality. The various medicines are all like this, so medicines always contain poison. Because they have poison, they are able to cure illness. Although there are differences between greater and lesser poisons, there are no medicines that do not contain poison. When doctors make good use of these, the various medicines all cure illness, but when they make poor use of them, even ginseng and atractylodes rhizome harm people. Although when treating an illness one uses even extremely poisonous medicines, in the absence of illness there is no benefit to using medicines even when they are minor poisons or not poisons at all.

The kinds of medicines I have been discussing are not things that one should consume every day, but doctors make use of them because their effectiveness in treating illness cannot be equaled even by the five grains. The Ways of people like Laozi resemble this. Although they are not the ordinary Way for governing the realm and state, in a later age when various illnesses arise in the state, the Ways discussed by the various philosophers, such as the non-action of Laozi, the universal love of Mozi, and the punishments and legal techniques of Shen Buhai and Hanfeizi, all have their respective uses. When one uses them well, they are all good medicines and will not fail to treat the illnesses of the country. One who sees the various philosophers in this manner is considered a person well versed in scholarship. Even among the various philosophers, the non-action of Laozi is a particularly mild and moderate Way, so it is an exceedingly good Way for managing the weary people of an age in decline. In the present age as well, ever since the Genroku era [1688–1704], the samurai and common people in the land have been destitute and the vital force of the state has been in decline, so the present age is a time when one should stop everything and exclusively practice non-action.

The Way of Changes

Those who govern the realm and state must understand the Way of Changes [*ekidō*].[13] Although it is not easy to study the *Classic of Changes*, it is not that difficult to understand the general meaning of the Way of Changes. In the Way of Changes there are three fundamental matters: one is the times, the second is number, and the third is yin and yang. To understand these three is to understand the Way of Changes.

As for the first, the times, in the Changes there are sixty-four hexagrams. Each hexagram is made up of six lines, so in the sixty-four hexagrams there are 384 lines. The sixty-four hexagrams and 384 lines all clarify the times. In the human affairs of the realm, there are various alterations. These alterations are all "the times." In managing the state, observing the people, and governing affairs, it is considered wise to understand the times and respond to alterations. In society there is prosperity and decline, in countries there is good governance and chaos, in houses there is tranquility and danger, in human rulers there is the good and the bad, and in the progression of affairs there is that which is possible and that which is impossible. These kinds of things are called "the times." Those who govern the state must discern what kind of time the present is and practice an appropriate form of government for that time. If one governs without understanding the times, then even if one uses the Way of Yao and Shun and the Three Kings, when it clashes with the times one will certainly not be able to practice it. The sixty-four hexagrams and 384 lines of the Changes are a teaching that allows humans to know of this. This is what is meant when the term "the times" is used to represent the essence of the *Classic of Changes*. If one studies the *Classic of*

---

13 I capitalize "Changes" as a translation for the Japanese *eki* (Ch. *yi*) to refer to the system of divination indicated by this Japanese term.

10 The Way of Changes

Changes, one will understand what this means. Even if one does not study it, though, when one has the intention of observing the times and governs by considering what is appropriate and inappropriate to the times, then even if it does not hit the mark, it will surely not be far off.[14] I have already discussed this point in abbreviated form in the "General Discussion of Political Economy"[15] that constitutes volume one of the present book.

The second element, number, comes from the original emergence of the Changes from numbers. Heaven is one and earth is two, heaven is three and earth is four, heaven is five and earth is six, heaven is seven and earth is eight, heaven is nine and earth is ten – these are the numbers of the River Chart.[16] The Changes were created based on the numbers of the River Chart. One, three, five, seven, and nine are numbers of heaven, and two, four, six, eight, and ten are numbers of earth. Adding up one, three, five, seven, and nine gives twenty-five, and adding up two, four, six, eight, and ten gives thirty, so the numbers of heaven and earth together are fifty-five. Fuxi created the eight trigrams based on these numbers.[17] Combining the eight trigrams with each other he made sixty-four hexagrams, exhausting the principle of heaven and earth and the myriad things.

Everything within heaven and earth has its particular number. When it comes to humans, from the time they are born until the time they die, their good and bad fortune and prosperity and decline all have their number. When it comes to the myriad things, the life and death of birds and beasts and fish and turtles, as well as the flourishing and withering of grasses and trees, all have their number. Let us consider, for a moment, a single ceramic piece. When a potter creates various pieces, making many

---

14 *Great Learning* 9.2: "In the 'Kang gao' ['Announcement to Kang'] it says, 'Act as if looking after an infant.' If [a mother] truly seeks in her heart after the infant's needs, then although she may not hit the mark, she will not be far off."
15 See above, p. 28.
16 The River Chart (Ch. *hetu*, Jp. *kato*) is a diagram that was said to have appeared on the back of a dragon horse that Fuxi saw emerge from the Yellow River. Early sources do not give any description of what exactly the River Chart looked like, but from the Song dynasty it was represented as an arrangement of strings of dots, either white (for odd numbers, "numbers of heaven") or black (for even numbers, "numbers of earth"). An even and an odd number are paired in each position of the chart, with the numbers five and seven in the center, two and seven at the top (south), four and nine on the right (west), one and six at the bottom (north), and three and eight on the left (east).
17 Fuxi is a deity in Chinese mythology who is credited with creating humans and teaching them such things as fishing, hunting, and the domestication of animals. He is said to have been inspired by the River Chart to create the eight trigrams, although the exact connection between the River Chart and the trigrams is not always explained, and sources that do present theories about it are not all in agreement.

of the same form out of the same type of clay, upon their completion he will find that as a matter of course these include both good ones and bad ones. There are those that break immediately upon completion, those that break after one sells them to others, those that break after one, two, five, or ten years, and those that remain undamaged after several dozen or a hundred years. There are also those that burn up in fires and those that are lost underwater. Although these were all produced and completed at the same time, each of the many pieces has its particular fixed number that determines when it comes into being and when it is destroyed. Even the potter does not know what this is, and nor do the buyer and seller. This is a number that each thing is furnished with and is natural to the myriad things of heaven and earth. This number cannot be altered even with the power of extraordinary sageliness.

To turn the discussion to the fate of humans, for warriors to go into battle is dangerous in the extreme. However, even when warriors of an age of unrest repeatedly experience peril in heading onto the battlefield, there are those who do not die at that time, but instead survive to old age and only then die of illness. One should observe the example of Cao Shen of the Han dynasty, who was wounded seventy times but did not die on the battlefield, instead governing the realm and dying in his bed after he had grown old.[18] There are also those who meet unexpected misfortune and die at an ordinary time when nothing is amiss, as well as those who fall severely ill and are in a perilous state where they are on the verge of death, and yet do not die at that time, but die later from such things as drowning or falling from a horse. When hundreds or thousands of people die all at once in a flood or fire, there will be one person in a hundred who escapes harm. Similarly, when dozens of people escape a disaster, there will be one or two who die. These things all come from the numbers attached to people's fates. When their number is up, they die, but as long as their number is not up, they will not die, no matter what happens. People whose number is up cannot be revived even by a superbly skilled doctor, but people whose number is not up cannot be killed even by a cruel official. Through these examples one should understand how this works. All affairs of the realm are like this. The peaceful government and unrest, rise and decline, and existence and disappearance of a state from the start

---

18 See the "Biography of Xiao He" in volume 39 of the *History of the Former Han* and the "Hereditary House of Prime Minister Xiao" in chapter 53 of the *Records of the Grand Historian*.

all have the numbers that are natural to them. This is not something that can be affected by humans. A country that is going to be well governed will be well governed even if nobody governs it. If a country is going to fall into unrest, even sages and wise men will not be able to govern it and keep it from descending into unrest.

Buddhists provide a useful framework for thinking about this when they speak of birth, old age, sickness, and death, dividing the life of a human into four stages and clarifying their order. In the realm and state, too, one finds birth, old age, sickness, and death. When a state is first established, this is birth. When it passes its midpoint and heads toward its latter days, this is old age. In the latter days of a state there are always things that occasion unrest, such as rulers who die early and leave the throne to a child, female rulers who preside over the court, rulers who lack a successor, rulers who are ignorant and are manipulated by wicked ministers, rulers who are violent and harm the people, rulers who are arrogant and licentious and cause suffering to the peasants, or natural or human disasters that lead the people to rise up and the land to become destitute. These correspond to illnesses. When a state collapses, this is its death.

Setting aside for a moment the most ancient past, the Three Dynasties of the Xia, Yin, and Zhou were all states established by sages, yet none were without birth, old age, illness, and death. From the Han dynasty onward, the founding rulers of dynasties were not sages like the Two Emperors and Three Kings, but they received the mandate of heaven and established countries, the maintenance of which by their descendants sometimes lasted for one or two hundred years and sometimes for three or four hundred years. In those ages as well, there always existed birth, old age, illness, and death. Even the realms of the Three Dynasties never failed to perish, just as there is no such thing as an immortal human. The only difference with the Three Dynasties is that they were states founded by sages, so they lasted for a long time, as opposed to later dynasties, which, due to their inferior virtue, did not last as long as the Three Dynasties. This is the number corresponding to their birth, old age, illness, and death, which is fixed and unchanging. Even with the extraordinary wisdom of the sages, one cannot turn back the time of old age and illness to its origin and make it the time of birth, nor can one transform death into immortality. If without knowing this number one pursued a form of government that went against the times, not only would it not be effective, it would in fact cause harm. People who clarify this principle are considered accomplished in the numbers of the Changes. The sixty-four hexagrams and 384 lines of the Changes all clarify these numbers.

The third element, yin and yang, is what the *Xici zhuan* [*Commentary on the Appended Phrases*] to the *Classic of Changes* describes when it states, "In the Changes there is the supreme ultimate, which gives birth to the two basic forms."[19] The two basic forms are yin and yang. The supreme ultimate divides and becomes the two basic forms, and the two basic forms divide and become the four images. The four images are greater yang, lesser yin, lesser yang, and greater yin.[20] Greater yang corresponds to summer, lesser yin to autumn, lesser yang to spring, and greater yin to winter. The four images are thus the four seasons. The four figures divide and become the eight trigrams, the eight trigrams divide and become the sixty-four hexagrams, and this brings the Way of Changes to completion. The Way of Changes, then, consists of yin and yang. The myriad words of the *Classic of Changes* simply speak of the principle of yin and yang. When Zhuangzi says, "The *Classic of Changes* speaks of yin and yang," this truly shows an understanding of the Changes.[21]

Heaven and earth are the father and mother of the myriad things. Heaven is yang and earth is yin. Because the myriad things come into being out of the two material forces of heaven and earth, which are yin and yang, a single thing is always endowed with the material forces of both yin and yang, just as a person is born with a single body that is endowed with the material forces of both his father and his mother. When one says that heaven is father and earth is mother, this is a general division. When one makes finer divisions, yin and yang each in turn have their own yin and yang. Even if one divides into two, eight, or an extremely large number, one will not reach the end of this principle. The two basic forms, four images, and eight trigrams of the Changes manifest this principle. To give a brief summation, cold and heat and day and night are the yin and yang of heaven. South and north and light and dark are the yin and yang of earth. Male and female and life and death are the yin and yang of humans. With animals there is male and female, with grasses and trees there is flourishing and withering, and with soil and stone there is dryness and dampness and cold and heat. Among all the things that exist within

---

19 The *Commentary on the Appended Phrases* is one of the "Ten Wings" to the *Classic of Changes*, a series of commentaries that were traditionally attributed to Confucius.
20 These are represented by the digrams ⚌ (greater yang), ⚍ (lesser yin), ⚎ (lesser yang), and ⚏ (greater yin).
21 The quotation is from the "Tianxia" ("All under Heaven") chapter of *Zhuangzi*.

heaven and earth, none lacks its yin and yang. In addition, each thing or affair has its diminishment and generation and its waxing and waning; this too is yin and yang. As for diminishment and generation, "diminishment" is disappearing; it refers to when things vanish. "Generation" is coming into being. For example, from the time a person is born until he reaches middle age, his life force, blood, muscles, and bones all grow; this is generation. After the age of fifty, his vital force, blood, muscles, and bones weaken; this is diminishment. With things like grasses and trees, there is diminishment and generation within the course of a single year. As for waxing and waning, waxing is growing full and waning is diminishing. This can be seen in such things as the waxing and waning of the moon and the ebb and flow of tides.

There is also decay and flourishing when it comes to two things that exist in relation to each other, one thing being yang and the other yin. To decay is to decline, and to flourish is to prosper and develop. When yin flourishes, yang decays, and when yang flourishes, yin decays. This is like the coming and going of cold and heat within the space of a year; it is the flourishing and decay of yin and yang. In the context of the realm and state, when the Way of the gentleman prospers, the Way of the petty man declines, and when the Way of the petty man prospers, the Way of the gentleman declines; this is the decay and flourishing of the gentleman and the petty man. Yin and yang by their nature decay and flourish, so they never stand in equal relation to each other as the horns of a bull do. In all the affairs of the realm, there is never a lack of decay and flourishing and waxing and waning; this is the decay and flourishing of yin and yang. The existence within the state of peaceful government and unrest, as well as rising and falling fortunes, is the decay and generation and waxing and waning of the state. The existence for an individual person of good and bad luck, fortune and misfortune, prosperity and adversity, and honor and disgrace are the decay and generation and waxing and waning of a single person. Within a person's lifetime, too, there are those who start out prosperous and later become poor, and those who start out poor and later become prosperous. During a period of several years, there are years with much good luck and years with much bad luck. Within the space of a single year, there are months when one is lucky and months when one is unlucky. Within a single month, there are days of pleasure and days of suffering, and days of joy and days of sorrow. Even within a single day, there are days when one has good luck in the morning and bad luck in the evening, or when one suffers in the morning and enjoys pleasure in the evening. These represent the decay and generation and waxing and waning of humans. In addition, within a single province or district there are times when the eastern portion prospers and the western portion declines, or when the southern portion prospers and the northern portion declines. This is the decay and flourishing of a single province or district. All the myriad things and affairs within heaven and earth are furnished with yin and yang, so there is nothing that does not have decay and generation and waxing and waning. When there are two things that are paired, they never fail to decay and flourish in relation to each other. This is the alternation of yin and yang.

In this process of alternation, though, there will be no transformation if something is not brought to its limit, and there will be no beginning without something ending.[22] For this reason, generation begins when decay ends, and decay begins when generation ends. When waxing reaches its limit there is waning, and when waning reaches its limit there is waxing. Decay and flourishing are also like this. With the peaceful government and unrest of the realm, too, when peaceful government reaches its limit unrest erupts, and when unrest reaches its limit peaceful government appears. In decay and generation and waxing and waning, there are the major and the minor. Such things as the peaceful government and unrest of the realm and the increase and decrease in the population are examples of major decay and generation and major waxing and waning. The good and bad luck and fortune and misfortune that occur within a single year or month are examples of minor decay and generation and minor waxing and waning. In the context of a state, its ruler in one reign being benevolent and in another being cruel, or in one reign being fond of luxury and in another being fond of frugality, are matters that also belong to the category of decay and generation and waxing and waning and that represent the alternation of yin and yang.

When it comes to the alternation of yin and yang, there is nothing more clearly evident than cold and heat and day and night. Those who understand the principle of yin and yang view all the decay and generation and waxing and waning of the myriad things as if they were cold and heat and day and night. Even with powers of extraordinary sageliness, it is impossible to make summer cold, winter hot, day into night, or night into day. Wise people understand on summer days that winter will surely be cold,

---

22 A similar statement appears in the *Commentary on the Appended Phrases* to the *Classic of Changes*: "When changes reach their limit, then there will be a transformation."

and gentlemen do not forget in winter that the summer was hot. The same is true when it comes to day and night. Just as one understands that there is coming and going in heat and cold and day and night, one understands that there is also coming and going in a person's honor and disgrace, rise and fall, suffering and pleasure, sorrow and joy. For this reason, when a gentleman is at ease, he does not forget distress. He exercises prudence, understands in times of distress that he will surely enjoy ease again, and is tranquil without any stirring of his heart. Just as one understands that there is coming and going in an individual person's honor and disgrace, rise and fall, suffering and pleasure, and sorrow and joy, one understands that there is also coming and going in the peaceful government and unrest and rising and falling fortunes of a state. Therefore, wise people in peacefully governed ages do not forget about unrest, and in ages of unrest they simply give thought to the business right before them, understanding that if unrest does not reach its limit, there will be no return to peaceful governance. Understanding that when one person rises another falls, and that when one person falls another rises, he finds a course of action, responding to changes and discharging his duties. Such a person is considered one who understands the principle of the decay and generation of yin and yang. Ignorant people do not understand this principle, so in times of ease they think they will always be at ease, and do not consider that distress is surely to come. When in the end they encounter distress, they immediately lose all resolve and think to take their lives. Not making any preparations for the unexpected, they are simply left at a loss when they face difficulties.

In the Way of decay and generation of yin and yang, when a limit is reached there will be a transformation, and when a limit is not reached there will not be a transformation. There never fails to be a transformation when a limit is reached, and a transformation never occurs if a limit is not reached. In the affairs of the realm, there is nothing that is without decay and generation and waxing and waning. Among these, such things as the waxing and waning of the moon or the ebb and flow of the tides are clearly evident, so even ignorant people are able to understand them. The decay and generation and waxing and waning of human affairs has a very subtle principle, though, so one cannot understand this if one is not wise. When one is well-versed in this principle, then one will commit few errors when conducting affairs. Even when merely governing one's individual person, one must not fail to understand this. All the more, how could it be acceptable for those who govern the realm and state not to understand it? It was with this in mind that Confucius said, "At fifty let me study the Changes, and then I could be free of major errors."[23]

The Way of Changes is vast, however. Even those who are Confucians by occupation find it difficult to exhaustively study it, to say nothing of the fact that ordinary gentlemen cannot be expected to master it. Nevertheless, it is simply time, number, and yin and yang that constitute the general framework of the Way of Changes, and an understanding of these can be attained even by those who do not engage in profound study. If those who preside over the state and practice government understand the meaning of these three things, then they will surely be able to avoid major mistakes.

The Way of the ancient kings exists entirely within the Six Classics. These are the *Classic of Poetry*, the *Classic of Documents*, ritual, music, the *Classic of Changes*, and the *Spring and Autumn Annals*.[24] The Way of the ancient kings is the Way of governing the realm, and the Six Classics are tools for governing the realm. The *Classic of Poetry* exhaustively presents the human feelings of the realm. If in governing the realm one does not understand human feelings, then even though one may issue edicts, they will not be carried out by those below; this is because they clash with human feelings. By making use of the *Classic of Poetry*, one becomes versed in the human feelings of the realm and understands the merits and demerits of governmental matters as well as the good and bad of customs; this is crucial for the Way of governing. The *Classic of Documents* provides a record of the Two Emperors and Three Kings and the Way with which they governed the realm. In practicing government, one should above all give attention to using the Way of the Two Emperors and Three Kings as one's basis, while at the same time giving consideration to the affairs of the present age. The Way of the sages is the constant Way of all ages, so those who follow it do not make errors. Moreover, the *Classic of Poetry* and *Classic of Documents* exhaustively present the correct principles of the realm, so when one studies these texts and becomes versed in these correct principles, one's heart will become clear and one will grow in wisdom. Ritual consists of the conventions of the state and the formalities

---

23 *Analects* 7.16.
24 I translate *rei* and *gaku* here simply as "ritual" and "music," rather than the *Classic of Ritual* and *Classic of Music*, because of the primacy Shundai gives to the practices of ritual and music, as opposed to the texts that discuss them. In a later work, *A General Outline of the Six Classics*, Shundai discusses at greater length his view that the term "Classic" (*kei*) does not necessarily refer to a text.

10 The Way of Changes

that govern human affairs. These formalities are something established by the sages, and to violate them is the same as behaving like a beast. Ritual is the constant standard of heaven and earth, so it is esteemed in the Way of the sages. Music is the Way of harmonious enjoyment, and the strict aspects of ritual are moderated with music. Like the two wheels of a cart or a person's two hands, ritual and music are never separated. Even today there still exist the Classics of Ritual.[25] The book called the *Yue jing* [*Classic of Music*] no longer exists in its entirety, but fragments of it can be found scattered in ancient books. I have already discussed the significance of ritual and music earlier in the present book.[26] The *Spring and Autumn Annals* presents the Way of rewards and punishments. Rewards and punishments are a critical task of the state and a technique for encouraging virtue and chastising vice [*kanzen chōaku*].

The Five Classics discussed above are the Way for governing the state in the immediate moment. If one practices government with these five, then there ought not to be anything lacking. Why, then, is the *Classic of Changes* added to these, resulting in what are called the "Six Classics"? To answer this, the Five Classics are the ordinary Way with which the ancient kings governed the realm, so one might conclude that if one used them to govern the state, then even after a hundred reigns there would be no vice in government and the country would be in no danger of descending into unrest. However, even in the realm as it was governed by the ancient kings, in later ages vices emerged in government and rebellious ministers and unfilial sons appeared. These put the state in peril, and in the end disturbances erupted and the state collapsed. Such things happen according to the principle of the decay and generation of yin and yang and result from the fact that heaven and earth have a fixed number that determines how things go to their limit and then transform. This is namely the Way of Changes. It is not possible to understand this principle without studying the Changes, and the *Classic of Changes* exhaustively presents this principle. When the people who govern the state do not understand this principle, doubts arise in them when presiding over affairs and they sometimes commit great errors. Because of this, the sages

---

25 I am interpreting this as a collective reference to the *Rituals of Zhou*, *Book of Ceremonies and Rituals*, and *Record of Ritual*. It is also possible that Shundai is using "Classic of Ritual" as an alternate title for one of these texts alone (the original Japanese here does not distinguish between singular and plural); this was an older title for the *Book of Ceremonies and Rituals* and was also sometimes used as an alternate title for the *Record of Ritual*.

26 See vol. 2 above.

wrote of these things in the *Classic of Changes* to show them to people of later times. When we add the *Classic of Changes* to the above Five Classics to make the Six Classics, then, there is nothing at all missing from the Way of governing the realm and state. Those who clarify the meaning of these things and grasp that knowledge of the Way of Changes is indispensable are considered to understand the Way of Changes.

An Addendum to "On Political Economy"

Addendum to "Food and Goods" (Volume 5)

Question: In recent times, both major and minor feudal lords lack sufficient funds for their countries and are in extreme poverty. They borrow from their retainers' stipends amounts ranging from 10 percent on the low end to 50 or 60 percent on the high end.[1] When this is not enough, they rescue themselves from emergency situations by extracting money from the common people of their countries. When that is still not enough, they borrow money from wealthy merchants in Edo, Kyoto, and Osaka, which goes on year after year with no end in sight. They constantly borrow and seldom repay, so interest gives rise to more interest, and overdue loans pile up without them realizing that they have grown to several times their original amount. In the past, when Kumazawa Banzan [1619–1691] said that the amount of debt owed by all the feudal lords in Japan must be a hundred times the total amount of money in the entire country, this was in reference to the Kanbun [1661–1673] and Enpō [1673–1681] eras.[2] Now that seventy years have passed since then, the amount must have grown to a thousand times. If today the feudal lords tried to repay this quantity of debt, where would they find the money that exists in name but not in reality? Therefore, they have no plans that go beyond merely rescuing themselves somehow or other from the emergency that is right before them and surviving the moment at hand.

---

1 As discussed in vol. 5 n. 32, this refers to a practice in which daimyo supposedly borrowed a portion of their retainers' stipends until they could pay them in full, but which in practice was simply a reduction in the retainers' stipends.
2 Banzan discusses this in volume 2 of *Daigaku wakumon* (*Some Questions on Greater Learning*).

An Addendum to "On Political Economy"

Among the retainers of the feudal lords there are those who lament this situation and apply wise techniques to devise strategies to resolve it. Sometimes, though, they do not think them through adequately and so do not achieve their intent. Sometimes they put themselves at odds with lofty personages and great ministers and back off from their plans after being punished. Sometimes they are despised by the lowly masses and their plans fall apart halfway.[3] Sometimes they unreasonably extort taxes from the common people of their countries and provoke a revolt. Sometimes the ruler is unceasing in his extravagance and his ministers' plans cannot be carried out. Sometimes the ruler prefers to enact policies on his own and does not delegate them to his ministers. If there is even one of these obstacles, then one may have the talent of Guan Zhong or Yanzi and the loyalty of Bi Gan or Wu Zixu, but one will still be unable to achieve one's goals.[4] Sometimes there are people who perceive a problem before it comes to a head and put forth a well-advised policy, but as long as nothing is amiss neither the ruler nor his officials will pay any heed.

When the situation becomes urgent, someone skilled at persuasion will provide relief from the immediate emergency by wheedling merchants, hoodwinking lenders, and borrowing money and grain. Both rulers and their officials will laud him for his distinguished service and immediately grant him a reward, raise his stipend, and promote him in rank. This can be compared to the story from ancient times of a certain person's house where the chimney of the kitchen stove was built straight and firewood was piled up next to it.[5] Someone saw this and said that he should bend the chimney and move the firewood elsewhere, lest there be an accidental fire, but the owner of the house did not pay any heed. While time passed with things left as they were, suddenly one evening there was an accidental fire. As it burned the neighbors came rushing in to help and the fire was put out. Overjoyed, the owner bought meat and liquor, put on a feast, and gave rewards to the people who had saved him from the fire. If he

---

3 From the poem "Bo Zhou" ("Cypress Wood Boat") in the *Classic of Poetry*: "My troubled heart is full of anxiety / I am despised by the lowly masses."
4 The political ability of Guan Zhong (c. 720–645 BC) and Yanzi (or Yan Ying; c. 578–500 BC) is mentioned in *Mencius* 2.1.1. Both of these served as prime ministers of the country of Qi. Bi Gan was an uncle of King Zhou, the last ruler of the Shang dynasty. He is praised by Confucius in *Analects* 18.1. Wu Zixu (d. 484 BC), a political advisor and military commander of the Spring and Autumn period, is a famous model of loyalty. He is discussed in the *Records of the Grand Historian* and various other sources.
5 The story that follows comes from the "Biography of Huo Guang" in volume 68 of the *History of the Former Han*.

Addendum to "Food and Goods"

had instead, following the instructions of the person mentioned earlier, bent the chimney and moved the firewood elsewhere, there would have been no accidental fire in the first place, nor would there have been any need for the expense of buying meat and liquor. Instead of making use of good teachings, though, the owner suffered an accidental fire and gave credit to those who rescued him from it. This is the same kind of thing as what I was discussing earlier. When one makes inept plans without governing the root and is later faced with a momentary emergency, then even though one may borrow a huge sum of money, this will only be enough to handle the temporary needs of what one is immediately faced with, but will not make good the overall losses, so it is like pouring water on a hot stone. Once one makes it through that moment, one's poverty is even worse than before. Banzan said that the feudal lords would surely be driven into a corner fiscally, something that can truly be seen in the present day.[6] No matter what techniques one uses, it seems that the situation cannot be salvaged. I would like to know whether there is a technique that can be used to salvage even this.

Answer: Techniques of political economy are like the treatment of an illness by a doctor. In treating an illness, the best method is to seek out its root, but in an emergency, there are times when one merely treats its symptoms. Political economy is the same. Establishing institutions in the state is its root. Without institutions, customs decline and there are insufficient funds for the country. To leave this situation just as it is, while seeking rescue from the emergency that is right before one's eyes, is to deal only with the branches. Reforming the institutions of the realm, though, is not something that can be achieved by a single feudal lord's country. One cannot practice proper political economy without a reform of the institutions of the realm, and yet a single feudal lord's country has its own political economy, so it shows a lack of wise techniques to cast aside all possible courses of action and let oneself be driven into a corner. Just as how in an emergency doctors treat the symptoms, one should look at what is critical in the current illness and seek salvation from this.

In ancient times in Japan, gold and silver were scarce and there was no minting of copper coins, so among both high and low it was rare to make use of gold and silver. Using only the copper coins of foreign countries, there was sufficient coinage for people's needs. From the middle of the

---

6 Banzan discusses this in volume 13 of *Shūgi washo* (*Collection of Writings in Japanese*).

An Addendum to "On Political Economy"

Keichō [1596–1615] era, though, gold and silver became plentiful,[7] and in the Kan'ei [1624–1645] era copper coins were minted.[8] From this point on, gold and silver sufficed for large transactions, while copper coins sufficed for small transactions. In addition, the people of the realm at that time, both lofty and lowly, all gathered in Edo and lived like travelers, so it became the custom to use gold and silver to fulfill all their needs. Even those who were not travelers behaved like travelers in that they did not value rice, grain, cloth, or silk, but instead valued gold and silver. They thought that even if they were in the countryside or the mountains, as long as they had gold and silver it would be easy to obtain rice, grain, cloth, and silk. For this reason, the world of today is only a world of gold and silver, and people are satisfied as long as they have enough rice and grain to feed themselves in the morning and evening and enough cloth and silk to clothe themselves. Beyond that, they only care about gold and silver. These can be used to handle the necessary expenses of the moment in both large and small matters, so the people of the realm value gold and silver a hundred times more than they did in the past. For this reason, in the present age, even though one may have rice, grain, cloth, and silk, when one is short of gold and silver it will be difficult to establish oneself in the world. This does not apply only to lowly people from the commoner class; officials and feudal lords are the same in this regard, so in the present age, even stipendiary officials and feudal lords fulfill their various needs entirely with gold and silver, just like merchants, leading them to hatch plans to somehow or other obtain these. This appears to be the urgent business of the present.

When it comes to techniques for obtaining gold and silver, there is none more effective than trade. In the present age, too, there are feudal lords whose countries have long used trade to fulfill their fiscal needs and substitute for rice as a source of income. The feudal lord of Tsushima possesses a small country with an official rice output of only 20,000 *koku*, but he purchases Korean ginseng and various other goods cheaply, monopolizes trade in these, and sells them at a high price, so he has wealth greater than that of feudal lords with countries of 200,000 *koku*.[9] The feudal lord

---

7   Ieyasu oversaw a large expansion in gold and silver mining in Japan, as well as the creation of new forms of standardized gold and silver currency.
8   "Kan'ei currency" (*Kan'ei tsūhō*) was a widely circulated form of copper coinage minted from 1636 until the end of the Tokugawa period.
9   The location of Tsushima in the Sea of Japan between Japan and Korea led it to play a central role in Japanese trade with Korea.

Addendum to "Food and Goods"

of Matsumae possesses a country with an official rice output of 7,000 *koku*, but he monopolizes trade in the products of his country as well as in the goods of Ezo, selling these at high prices, so he has wealth that is not attained even by feudal lords with countries of 50,000 *koku*.[10] The feudal lord of Tsuwano in Iwami province has an official rice output of upwards of 40,000 *koku*, but he produces paper and monopolizes its sale, so his income is equivalent to 150,000 *koku*.[11] The feudal lord of Hamada in the same province, following the example of the feudal lord of Tsuwano, also produces paper, so it is said that with an official rice output of 50,000 *koku*, he in fact creates wealth of more than 100,000 *koku*. Satsuma is a large country to begin with, but on top of that it monopolizes the sale of goods from Ryukyu, so it is among the wealthiest in all Japan. Goods from China also often come to Satsuma via Ryukyu, and from Satsuma circulate to the various regions of Japan. Tsushima, Satsuma, and Matsumae all monopolize the goods of foreign countries and sell a disproportionate share of these, so this is not something that other feudal lords can imitate. Countries like Tsuwano and Hamada monopolize the products of their own soil and sell a disproportionate share of them, creating fiscal abundance. The feudal lord of Shingū is a senior retainer of the feudal lord of Kii and has an official rice output of 30,000 *koku*, but he has a monopoly on the sale of products from the mountains and seas of Kumano, giving him income reputed to be equivalent to 100,000 *koku*. When one makes use of policies modeled on these examples of political economy, one finds that in the countries of both major and minor feudal lords there is never a lack of products of the local soil ready at hand. These products are sometimes numerous and sometimes scarce. Where they are scarce, one should instruct the common people and press them on, plant useful things in keeping with the qualities of the land, not just grains but also trees and other plants, and thus create abundance in products of the local soil. In addition, one should teach appropriate crafts to the common people of one's country, have them produce all manner of useful things when they are not occupied with farm work, barter these with other countries, and by doing so meet the fiscal needs of one's own country. This is the technique for enriching a country.

10 Matsumae domain was on the island of Hokkaido, giving it an advantageous position for trade with the areas north of Japan, broadly referred to as "Ezo," which were inhabited by the Ainu.
11 Tsuwano set up a papermakers' guild in 1646, and in 1665 the sale of paper became a state monopoly.

An Addendum to "On Political Economy"

In the countries of feudal lords, there is a fixed tax on rice. The various other products that come from the mountains and seas, as well as the crafts produced in the houses of the common people, such as cloth, silk, thread, cotton, wicker, rush matting, straw raincoats, and sedge hats, are all goods, so when they are sold by the common people, there is always a certain portion given as tribute to the ruler, which is considered a tax. The amount given is sometimes one part in twenty or thirty, and sometimes one part in fifty or a hundred. Also, sometimes it is paid in cash rather than in kind. In the customs of Japan, this is referred to as a "business tax." Once this tax is paid, the remaining goods are all the private property of the common people, so when they sell these to merchants, the money they receive in return is entirely theirs to keep. This is the ancient method.

Today, though, there are many cases where the countries of feudal lords do not have such taxes. The reason for this change is that in ancient times rulers, considering the people to be farmer-soldiers, conscripted horses and men from among the commoners for military duty, so under what was called the "one-tenth" system they took one part in ten of the harvest as the field tax. For example, from a field that produces 100 *koku*, they would take 10 *koku* of unhulled rice. They did not make a practice of maintaining horses and men for military purposes, so the one-tenth tax sufficed for the fiscal needs of the country. Now, though, under what is known as "government troops," it is standard practice for horses and men to be maintained by landholders for military purposes, so it is customary to take four parts in ten as the field tax.[12] From a field that produces 100 *koku*, they take 40 *koku* of unhulled rice. When in addition to collecting a large amount of field tax in this way, they also force people to pay tax on the products of the mountains and the seas, as well as on other goods, the common people suffer, so generally they do not levy such taxes. In recent times it has been common that, suffering from a lack of necessary funds, the countries of feudal lords start to impose new taxes on various things

---

12 That is, the higher tax rate is necessary because the tax on rice and grain now must pay for the expenses of maintaining a standing army. It is unclear what Shundai is referring to by "conscription" in the Tokugawa context; his assertion is perhaps best understood as a general reference to the creation of a clear distinction between the farmer and warrior classes, a process that in Tang dynasty China did involve conscription. In Japan, the creation of this distinction between farmers and warriors was one element of the consolidation of power at the outset of the Tokugawa regime.

Addendum to "Food and Goods"

that had long been untaxed, leading the common people to rebel and riot. One must exercise caution in this.

Because of what I discussed above, in the political economy of the present, feudal lords should make outlays to buy up all the local products and various goods of their countries. If there are buyers at hand for these things, the feudal lords should sell to these people. If there are no buyers, they should put the goods on boats or load them on horses and transport them to Edo, Kyoto, and Osaka to sell them. When the common people of a country transport local products elsewhere to sell them themselves, there are considerable travel expenses. With boats, there is the fee for using the boat. With horses, there is the fee for horse transport. When one goes elsewhere to sell goods, there are wholesalers and middlemen. When one lodges with wholesalers, there are expenses for food. When selling things to shopkeepers, there are commissions to the wholesaler. With middlemen, there are labor fees. For the shrine of the wholesalers' deity, one must make a contribution for lamp oil. After one's business is concluded, one must offer a gratuity to the wholesaler to express thanks. In this way, one incurs various expenses. The seller is left with what remains after subtracting these expenses from the price of the goods, so his profits are not great. There are also cases where merchants come from other countries, buy up various local products, and then take them to sell to wholesalers elsewhere. These merchants incur considerable travel expenses in their coming and going. They lodge for several days at the source of the goods, so they incur expenses for food. When they buy goods net of these various expenses, pay fees for transport by boat or horse, and take the goods elsewhere to sell to merchants, they aim to make a considerable profit, so when they originally purchase the goods they always pay a very low price. The original holder of the goods does not travel, so he has neither trouble nor expenses, but because he sells cheaply his profits are not great.

If the feudal lords, in making outlays to buy up all the local products and goods of their countries, considered the prices received when the common people of their countries stay at home and sell to merchants from elsewhere, as well as the prices received when they travel elsewhere and sell to wholesalers there, then even if they bought from the common people at a slightly higher price than these merchants, they would be able to gather many goods in one place, send them to such cities as Edo and Osaka, warehouse them in their mansions there, and sell them when the market price is high, so there would be more profit than when the

An Addendum to "On Political Economy"

common people of their countries sell their goods privately. The common people of their countries would have no need to travel or to go through any trouble, nor would they incur the various kinds of expenses I discussed earlier. For this reason, they should take joy in receiving more profit than when they sold to merchants, so they should surely offer up for sale all the goods they have, without hiding any away.

However, in the rare cases of corrupt officials who attempt to buy at a price lower than that which the common people of their countries can get from selling privately, the common people will surely not feel joy, but instead will hide away their goods and secretly sell them on their own. If such a thing happens and one uses laws from above to try to prohibit it, then many lawbreakers will emerge and the common people will surely cause disturbances. When it comes to the goods on which business tax is levied in various countries, the common people will find it natural that the feudal lord has a fixed stipend and collects taxes. However, they will consider it unreasonable for there also to be taxes on the other local products and goods that are produced by the common people. Sometimes they will be delinquent in paying their business taxes, and sometimes they will provide their lower-quality goods for their business taxes while selling their higher-quality goods to merchants from elsewhere. When such things come to light, officials will punish them and try to prohibit such abuses, in the process causing criminals to emerge, which also becomes troubling for the common people. When it comes to business taxes, there are these kinds of improper practices. In the customs of later ages, wicked officials rule over dishonest common people, so various abuses come about in government.

If feudal lords, though, made outlays to buy up all the various products of their countries, and made this more profitable to the common people than the way in which they previously sold their goods privately to merchants from elsewhere, then the common people would surely find this beneficial and rejoice. After buying up all the goods, feudal lords should barter anything appropriate with neighboring countries. They should send the bulk of the goods to Edo and Osaka and warehouse them in their mansions. They should then choose people[13] from their own country who are skilled at trade, have them reside in Edo and Osaka, make them overseers of their storehouses, and have them collect

---

13 The text says "one person" here, but Shundai seems to be describing a system in which there is one trade representative in Edo and a different one in Osaka.

bids from other merchants and sell at a favorable price. One should select one or two upright people from among the stipendiary samurai and have them supervise these affairs. Today, the feudal lords of both the east and the west sell their warehoused rice in Osaka. For this they typically use the method I have described. This practice is reflected in the common use of the term "warehouse chopping block paper" for the chopping block paper of Iwami province, a term that derives from the fact that this all comes from the warehouses of two feudal lords.

The feudal lords of today cannot satisfy the fiscal needs of their countries without gold. Even their official duties are difficult to perform, so they should simply carry out plans for amassing gold in whatever way possible. When it comes to techniques for amassing gold, there is none more effective than profiting from commerce. As a feudal lord, to seek profit from commerce is not the ideal method for governing the state, but it is one technique for finding salvation from a present emergency.

In ancient times, when Guan Zhong governed the country of Qi, there was a system similar to this.[14] In the Han dynasty, Sang Hongyang [c. 152–80 BC] had a method called "equalized transport" [Ch. *junshu*, Jp. *kinshu*].[15] Even people in his own time criticized this, as did many later scholars of political economy, but Jiao Ruohou [1540–1620] of the Ming dynasty said that it was beneficial to the state and caused no harm to the common people, so one should not necessarily condemn Sang Hongyang.[16] Sang Hongyang was originally a merchant, and "equalized transport" is a method of conducting trade. He, too, did what was unavoidable in order to rescue his age. In our degenerate age today, it would be of the utmost benefit to make gold and silver, as well as copper coinage, as scarce as they were in ancient times, and thus have sufficient finances for the country and avoid trouble for the samurai and commoners, but it is

---

14 Duke Huan appointed Guan Zhong as prime minister when he became marquis of Qi in 685 BC. He promoted a method of price stabilization in which the government bought goods when prices fell and sold them when prices rose. He also introduced state monopolies on salt and iron.
15 Sang Hongyang was an official who served under emperors Wu and Zhao of the Western Han. He is known for his economic policies, which included a tax on assets and state monopolies on salt and iron. The method of "equalized transport" that Shundai mentions here was introduced in the reign of Emperor Wu. It aimed to stabilize prices, restrict merchants' profits, and increase government revenues by imposing levies in kind on the goods particular to each region, which the government then sold to other regions.
16 This argument appears in volume 22 of Jiao Ruohou's *Jiao Danyuan ji* (*Collection of Jiao Danyuan*).

difficult to attain this without reforming the institutions of the realm and changing the customs of the people. Therefore, there is nothing to do but simply to make gold and silver plentiful through the strategic planning of a single feudal lord's country. When it comes to techniques for amassing gold and silver, there is none more effective than commerce. When there are wise men like Guan Zhong and they are employed by rulers like Duke Huan of Qi, then it will surely be possible to practice such techniques. Within the space of three to five years one will surely enrich one's country. Today, the government office in Nagasaki buys up the goods shipped by sea and sells them throughout the land; this is the proper manner of conducting commerce.[17] What is keeping feudal lords from using the local products of their own countries to conduct commerce with other places?

...

---

17 Shundai does not give the name of the office, but this is a reference to the Nagasaki Kaisho, which controlled trade with Holland and China. It began operations in 1698 and was operated by the *bakufu* under the supervision of the Nagasaki Magistrate. Some of its profits were distributed locally in Nagasaki, with the remainder going to the *bakufu*.

Character List

Arai Hakuseki	新井白石
Asano	浅野
Ashikaga Takauji	足利尊氏
Ashikaga Yoshimitsu	足利義満
Azuma uta (Songs of the East)	東歌
Ban Gu	班固
bazhe (hegemon)	覇者
Bendō (*On Distinguishing the Way*)	弁道
Bendōsho (*A Treatise on the Way*)	弁道書
Benmei (*On Distinguishing Names*)	弁名
Bi Gan	比干
"Bi ming" ("Charge to the Duke of Bi")	畢命
Bian He	卞和
"Bian yue jie" ("Explanation of Discussions of Music")	弁楽解
Bing	昺
Bo I	伯夷
Bo Yi	伯益
"Bo Zhou" ("Cypress Wood Boat")	柏船
Bu Shi	卜式
Buke Shohatto (Laws for Military Houses)	武家諸法度
Bunron (*A Discourse on Literary Writing*)	文論
butsuri (principles of things)	物理
"Cai Zhong zhi ming" ("Charge to Zhang of Cai")	蔡仲之命

Cao Shen	曹参
Chao Cuo	晁錯
Chen Liang	陳亮
Cheng	成
Cheng Hao	程顥
Cheng Yi	程頤
Chiyou	蚩尤
Chōsokabe	長宗我部
Chōsokabe Morichika	長宗我部盛親
Chui	倕
Chunqiu (*Spring and Autumn Annals*)	春秋
chūyō (mean)	中庸
da guo ("Great Exceeding" hexagram)	大過
Da Ming yi tong zhi (*Comprehensive Gazetteer of the Great Ming*)	大明一統志
"Da Yu mo" ("Counsels of the Great Yu")	大禹謨
Daigaku wakumon (*Some Questions on Greater Learning*)	大学或問
daitai (general outline)	大体
Dan	旦
dao (Way)	道
Dao de jing (*Classic of the Way and Its Virtue*)	道徳経
Daxue (*Great Learning*)	大学
Daxue zhangju (*Sentence and Section Annotations on the "Great Learning"*)	大学章句
Dazai Jun	太宰純
Dazai Ken'ō	太宰謙翁
Dazai Shundai	太宰春台
Dazhidu lun (*Treatise on the Great Perfection of Wisdom*)	大智度論
"Di guan si tu" ("Office of Earth")	地官司徒
Dokugo (*Solitary Words*)	独語
Dong Zhongshu	董仲舒
Dongguo Xianyang	東郭咸陽
dōri (principles of the Way)	道理
"Etenraku" ("Music from Heaven")	越天楽

Feng	封
Feng Yi	馮異
Fu Yue	傅説
Fujiwara no Fuhito	藤原不比等
Fujiwara no Kintō	藤原公任
Fuke	普化
fukoku kyōhei (enriching the country and strengthening the military)	富国強兵
fūzoku (customs)	風俗
ga (refined)	雅
Gai Gong	蓋公
Gan De	甘徳
Gan Pan	甘盤
Gan Shi xing jing (*Classic of Celestial Bodies of Gan and Shi*)	甘石星経
Gao Yao	皋陶
Gaozong	高宗
Gaozu	高祖
ge ("Revolution" hexagram)	革
Geng Shouchang	耿壽昌
Genji monogatari (*Tale of Genji*)	源氏物語
Genkō	元弘
Genpei	源平
Genroku	元禄
gi (rightness)	義
gisō (public welfare granary)	義倉
Go-Daigo	後醍醐
Gongshu Ban	公輸班
Gongyong zhuan (*Gongyong Commentary*)	公羊伝
Goseibai Shikimoku (Formulary of Adjudications)	御成敗式目
Go-Shirakawa	後白河
"Goshōraku" ("Song of the Five Constant Virtues")	五常楽
Go-Toba	後鳥羽
Go-Yōzei	後陽成
Guan Zhong	管仲

"Guang yao dao" ("Amplification of the Essential Way")	広要道
"Gu ming" ("Testamentary Charge")	顧命
gunken (districts and prefectures)	郡県
"Guo feng" ("Airs of the States")	国風
Guo Shoujing	郭守敬
gyo (honorable)	御
Hachisukashi	蜂須賀氏
Hanfeizi	韓非子
hasha (hegemon)	覇者
Hashiba	羽柴
He	和
"He shi" ("Mr. He")	和氏
Heiji	平治
heijun (leveling)	平準
Heike monogatari (*Tale of the Heike*)	平家物語
hetu (River Chart)	河図
Hirata Atsutane	平田篤胤
Hirate Masahide	平手政秀
Hisamatsu	久松
Hōei	宝永
Hōgen	保元
Hōjō	北条
Hōjō Tokimasa	北条時政
Hōjō Yasutoki	北条泰時
hōken (feudal)	封建
Honda Masanobu	本多正信
Honda Toshiaki	本多利明
"Hong fan" ("Great Plan")	洪範
Hong fan wuxing zhuan (*Transmission on the Five Elements in the "Great Plan"*)	洪範五行伝
Hongwu	洪武
Honjō Munesuke	本庄宗資
Hou Han shu (*History of the Latter Han*)	後漢書
Hu	忽
Huan	桓

Character List

Huangdi	黄帝
Hui	惠
Huizong	徽宗
Huo Guang	霍光
Ikeda	池田
ikioi (force)	勢
Inuzuka Katsutarō	犬塚勝太郎
Ishida Baigan	石田梅岩
Ji	稷
ji ji ("Already Fording" hexagram)	既済
Ji kokkan kongen (*The Basis of Governing the State*)	治国家根元
Jia Yi	賈誼
Jiao Danyuan ji (*Collection of Jiao Danyuan*)	焦澹園集
Jiao Ruohou	焦弱侯
Jing	景
Jinmu	神武
Jōei	貞永
Jōgan	貞観
jōheisō (stabilization granary)	常平倉
Jōkyō	貞享
Jōruri	浄瑠璃
Jōruri monogatari (*Tale of Jōruri*)	浄瑠璃物語
Kaiho Seiryō	海保青陵
Kaihuang	開皇
"Kaikotsu" ("Turn Abruptly")	回忽
Kaitokudō	懐徳堂
Kaiyuan	開元
Kamo no Mabuchi	賀茂真淵
Kamōsho (*Rebuking Absurdities*)	呵妄書
kan ("Gorge" hexagram)	坎
Kan'ami	観阿弥
Kanbun	寛文
Kan'ei	寛永
"Kang gao" ("Announcement to Kang")	康誥
kato (River Chart)	河図

Keichō	慶長
Keiko dan (*Reflections on the Past*)	稽古談
keizai (political economy)	経済
Keizai yōryaku (*An Outline of Political Economy*)	経済要略
Keizairoku (*On Political Economy*)	経済録
Keizairoku shūi (*An Addendum to "On Political Economy"*)	経済録拾遺
Kenmu	建武
Kohōha (School of Ancient Methods)	古方派
Kokugaku (National Learning)	国学
Kokuikō (*Reflections on the Meaning of Our Country*)	国意考
kokumin dōtoku (national ethics)	国民道徳
Kondō hisaku (*A Secret Plan for Unification*)	混同秘策
Kongzi jiayu (*School Sayings of Confucius*)	孔子家語
kōri (utility)	功利
Kōwaka	幸若
Kui	夔
Kumazawa Banzan	熊沢蕃山
Kuroda	黒田
Kusunoki Masashige	楠木正成
Kyōhō	享保
Laozi	老子
li (principle)	理
Li	李
Li ji (*Record of Ritual*)	礼記
Li Kui	李悝
Li Lou	離婁
Li Shiji	李世勣
Li Shimin	李世民
Li Si	李斯
"Li yun" ("Ritual Usages")	礼運
"Lie Yukou"	列禦寇
Lin Xiangru	藺相如
Ling Lun	伶倫
"Ling Tai" ("The Wondrous Tower")	霊台

Character List

"Lie Yukou"	列禦寇
Liu	劉
Liu Bang	劉邦
Liu Gongfu	劉貢父
Liu Jing	劉敬
Liu tao (*The Six Secret Strategies*)	六韜
Liu Xiang	劉向
Long	竜
Lü	呂
Lu Ban	魯班
Lü Jing	婁敬
Lü Wang	呂望
Lu Xiangshan	陸象山
Lu Xiufu	陸秀夫
Ma Xian	馬顕
Maeda	前田
Man'yōshū	万葉集
Mao	毛
Maoshi (*Mao Poems*)	毛詩
Maoshi zhuan (*Transmissions on the Mao Poems*)	毛詩伝
Matsudaira	松平
michi (Way)	道
Minamoto	源
Minamoto no Yoritomo	源頼朝
Minamoto no Yoshitsune	源義経
Mizuno Genrō	水野元朗
Momonoi Naoakira	桃井直詮
Monmu	文武
Mōri	毛利
Motoori Norinaga	本居宣長
Mozi	墨子
mui (non-action)	無為
mujinzō (inexhaustible storehouse)	無尽蔵
Nabeshima	鍋島
Nagasaki Kaisho	長崎会所

Character List

Naobi no mitama (*The Spirit of the Gods*)	直御霊
ninjō (human feelings)	人情
Nitta Yoshisada	新田義貞
ō (king)	王
Oda Nobuhide	織田信秀
Oda Nobunaga	織田信長
Ogasawara	小笠原
Ogyū Sorai	荻生徂徠
"Ōjō"	皇麞
Ōnin	応仁
Ono Otsū	小野お通
Pingjin	平津
Qian Han shu (*History of the Former Han*)	前漢書
Qin Shi Huang	秦始皇
Qinzong	欽宗
"Qu li shang" ("Summary of Rituals, Part I")	曲礼上
ri (principle)	理
riken (interests and privileges)	利権
Rikukei ryakusetsu (*A General Outline of the Six Classics*)	六経略説
rōnin (masterless samurai)	浪人
Sakai	酒井
Sakanoue	坂上
Sang Hongyang	桑弘羊
sankin kōtai (alternate attendance)	参勤交代
Satō Nobuhiro	佐藤信淵
sei (innate qualities, inborn nature)	性
seido (institutions)	制度
Seigaku mondō (*Dialogue on the Learning of the Sages*)	聖学問答
Seiiki monogatari (*Tales of the West*)	西域物語
Seiwa	清和
Sekimon Shingaku (Heart Learning movement of Ishida Baigan)	石門心学
Senju	千寿
Shan	禅
Shang jun shu (*The Book of Lord Shang*)	商君書

Character List

Shang Yang	商鞅
Shanhai jing (*Classic of Mountains and Seas*)	山海経
Shen Buhai	申不害
"Shi hun li" ("Ritual of Marriage for a Scholar-Official")	士昏礼
Shi ji (*Records of the Grand Historian*)	史記
Shi jing (*Classic of Poetry*)	詩経
Shi Shen	石申
Shibukawa Shunkai	渋川春海
Shimazu	島津
shinbō (heart methods)	心法
Shingaku (Heart Learning)	心学
Shiron (*A Discourse on Poetry*)	詩論
shizen (natural state)	自然
Shōbutsu	生仏
Shōtoku (era name)	正徳
Shōtoku (prince)	聖徳
Shoushi	授時
Shu jing (*Classic of Documents*)	書経
Shūgi washo (*Collection of Writings in Japanese*)	集義和書
Shun	舜
"Shun dian" ("Canon of Shun")	舜典
"Shuning"	数寧
Shunzhi	順治
Shusun Tong	叔孫通
Sima Qian	司馬遷
Soga	曽我
Song shi (*History of the Song*)	宋史
Sorai sensei tōmonsho (*Master Sorai's Responsals*)	徂徠先生答問書
Suiko	推古
Sunzi	孫子
"Tai shi shang" ("Great Proclamation, Part I")	泰誓上
Taihō	大宝
Taihō Ritsuryō (Taihō Code)	大宝律令
Taika	大化

Taira	平
Taira no Kiyomori	平清盛
Taira no Shigehira	平重衡
Taizong	太宗
Taizu	太祖
Tako	多湖
"Tan Gong xia" ("Tan Gong, Part II")	檀弓下
Tang	湯
Tenna	天和
"Tianxia" ("All under Heaven")	天下
Toda	戸田
Tohi mondō (Dialogue of the City and the Country)	都鄙問答
toki (times)	時
Tokugawa Ienobu	徳川家宣
Tokugawa Ietsugu	徳川家継
Tokugawa Ieyasu	徳川家康
Tokugawa Mitsukuni	徳川光圀
Tokugawa Tsunayoshi	徳川綱吉
Tokugawa Yoshimune	徳川吉宗
Tōshōgū (Light of the East)	東照宮
Toyotomi Hideyori	豊臣秀頼
Toyotomi Hideyoshi	豊臣秀吉
Tsurezuregusa (Essays in Idleness)	徒然草
Tuan zhuan (Tuan Commentary)	彖伝
Urabe Kanetomo	卜部金朋
Wadō	和銅
Wadoku yōryō (A General Outline of Reading in Japanese)	和読要領
Wakan rōei shū (Japanese and Chinese Poems to Sing)	和漢朗詠集
wang (king)	王
Wang Anshi	王安石
Wang Sunjia	王孫賈
Wang Tong	王通
Wang Yangming	王陽明
"Wang zhi" ("Kingly Regulations")	王制

wei ji ("Not Yet Fording" hexagram)	未済
Wen	文
Wenzhongzi	文中子
Wu	武
"Wu cheng" ("Completion of the War")	武成
Wu Ding	武丁
Wu Qi	吳起
Wu Zixu	伍子胥
Xi (family of astronomers)	羲
xi (duke)	僖
"Xia shu" ("Books of Xia")	夏書
Xiang	襄
"Xiang yin jiu yi" ("Meaning of Drinking Festivities in the Country Districts")	鄉飲酒義
Xiao	孝
Xiao He	蕭何
Xiao jing (*Classic of Filial Piety*)	孝経
Xici zhuan (*Commentary on the Appended Phrases*)	繋辞伝
Xie	契
Xin shu (*New Writings*)	新書
Xing jing (*Classic of Celestial Bodies*)	星経
Xu Shiji	徐世勣
Xuan	宣
Xuanming	宣明
Xuanzong	玄宗
Xunzi	荀子
Yamanouchi	山内
Yan Ying	晏嬰
Yan Yuan	顔淵
Yanagisawa Yoshiyasu	柳沢吉保
Yanzi	晏子
Yao	堯
"Yao dian" ("Canon of Yao")	堯典
Yasui Santetsu	安井算哲
Yi jing (*Classic of Changes*)	易経

Yi li (*Book of Ceremonies and Rituals*)	儀礼
Yi Yin	伊尹
Yin	隠
Yongle	永楽
Yōrō Ritsuryō (Yōrō Code)	養老律令
Yoshida Kanetomo	吉田金朋
Yoshida Kenkō	吉田健康
Yu	禹
"Yu gong" ("Tribute of Yu")	禹貢
"Yue ji" ("Record of Music")	楽記
Yue jing (*Classic of Music*)	楽経
"Yue ming xia" ("Charge to Yue, Part III")	説命下
Yukinaga	行長
Zengzi	曽子
Zhang Yan	張嫣
Zhangsun Ping	長孫平
Zhao	昭
Zhao Kuo	趙括
Zhaoxiang	昭襄
Zhili Yi	支離益
"Zhonghui zhi gao" ("Announcement of Zhonghui")	仲虺之誥
Zhongshuo (*Explanation of the Mean*)	中説
Zhongyong (*Doctrine of the Mean*)	中庸
"Zhou guan" ("Officers of Zhou")	周官
Zhou li (*Rituals of Zhou*)	周礼
Zhu Pingman	朱泙漫
Zhu Xi	朱熹
Zhuangzi	荘子
Zhufu	主父
zhun ("Sprouting" hexagram)	屯
Zigong	子貢
zoku (vulgar, common, popular)	俗
Zuo zhuan (*Zuo Commentary*)	左伝

Bibliography

Note: The place of publication of all modern Japanese works is Tokyo unless otherwise specified.

Texts of *Keizairoku* 経済録 and *Keizairoku shūi* 経済録拾遺

Dazai Shundai 太宰春台. *Keizairoku* 経済録. 1729. [Wooden movable type edition in the collection of Kobe University Library; digital microfilm, National Institute of Japanese Literature.]

Keizairoku 経済録. In *Nihon keizai taiten* 日本経済大典, vol. 9, edited by Takimoto Seiichi 滝本誠一, 377–671. Shishi Shuppansha, 1928.

Keizairoku 経済録. In *Sorai gakuha* 徂徠学派, *Nihon shisō taikei* 日本思想大系, no. 37, edited by Rai Tsutomu 頼惟勤, 7–44. Iwanami Shoten, 1972.

Keizairoku shūi 経済録拾遺. In *Sorai gakuha* 徂徠学派, *Nihon shisō taikei* 日本思想大系, no. 37, edited by Rai Tsutomu 頼惟勤, 45–56. Iwanami Shoten, 1972.

English Translations of *Keizairoku* 経済録 and *Keizairoku shūi* 経済録拾遺

Kirby, Richard J. "Dazai on Japanese Music." *Transactions of the Asiatic Society of Japan*, vol. 28 (1900): 46–58. [A partial, unannotated translation of volume 2 of *Keizairoku*.]

"Dazai Jun on Bubi or Preparation for War." *Transactions of the Asiatic Society of Japan*, vol. 32 (1905): 24–47. [A partial, minimally annotated translation of volume 7 of *Keizairoku*.]

"An Essay by Dazai Jun Relating to Adoption and Marriage." *Transactions of the Asiatic Society of Japan*, vol. 36, no. 1 (1908): 97–135. [A full, unannotated translation of volume 9 of *Keizairoku*.]

"Food and Wealth. An Essay by Dazai Jun." *Transactions of the Asiatic Society of Japan*, vol. 35, no. 2 (1908): 113–190. [A full, unannotated translation of volume 5 of *Keizairoku*.]

"Translation of Dazai Jun's Essay on Gakusei (Educational Control)." *Transactions of the Asiatic Society of Japan*, vol. 34, no. 4 (1906): 133–144. [A partial, unannotated translation of volume 6 of *Keizairoku*.]

"Translations of Dazai Jun's Economic Essays upon 'Doing Nothing' and 'Divination.'" *Transactions of the Asiatic Society of Japan*, vol. 41 (1913): 195–213. [A full, unannotated translation of volume 10 of *Keizairoku*.]

Najita, Tetsuo, ed. "*Keizairoku Shūi*: Addendum to 'On the political economy.'" In *Tokugawa Political Writings*. Cambridge: Cambridge University Press, 1998, 141–153. [A full, unannotated translation of *Keizairoku shūi*.]

Works Cited

Bellah, Robert N. "Baigan and Sorai: Continuities and Discontinuities in Eighteenth-Century Japanese Thought." In Tetsuo Najita and Irwin Scheiner, eds. *Japanese Thought in the Tokugawa Period, 1600–1868: Methods and Metaphors*, 137–152. Chicago: University of Chicago Press, 1978.

―――. *Tokugawa Religion: The Values of Pre-industrial Japan*. Glencoe, IL: Free Press, 1957.

Dazai Shundai 太宰春台. *Rikukei ryakusetsu* 六経略説. In Inoue Tetsujirō 井上哲次郎 and Kanie Yoshimaru 蟹江義丸, eds. *Nihon rinri ihen* 日本倫理彙編, vol. 6, 301–330. Ikuseikai, 1903.

Honda Masanobu 本多正信. *Ji kokka kongen* 治国家根元. In Naramoto Tatsuya 奈良本辰也, ed. *Kinsei seidōron* 近世政道論, *Nihon shisō taikei* 日本思想大系, no. 38, 7–20. Iwanami Shoten, 1976.

Honda Toshiaki 本多利明. *Seiiki monogatari* 西域物語. In Tsukatani Akihiro 塚谷晃弘 and Kuranami Seiji 蔵並省自, eds. *Honda Toshiaki・Kaiho Seiryō* 本多利明・海保青陵, *Nihon shisō taikei* 日本思想大系, no. 44, 87–163. Iwanami Shoten, 1970.

Ishida Baigan 石田梅岩. *Tohi mondō* 都鄙問答. In Ienaga Saburō 家永三郎 et al., eds. *Kinsei shisōka bunshū* 近世日本思想家文集, *Nihon koten bungaku taikei* 日本古典文学大系, no. 97, 349–516. Iwanami Shoten, 1966.

Kaiho Seiryō 海保青陵. *Keiko dan* 稽古談. In Tsukatani Akihiro 塚谷晃弘 and Kuranami Seiji 蔵並省自, eds. *Honda Toshiaki・Kaiho Seiryō* 本多利明・海保青陵, *Nihon shisō taikei* 日本思想大系, no. 44, 215–346. Iwanami Shoten, 1970.

Kumazawa Banzan 熊沢蕃山. *Daigaku wakumon* 大学或問. In Gotō Yōichi 後藤陽一 and Tomoeda Ryūtarō 友枝龍太郎, eds. *Kumazawa Banzan* 熊沢蕃山, *Nihon shisō taikei* 日本思想大系, no. 30, 405–463. Iwanami Shoten, 1971.

―――. *Shūgi washo* 集義和書. In Gotō Yōichi 後藤陽一 and Tomoeda Ryūtarō 友枝龍太郎, eds. *Kumazawa Banzan* 熊沢蕃山, *Nihon shisō taikei* 日本思想大系, no. 30, 7–403. Iwanami Shoten, 1971.

Morris-Suzuki, Tessa. *A History of Japanese Economic Thought*. London: Routledge, 1989.

Najita, Tetsuo. "Political Economism in the Thought of Dazai Shundai (1680–1747)." *Journal of Asian Studies*, vol. 31, no. 4 (November 1972): 821–839.

Visions of Virtue in Tokugawa Japan: The Kaitokudō Merchant Academy of Osaka. Chicago: University of Chicago Press, 1987.

Nakai, Kate Wildman. *Shogunal Politics: Arai Hakuseki and the Premises of Tokugawa Rule*. Cambridge, MA: Harvard University Press, 1988.

Ogyū Sorai 荻生徂徠. *Bendō* 弁道. In Yoshikawa Kōjirō 吉川幸次郎 et al., eds. *Ogyū Sorai* 荻生徂徠, *Nihon shisō taikei* 日本思想大系, no. 36, 9–36. Iwanami Shoten, 1973.

Benmei 弁名. In Yoshikawa Kōjirō 吉川幸次郎 et al., eds. *Ogyū Sorai* 荻生徂徠, *Nihon shisō taikei* 日本思想大系, no. 36, 37–185. Iwanami Shoten, 1973.

Sorai sensei tōmonsho 徂徠先生答問書. In *Ogyū Sorai zenshū* 荻生徂徠全集, vol. 1, 421–486. Misuzu Shobō, 1973.

Roberts, Luke S. *Mercantilism in a Japanese Domain: The Merchant Origins of Economic Nationalism in 18th-Century Tosa*. Cambridge: Cambridge University Press, 1998.

Satō Nobuhiro 佐藤信淵. *Keizai yōryaku* 経済要略. In Bitō Masahide 尾藤正英 and Shimazaki Takao 島崎隆夫, eds. *Andō Shōeki • Satō Nobuhiro* 安藤昌益・佐藤信淵, *Nihon shisō taikei* 日本思想大系, no. 45, 519–570. Iwanami Shoten, 1977.

Kondō hisaku 混同秘策. In Bitō Masahide 尾藤正英 and Shimazaki Takao 島崎隆夫, eds. *Andō Shōeki • Satō Nobuhiro* 安藤昌益・佐藤信淵, *Nihon shisō taikei* 日本思想大系, no. 45, 425–485. Iwanami Shoten, 1977.

Sawada, Janine Anderson. *Confucian Values and Popular Zen: Sekimon Shingaku in Eighteenth-Century Japan*. Honolulu: University of Hawai'i Press, 1993.

Tillman, Hoyt Cleveland. *Confucian Discourse and Chu Hsi's Ascendancy*. Honolulu: University of Hawai'i Press, 1992.

Yamamura, Kozo. *A Study of Samurai Income and Entrepreneurship: Quantitative Analyses of Economic and Social Aspects of the Samurai in Tokugawa and Meiji Japan*. Cambridge, MA: Harvard University Press, 1974.

Further Reading

Ansart, Olivier. "The Philosophical Moment between Ogyū Sorai and Kaiho Seiryō: Indigenous Modernity in the Political Theories of Eighteenth-Century Japan?" In Chun-chieh Huang and John Allen Tucker, eds. *Dao Companion to Japanese Confucian Philosophy*, 183–214. Dordrecht: Springer, 2014.

Flueckiger, Peter. "Human Nature and the Way in the Philosophy of Dazai Shundai." In Chun-chieh Huang and John Allen Tucker, eds. *Dao Companion to Japanese Confucian Philosophy*, 215–232. Dordrecht: Springer, 2014.

Lidin, Olof G. "Ogyū Sorai: Confucian Conservative Reformer: From *Journey to Kai* to *Discourse on Government*." In Chun-chieh Huang and John Allen

Tucker, eds. *Dao Companion to Japanese Confucian Philosophy*, 165–182. Dordrecht: Springer, 2014.

McEwan, J. R. *The Political Writings of Ogyū Sorai*. Cambridge: Cambridge University Press, 1962.

Morris-Suzuki, Tessa. *A History of Japanese Economic Thought*. London: Routledge, 1989.

Najita, Tetsuo. "History and Nature in Eighteenth-Century Tokugawa Thought." In John Whitney Hall, ed. *The Cambridge History of Japan, Volume 4: Early Modern Japan*, 596–659. Cambridge: Cambridge University Press, 1991.

——— "Political Economism in the Thought of Dazai Shundai (1680–1747)." *Journal of Asian Studies*, vol. 31, no. 4 (November 1972): 821–839.

Nakai, Kate Wildman. "The Naturalization of Confucianism in Tokugawa Japan: The Problem of Sinocentrism." *Harvard Journal of Asiatic Studies*, vol. 40, no. 1 (June 1980): 157–199.

Nishioka Mikio. "Economic Thought and Public Welfare in Early Modern Japan: Dazai Shundai's Idea of Political Economy and Joheiso." *The Japanese Society for the History of Economic Thought*, vol. 52, no. 1 (2010): 1–19.

Tucker, John A. *Ogyū Sorai's Philosophical Masterworks: The "Bendō" and "Benmei."* Honolulu: University of Hawai'i Press, 2006.

Yamashita, Samuel Hideo. *Master Sorai's Responsals: An Annotated Translation of "Sorai sensei tōmonsho."* Honolulu: University of Hawai'i Press, 1994.

Index

An Addendum to "On Political Economy" (Keizairoku shūi, Dazai Shundai), xiii, xxix, xxxii; publication of, vii; translation by Tetsuo Najita, viii
adoption, xiii, 151–154
agrarian society: breakdown in Tokugawa Japan, xii, xxxi, 157; and country samurai *(gōshi),* 134–136; and the government of the sages, xxxi, 157, 163
alternate attendance *(sankin kōtai),* xv, 28, 28 n. 56, 71, 71 n. 17
Analects, 21; on changes between dynasties, xxiii, 22; Dazai Shundai's studies of, xiv; on food and the military, 21; on non-action, 166; on profit, 116. *See also* Confucius
ancestral temples, 40, 119; in China, 44, 121; in Japan, 121–123
ancient kings. *See* sage kings
Arai Hakuseki, xxviii, xxviii n. 35, 10 n. 28
artisans, 30, 33, 36, 86, 88–89, 101, 161; in Tokugawa Japan, xvi, 89, 100–102, 104, 116, 157
Ashikaga (Muromachi) shogunate, 8, 8 n. 19, 26, 26 n. 46, 26 n. 48, 53 n. 33, 54
Ashikaga Takauji: as founder of the Ashikaga shogunate, 26 nn. 43–44, 53 n. 33; as musician, 53
Ashikaga Yoshimitsu: as "king of Japan," 8; as patron of noh theater, 54 n. 34
astronomy: in ancient China, 72–76; in European learning, xxxiv; in Japan, 76, 78–79
authoritarianism, xvii, xxii

Ban Gu, 21, 22, 83
barter, 87, 93; practiced by daimyo, 190, 192; as teaching of the sages, 85. *See also* commerce, trade
The Basis of Governing the State (Ji kokka kongen, Honda Masanobu), xxvi
Bellah, Robert N., xxx n. 41
biwa hōshi (biwa priests), 54, 54 n. 38
biwa lute, 50–54, 57
Book of Ceremonies and Rituals (Yi li), 45, 45 n. 7, 62 n. 2, 181 n. 25
Book of Lord Shang (Shang jun shu), xxviii n. 34
brotherly obedience, 46, 60, 90, 122; promotion through ritual, 46
Buddhism, 14–15, 39, 55, 121, 158, 162, 175; Dazai Shundai's criticisms of, xiv, xxvii; and funerals, 55, 121–123; Ishida Baigan's use of, xxx, 4 n. 7; ritual and music of, 39, 48; and *yamabushi,* 159, 159 n. 18. *See also* Buddhist monks
Buddhist monks, 5, 130; and Buddhist rites, 39, 48; and funeral services, 121–123; as scholars, xvii, 125; sermons of, 55; and the *shakuhachi,* 52; state regulation of, 158–159, 162. *See also* Buddhism
Bunron. See A Discourse on Literary Writing
bureaucratic offices, 61–71; adoption of Chinese system in Japan, 66; in China, 61–69; in Tokugawa Japan, 67, 69–71
Bu Shi, 117

211

Index

calendars, 20, 73, 78–79, 127
Cao Shen, 169 nn. 10–11, 170 n. 12, 174; and governing through "non-action," 169–170
ceremonial guards, 130–132
Chao Cuo, 88, 88 n. 10
Chen Liang, xxvii, xxvii n. 32
Cheng, King, 34, 62
Cheng brothers, 4 n. 7, 75. *See also* Cheng Hao, Cheng Yi
Cheng Hao, 4. *See also* Cheng brothers
Cheng Yi, 4. *See also* Cheng brothers
Christianity, 122, 122 n. 5
civil service examinations, 125
clans. *See* surnames
Classic of Celestial Bodies of Gan and Shi (*Gan Shi xing jing*, Ma Xian), 76, 76 n. 11
Classic of Changes (*Yi jing*), 3 n. 1, 16, 17, 85, 96, 139, 155, 172–173, 176, 180–182
Classic of Documents (*Shu jing*), 3 n. 1, 17, 20–22, 35, 61, 77, 78, 79, 83, 126, 166, 180
Classic of Filial Piety (*Xiao jing*), 49, 59 n. 52
Classic of Mountains and Seas (*Shanhai jing*, Liu Xiang), 79–80, 80 n. 21
Classic of Music (*Yue jing*), 3 n. 1, 180 n. 24, 181
Classic of Poetry (*Shi jing*), 3 n. 1, 17, 33, 33 n. 63, role in teaching human feelings, 180
clothing, 168: as economic good, 84–87, 89, 98, 100, 108, 116, 136; ritual use, 44, 149; as status marker, 10, 32, 129–130
colonialism, xxxv
commerce, 193–194; Confucian views of, xxix–xxx; and daimyo, 193–194; Dazai Shundai on, xii, xxix–xxx, xxxi, xxxiii; Ishida Baigan's defense of, xxx; Kaiho Seiryō's defense of, xxxiii–xxxiv; Ogyū Sorai on, xxxi; and the samurai, xiii, xxxiii. *See also* barter, merchants, trade
Comprehensive Gazetteer of the Great Ming (*Da Ming yi tong zhi*), 80
Confucianism, xxvi, xxvii; and the *Classic of Changes*, 180; Dazai Shundai's interpretation of, xii–xiv, xvii–xxiii, xxviii–xxix, xxix–xxx, xxxi, xxxiii; and "enriching the country and strengthening the military," 87; introduction to Japan, xvii, xix; learning, 82, 122, 124–127; of the Ming dynasty, xviii, 80; Ogyū Sorai's interpretation of, xv, xviii–xix, xxi–xxii, xxiv, xxxiii; Qin dynasty suppression of, 49; of the Song dynasty, xviii, xxiv, 43, 75; in Tokugawa Japan, xvii–xviii, xxix, xxx, 82, 122, 125–126; Tokugawa-period criticisms of, xxxiv; views of commerce and profit, xxix–xx; vs. Buddhism, xiv, xxviii; vs. Daoism, 166, 170–171; vs. non-Confucian methods of governance, xxviii–xix, xxxiii; vs. Shinto, xiv, xxviii; Zhu Xi's interpretation of, xviii, xxiv. *See also Analects*, Confucius
Confucius, 5, 15, 18, 46, 74, 98, 140, 151–152, 176 n. 19, 180; and "enriching the country and strengthening the military," 87; on food and the military, 21, 136; on Guan Zhong, xxvii, 18, 186 n. 4; on heaven, 75; on music, 49; on non-action, 166; on profit, 116; and the rectification of names, 9; on ritual and rightness, xxvii, 44; and the Six (Five) Classics, 3 n. 1, 63 n. 3; Way of, 3–5, 7. *See also Analects*, Confucianism
considerateness (*jo*), 139–140, 145
copper. *See* copper currency
corvée labor, 97–99, 102, 158
countries (*kuni*), 13, 13 n. 37, 23–25, 24 n. 37
court nobles: adoption of warrior customs by, 130; customs of, 82, 125, 130, 132, 135–136, 150; institutions of, 148; legal codes of, 144–145; loss of political power by, xxi, 8 n. 17, 25–26, 39, 67, 130; offices of, 66–67, 69, 159; period of governance by, xx, 8, 11, 26, 26 n. 43, 39, 76, 78, 125; preservation of ritual and music by, xxi, 39; treatment of Buddhism by, 158
currency: copper, 84, 87, 100 n. 22, 110–111, 110 n. 33, 115, 187–188, 193; gold, 5, 84, 87–89, 92, 99, 100–101, 102–103, 104, 110, 111–115, 138, 154, 157, 187–188, 188 n.7, 193–194; and grain, 21, 87–88, 104, 108–109; paper, 115–116; revision of, 103, 103 n. 25, 111–115; silver, 84, 84 n. 4, 87–89, 92, 99, 100–101, 102, 104, 110, 111–112, 114, 187, 188, 188 n.7, 193–194
customs, 26, 33, 43, 53, 55, 71, 79, 85, 101, 115, 122, 130, 141–142, 143, 145, 149, 151–152, 164, 165, 180, 187, 190, 192, 194; of barbarians, 151–152; of court

Index

nobles, 82, 135; Dazai Shundai and Ogyū Sorai on, xix; effect of music on, 49, 58–60; effect of ritual on, 43; Honda Toshiaki on, xxxiv; of Japan vs. China, 5, 66–67; of warriors, 135, 145

Da Ming yi tong zhi. See Comprehensive Gazetteer of the Great Ming
daigashira dance, 53, 53 n. 31
daimyo, xiv, xvii, xxvi, 12, 13 n. 35, 13 n. 37, 27; commercial ventures of, xxxii; Dazai Shundai's service to, xv; financial difficulties of, 110 n. 32, 187 n. 1; and the shogun, xiv–xv, xxi, 27 n. 54, 70 n. 13, 71 n. 17, 93 n. 16, 148 n. 1, 150 n. 8, 163 n. 22. *See also* feudal lords
Daxue. See Great Learning
Dazai Shundai: authoritarianism of, xxvii; on commerce, xii; on the Confucian tradition, xii, xvii–xviii; on economic prosperity and Confucian government, xiii, xxv–xxvi, xxix–xxx, xxxi–xxxiii; on empirical knowledge, xxiv–xxv; on "enriching the country and strengthening the military," xii, xxvii, xxxvi; family and upbringing, xv, 6 n. 13; on government as the purpose of Confucianism, xv–xvi, xvii–xviii; on human nature, xviii, xxii; on institutions, xvii, xix, xx, xxxiv; on *keizai* (political economy), xiii; Kokugaku criticisms of, xx n. 12; and Ogyū Sorai, xv, xviii–xix, xxiv; on political reform, xvii, xxiii–xxiv, xxix; pragmatism of, xii, xxvii, xxviii, xxxiii; on "rightness," xxiii–xxiv; on ritual and music, xiii, xviii–xix, xx; on the role of Chinese culture in Japan, xix–xx, xxi, xxii–xxiii; scholarly works of, xiv; on the shogun as "king of Japan," xxviii; on the Tokugawa shogunate, xx–xxi, xxix; on Zhu Xi, xviii, xxiv–xxv, xxvi–xxvii
deities, 38, 119–121, 191; creator, 93; of soil and grain, 40, 50, 119–120
dengaku ("field music"), 53, 53 n. 32, 78
Dialogue of the City and Country (*Tohi mondō*, Ishida Baigan), xxx
Dialogue on the Learning of the Sages (*Seigaku mondō*, Dazai Shundai), xiv
A Discourse on Literary Writing (*Bunron*, Dazai Shundai), xiv

A Discourse on Poetry (*Shiron*, Dazai Shundai), xiv
"districts and prefectures" (*gunken*) system of government, 67–68; in China, xx, 19, 23, 24, 28, 64, 66, 124, 148; in Japan, 24, 28, 66, 82. *See also* feudal system of government
Doctrine of the Mean (*Zhongyong*), 16, 18, 77, 166
Dong Zhongshu, 3
Dongguo Xianyang, 117
Duke of Zhou, 34, 34 n. 70, 34 n. 72, 62, 62 n. 2

Edo, 88, 100, 160, 161, 190; as center of trade and finance, xxxii, 101, 105–106, 117, 185, 191–193; daimyo presence in, xv, xxxii, 71, 71 n. 17, 107, 191–193; Dazai Shundai's residence in, xv; laborers in, 99, 160; licensed quarters of, 161, 161 n. 20; natural disasters in, 102; as Tokugawa seat of government, xv, 12; and urbanization of the samurai, xvi, xxxi
education. *See* learning
emperor (Japanese): political power of, xiv, xx, xxviii, xxxvi, 8 nn. 17, 23; relationship to shogun, xiv, xxviii, 8 n. 23, 9 n. 24; and Shinto, xx, xxxvi
empirical knowledge: Dazai Shundai on, xxiv–xxv, 28 n. 57; Honda Toshiaki on, xxxiv
"encouraging virtue and chastising vice" (*kanzen chōaku*), 181
England, xxxv
"enriching the country and strengthening the military" (*fukoku kyōhei*): Dazai Shundai on, xii, xxvii–xxviii, xxxi; and the hegemon, xxvii, 18–19, 87; as Meiji-era slogan, xxxvi; Satō Nobuhiro on, xxxvi; and the Way of the sages, xii, xxvii–xxviii, xxxi, 19, 87
Ezo, 189, 189 n. 10

faithfulness (*shin*), 60; and laws, 137, 143
farmers, xvi, 30, 84, 86, 88–90, 104; and rice prices, 99–101, 119; warriors as, 134, 157, 161, 190
feudal lords (*shokō*), 13–14, 73, 87, 90; adoption among, 153; celebrations conducted by, 119–121; commercial ventures of, 188–189, 191–194; "countries" as

territories of, 24; financial difficulties of, 110, 115, 157, 185–187; and learning, 124, 127; marriage among, 155, 157; of pre-Tokugawa Japan, 24, 66; processions of, 130–132; and "public welfare granaries," 107, 110; Qin dynasty elimination of, 19, 23, 63; and the shogun, 163; surnames of, 150–151; of Tokugawa Japan, xiv, 12–13, 69–71, 82, 88, 99, 100, 102, 115, 141–142, 145, 148, 150–151, 163, 185–194; of the Zhou dynasty and earlier, 12, 23, 63, 64. *See also* daimyo

feudal (*hōken*) system of government, xx, 23, 67–70; in China, xx–xxi, 23, 24, 28, 64; in Japan, xx–xxi, 27–28, 27 n. 52, 70 n. 13, 82, 145. *See also* "districts and prefectures" system of government, feudal lords

filial piety, 46, 90, 122, 149, 181; and adoption, 153; and ancestor worship, 153; and changing surnames, 149; depiction in theater, 58, 60; and funerals, 123; and mourning clothes, 149; promotion through ritual, 46

Five Classics, 3 n. 1, 181–182. *See also* Six Classics

food, 22, 32, 83–89, 91, 98, 100, 101, 116, 136; Confucius on, 21, 136. *See also* grain, rice

force (*ikioi*), xxiv, 23, 29–30, 32, 35; and relationship to principle, xxiv, 29–30

Formulary of Adjudications (Goseibai Shikimoku), 144, 144 n. 8

Fu Yue, 33–35, 34 n. 69

Fujiwara no Fuhito, 144, 144 n. 7

Fujiwara no Kintō, 52, 52 n. 26

funerals, 40, 47, 121–122

Fuxi, 173, 173 nn. 16–17

ga (refined), xxi, 57. *See also* refined music

gagaku, 49 n. 14, 53 n. 29, 56, 56 n. 44, 57 n. 47, 58. *See also* refined music

Gai Gong, 169

Gan Shi xing jing. See Classic of Celestial Bodies of Gan and Shi

Gaozong (King Wu Ding), 33, 34 n. 69

Gaozu, Emperor (Han dynasty), 38, 141, 149, 169

A General Outline of Reading in Japanese (*Wadoku yōryō*, Dazai Shundai), xiv

A General Outline of the Six Classics (*Rikukei ryakusetsu*, Dazai Shundai), 3 n. 2, 180 n. 24

Geng Shouchang, 101, 105

Genkō War, 25, 26 n. 43

Genpei War, xx, 8, 8 nn. 17–18, 25, 53 n. 28, 53 n. 30, 54 n. 38

Genroku era, xxix, 126, 172; currency of, 111–115; rice prices during, 101–104

gentleman (*kunshi*), 16, 37, 73, 75, 86 n. 9, 156, 165, 177, 179, 180; definition of, 14, 14 n. 42; and humaneness, 160; and profit, 118; and punishments, 143–144. *See also* petty man

geography, 79; in ancient Chinese texts, 21–22, 79–80; and commodity production, xxxii; as element of European learning, xxxiv; records in China, 80–82; records in Japan, 81–82; role in governing, 21, 80, 82, 94

Go-Daigo, Emperor, 26 n. 43

gokenin ("housemen"), 13 n. 39, 25 n. 40

gold. *See* gold currency

goods, 83–84, 87

Go-Shirakawa, Emperor, 25

Go-Yōzei, Emperor, 9 n. 24

grain, xxxvi, 83–85, 88–89, 91–95, 97, 99–102, 104–109, 120, 186, 188, 189; and currency, 21, 87–88, 104, 108–109; deities of, 40, 50, 119–120; as metaphor for the Way of the sages, xxviii, 143, 171

granaries. *See* public welfare granaries, stabilization granaries

Grand Historian. *See* Sima Qian

Great Learning (*Daxue*), xxvi n. 31, 4 n. 6, 31, 37

Guan Zhong, 19, 85–86, 186; and "enriching the country and strengthening the military," xvii, 18, 87; and the ruler as hegemon, xxvii, 18, 87; and state management of commerce, 193–194, 193 n. 14

Guo Shoujing, 79, 79 n. 19

Han dynasty, 3, 7, 8, 19, 20, 21–22, 65, 73, 80, 83, 124, 141, 145, 152, 170, 175; bureaucratic offices of, 63–65, 68–69; Confucianism of, 3, 3 n. 3, 50, 50 n. 17, 124; "districts and prefectures" system during, 19, 23–24, 28, 64, 148; dynastic name of,

Index

11; economic policies of, 88, 96–97, 101, 105, 116, 117–118, 193; rice prices during, 100–101; ritual and music of, 39, 50; Hanfeizi, xxviii, 19, 19 n. 19, 40, 60, 139, 171
hatamoto ("bannermen"), 13 n. 39, 136, 136 n. 10
heart learning (*shingaku*), 4, 4 n. 7
"heart methods" (*shinbō*), xviii, xxvii, 3, 4, 4 n. 4, 5
heaven, xxxv, 27, 72–76, 95–96, 153, 173, 176; fear of, 73, 75; mandate of, 175; unknowability of, xxiv, 74–76. *See also* astronomy
hegemon (Ch. *bazhe*, Jp. *hasha*): Arai Hakuseki's view of, xxviii, xxviii n. 35; Chen Liang's view of, xvii; in Chinese history, xxvii, 18; and "enriching the country and strengthening the military," xxvii, 18–19, 87; and the "king," xxvii–xxviii; Mencius' view of, 19, 19 n. 17; the shogun as, xxviii; Shundai's defense of, xxvii
hereditary status: of artistic practitioners, 78, 127–128; of military governors, 27 n. 52; of officials, xvii, 66, 91 n. 14, 125 n. 7, 159; of provincial governors, 150; of servants, 159–160; of stipends, 32, 125–126, 125 n. 7, 128, 135, 154, 165; of vassals, 150, 163, 163 n. 22
Hirata Atsutane, xx n. 12
Hirate Masahide, 6, 6 n. 10
History of the Former Han (*Qian Han shu*, Ban Gu), 21–22, 37, 64, 72, 76, 80, 83, 83 n. 2, 170
History of the Latter Han (*Hou Han shu*), 80
Hōjō regency, 25, 25 n. 41, 53, 53 n. 32, 144
Hokkaido, 189 n. 10. *See also* Ezo
Holland, xxxiii–xxxiv
Honda Masanobu, xxvi
Honda Toshiaki, xxxiv–xxxv
Honjō Munesuke, 151, 151 n. 9
Hou Han shu. *See History of the Latter Han*
Huan, Duke of Qi, 86; as hegemon, xxvii; and state management of commerce, 193 n. 14, 194
Huangdi, 76, 76 n. 13, 169, 170
Hui, Emperor (Han dynasty), 152, 152 n. 11
Huizong, Emperor (Song dynasty), 4, 4 nn. 5–6
human ethics (*jinrin*), 149, 152, 157; and marriage, 44, 154; and theater, 60

human feelings (*ninjō*), 31, 41, 48, 89, 126–127, 160; and the *Classic of Poetry*, 33, 180; Dazai Shundai on, xxiv, xxv; methods of understanding, 32–35, 180; and music, 48; and principle, xxiv, 23, 32, 35, 37, 40, 41, 44, 68; and ritual, 41–42; role in governing, xxiv, xxv, 23, 30–35, 37, 44, 180; universality of, 31, 40, 68
human nature, xiv, xvii; Dazai Shundai on, xviii, xxii, xxxiv; Honda Toshiaki on, xxxiv; Ogyū Sorai on, xviii, xxi–xxii, xxiv, xxv, xxxiv; relationship to the Confucian Way, xviii, xxi–xxii, xxiv–xxv; shaping by institutions, xxxiv; Zhu Xi on, xviii, xxiv, xxvi
humaneness, 122, 139–140, 145, 157, 160, 166
Hundred Schools, 19, 19 n. 18, 60, 60 n. 55

imayō song, 52, 52 n. 25
imperial court ranks: as established by Prince Shōtoku, 66 n. 6; as honorary status for warriors, 13, 13 n. 36, 13 n. 38, 67 n. 9, 69 nn. 11–12
institutions (*seido*), 19, 21, 22, 26, 129, 144, 147–149, 156–157, 164, 165, 187, 194; Dazai Shundai on, xvii, xix–xxi, xxiii, xxxiv; Honda Toshiaki on, xxxiv–xxxv; Ogyū Sorai on, xix, xxxiv; of the Tokugawa period, xvii, xx–xxi, 132, 141, 145, 148, 157
Inuzuka Katsutarō, vii
Ishida Baigan, xxx, xxx n. 41, xxxiii, 4 n. 7

Japanese and Chinese Poems to Sing (*Wakan rōei shū*), 52, 52 n. 26
Ji kokka kongen. *See The Basis of Governing the State*
Jia Yi, 3, 6, 6 n. 10; criticism of merchants by, 105, 105 n. 27
Jiao Ruohou, 193
Jin dynasty, 11
Jing, Emperor (Han dynasty), 88 n. 10, 170
Jinmu, Emperor, 24, 24 n. 36
Jōei Code, 25, 25 n. 42
jōruri, 55–57, 57 n. 49, 60

kabuki, 60
Kaiho Seiryō, xxxiii–xxxiv
Kaitokudō academy, xxx

Index

Kamakura period, 11, 131, 144, 148, 158. *See also* Kamakura shogunate
Kamakura shogunate, xiv, 8 n. 23, 25–26, 25 n. 41, 26 n. 43, 53 n. 32. *See also* Kamakura period
Kamo no Mabuchi, xx n. 12
Keizairoku shūi. *See An Addendum to "On Political Economy"*
Kenmu Restoration, 26 n. 43
king, 46–47, 49, 98, 158; shogun as, xxviii, 8–10, 10 n. 28; vs. hegemon, xxvii–xxviii, 19 n. 17. *See also* sage kings
Kirby, Richard J., viii
koban, 84, 84 n. 3, 111–113, 155; recoinage of, 112, 113 n. 44
Kokugaku (National Learning), xx n. 12
kokyū fiddle, 57–58, 57 nn. 45–46
komusō, 52, 52 n. 24
Korea: diplomatic communications with: 10, 10 n. 28; embassies from, 131; music of, 51; Tsushima domain trade with, 188, 189 n.9
kōwakamai dance, 53 n. 31, 54, 54 nn. 36–37
Kumazawa Banzan, xviii, xxxi, 185, 185 n. 2, 187, 187 n. 6
Kusunoki Masashige, 53
kyōgen theater, 58, 58 n. 50, 60
Kyōhō Reforms, xvi–xvii, xxx, 125
Kyoto, 99, 161; as Ashikaga seat of government, 8, 8 n. 9; as center of trade and finance, 117, 185, 191; Dazai Shundai's residence in, xv

land: attachment of samurai to, xxxi, 157, 163; economic potential of, xxvi, xxxiv, 90–97, 189; expansion of cultivation of, xvii, 93–96; types of, xxvi, 90–96;
Laozi, xxviii–xxix, 60, 60 n. 54, 165–167, 169–172
laws, 22, 24, 26, 28, 31, 122, 131, 134, 137–141, 142–143, 147, 148; in the government of the sages, 140; vs. ritual and music, 40. *See also* Legalism
Laws for Military Houses (Buke Shohatto), 28 n. 56, 148, 148 n. 1
learning, 18, 35, 67, 93, 96, 118, 123–128; Confucian, xxiv, 50 n. 17, 122, 124, 125, 127, 170; European, xxiv; merchant-class, xxx; military, 124, 127; of principle, 75; promotion in the Kyōhō reforms, xvii, xxx
Legalism, xxvii, xxviii n. 34, 19 nn. 19–21, 40 n. 3, 88 n. 10, 91 n. 14, 138–140. *See also* Hanfeizi, Li Si, Shang Yang, Shen Buhai
Legge, James, xxiii n. 21, 16 n. 4, 19 n. 17, 31 n. 61
Li Kui, 91–93, 91 n. 14
Li Si, 19, 19 n. 21, 40, 60
licensed quarters, 161
Ling Lun, 76–77
literary writing, 127; Dazai Shundai's writings on, xiv; inclusion in civil service examinations, 124; vs. government as application of learning, xv–xvi, 18, 117. *See also* poetry
Liu Gongfu, 95–96
Liu Xiang, 22 n. 32, 80 n. 21
Lord Shang. *See* Shang Yang
loyalty (*chū*), 60, 139, 160, 186
Lü, Empress Dowager, 152, 152 n. 11
Lu Xiangshan, 4 n. 7, 5, 5 n. 8
Lu Xiufu, 4, 4 n. 6

Ma Xian, 76 n. 11
Man'yōshū, 33, 33 n. 65
marriage, 108, 154–157; and human ethics, 44, 154; rituals of, 40, 44–45, 47, 154
material force (Ch. *qi*, Jp. *ki*), 5 n. 8, 48–49, 77, 96, 176
mean (*chū*, *chūyō*), xviii; and ritual, 41–43
Meiji era, xxxvi
Meiji Restoration, xiv
Mencius, 34, 36, 46, 86, 90, 153; criticism of the hegemon by, 19
merchants, xii, xvi, xxix, xxxii, 86, 88–89, 99, 100–101, 104, 116, 117, 185, 186, 188, 190, 191–193; Dazai Shundai on, xxix, xxxi, xxxii n. 45, xxxiii; Ishida Baigan's defense of, xxx; learning of, xxx; Ogyū Sorai on, xxx–xxxi; Tokugawa Confucian views of, xxix. *See also* shopkeepers, traders
military governors (*shugo*), 25–26, 25 nn. 39–40, 27, 27 n. 52, 27 n. 55
military learning, 124, 127. *See also* School of the Military, Sunzi
military preparations, 132–136, 163

216

Index

Minamoto no Yoritomo, 8, 8 n. 18, 25, 25 n. 39, 25 n. 41, 67, 82
Ming dynasty: adoption practices during, 152; bureaucratic offices of, 65; coinage of, 110, 110 n. 35; Confucianism of, xviii, 5; diplomatic relations with Japan during, 8; dynastic name use of, 11; geographic records of, 80–81
Mizuno Genrō, vii
moneylending: to samurai from merchants, xvi, xxxii, 185–187; to samurai from public welfare granaries, xxxii, 108
Monmu, Emperor 81, 107
Morris-Suzuki, Tessa, xiii n. 3
Motoori Norinaga, xx n. 12
mourning clothes, 149
Mozi: xxviii, 171
Muromachi period, 8, 9, 11–12, 12 n. 32, 27, 39, 131, 132, 144, 148
Muromachi shogunate. *See* Ashikaga shogunate
music, 20, 22, 32–33, 47–60, 76–78, 127, 131, 170, 181; of barbarians, 48; Buddhist, 39; of court nobles, xxi, 39, 50; Dazai Shundai on, xiv, xviii–xix, xx, xxi, xxviii–xxix; effect on customs, 49; licentious, xxi, 48–50, 56–59; Ogyū Sorai on, xviii–xix; refined, xxi, 49, 49 n. 14, 51–52, 53, 56–59, 78; and ritual, xviii–xix, xxi, xxviii–xxix, 20, 38–40, 45, 48, 49–51, 59–60, 148, 149; and the Six Classics, 3 n. 1, 180–181, 180 n. 24; transmission from China to Japan, 50–51; transmission from Korea to Japan, 51; vulgar, 39, 51, 53, 57, 59, 60, 78; of warriors, xxi, 39, 54

Nagasaki, 194, 194 n. 17
Najita, Tetsuo, viii, xiii n. 3, xxx n. 40
Nakai, Kate Wildman, xxviii n. 35
natural world: as economic resource, xxv–xxvi, xxxiii–xxxv; as repository of moral value, xviii, xxv, xxx, xxxiv
nine ministers, 65, 68–69
Nitta Yoshisada, 26 n. 43, 53
noh theater, 39 n. 2, 54 n. 34, 58 n. 50
non-action (*mui*): historical examples in China, 170; of Laozi, xxviii–xxix, 60, 165–167, 169, 171–172; as response to an age of decline, xxix, 165, 167, 169–172; of the sages, 165–167

ōban, 84, 84 n. 3, 111–113; recoinage of, 115
Oda Nobunaga, 8, 8 nn. 20–21, 26, 26 n. 48, 144, 148; Dazai Shundai's ancestor Hirate Masahide's service to, 6 n. 14
Ogyū Sorai, xv, xviii–xix, xxi–xxii, xxiv–xxv, xxx–xxxi, xxx n. 41, xxxiii–xxxiv, 151 n. 9
On Political Economy (*Keizairoku*, Dazai Shundai), xiii, xiv, xvi, xvii, xxiv–xxvi, xxix, xxxi, xxxiii; publication of, vii, xvi; translations by Richard J. Kirby, viii
Osaka, 99, 161; as center of merchant-class Confucian learning, xxx; as center of trade and finance, xvi, 117, 185, 191–193; Dazai Shundai's residence in, xv
An Outline of Political Economy (*Keizai yōryaku*, Satō Nobuhiro), xxxv

petty man (*shōjin*), 30, 156, 177; definition of, 14, 14 n. 42; and profit, 116. *See also* gentleman
pitch pipes, 20, 22, 76–78, 76 n. 12, 77 n. 15; as basis for other measures and standards, 20, 20 n. 24, 77–78. *See also* music
poetry: in Chinese, xiv, xv, 127; Dazai Shundai's writings on, xiv; popular, xiv; role in governing, xv, 124; *waka*, 33, 33 n. 65, 127. *See also* Classic of Poetry, literary writing
political economy (*keizai*), xiii, xiii n. 3, xiv, xvii, xxxvi, 3, 5, 7, 16–21, 16 n. 1, 23, 32, 35, 37, 110, 117, 136, 164–165, 187, 189, 191, 193
pragmatism: of Dazai Shundai, xii, xxii–xxiii, xxvii–xxviii, xxxiii; and "enriching the country and strengthening the military," xii; and the hegemon, xxvii; of Ogyū Sorai, xv
prices: manipulation by cartels, xxxi, 117; of rice, xvi, xxxi–xxxii, 99–106, 107, 116; stabilization through "equalized transport," 193, 193 n. 15; stabilization through "leveling" (*heijun*), xxxi, 116, 118, 193, 193 n. 14
principle (Ch. *li*, Jp. *ri*), 23, 28–30, 31, 32, 35, 37, 40, 41, 44, 68, 75, 79, 104, 127, 161, 173, 175, 176, 178–179, 180, 181; Dazai Shundai on, xxiv, xxv, 28 n. 57; Kaiho Seiryō on, xxxiv; learning of, 4 n. 7, 75; Lu Xiangshan on, 5 n. 8; Song dynasty Confucians on, 75; Zhu Xi on, xviii, xxiv, xxv; 4 n. 7, 5 n. 8, 28 n. 57, 75

profit, 89, 94–95, 101, 104, 113, 115–118, 126, 154, 191–192; Confucian views on the morality of, xxix–xxx, xxxiii–xxxiv; daimyo pursuit of, xxxii, 192–193; Dazai Shundai's views on, xxxi–xxxii; Ishida Baigan's defense of, xxx; Kaiho Seiryō's defense of, xxxiii–xxxiv; and the samurai, xvi, xxx, xxxi, xxxiv, 101, 102

provincial governors (*kokushi*), 24–26, 24 n. 37, 25 n. 38, 66; displacement by military governors, 25–26, 25 n. 39; as honorary title, 69

public welfare granaries (*gisō*), xxxii, 106–110

punishments, 31, 90, 117, 138–141, 143–146, 147, 164, 181; in the government of the sages, 140; historical use in China, 22, 65, 68, 138, 143–144, 152; historical use in Japan, 144–145; of Shen Buhai and Hanfeizi, xxviii, 19, 19 n. 19, 60, 139, 171. *See also* rewards

Qian Han shu. *See History of the Former Han*

Qin dynasty, 7, 19, 24, 63, 65, 140–141, 145; dynastic name of, 11; suppression of Confucianism during, 49, 50 n. 17, 124; and transition from feudalism to "districts and prefectures," xx, 19, 23, 28, 64, 148

Qin Shi Huang, 19 n. 21, 63; creation of system of "districts and prefectures" by, 19, 23; elimination of ritual and music by, 38; suppression of Confucian learning by, 50 n. 17

Qing dynasty, 11 n. 31; bureaucratic offices of, 65; dynastic name of, 11

Qinzong, Emperor (Song dynasty), 4, 4 nn. 5–6

Rai Tsutomu, vii

Rebuking Absurdities (*Kamōsho*, Hirata Atsutane), xx n. 12

Record of Ritual (*Li ji*), 3 n. 1, 45 n. 7, 56, 62 n. 2, 99, 140, 181 n. 25

Records of the Grand Historian (*Shi ji*, Sima Qian), 20, 37, 72, 76, 80, 116

Reflections on the Meaning of Our Country (*Kokuikō*, Kamo no Mabuchi), xx n. 12

Reflections on the Past (*Keiko dan*, Kaiho Seiryō), xxxiii

rewards, 90, 126, 138–139, 164, 181, 187; historical use in China, 138. *See also* punishments

rice, 83, 85, 87–89, 91, 97, 188–189, 193; interest charged when loaned, xxxiv, 108; price of, xvi, xxxi–xxxii, 99–106, 107, 116; samurai stipends paid in, xvi, xxxiv, 100, 107, 109; tax on, 190. *See also* food, grain

rightness (*gi*), 30–31, 85–87, 107 n. 31, 122, 145, 157, 160; as basis of ritual, xxiii–xxiv, 43–44

Rikukei ryakusetsu. *See A General Outline of the Six Classics*

ritsuryō system, 25 n. 38, 70 nn. 15–16, 144 n. 7

ritual, 9, 20, 22, 38–47, 65, 85, 126, 141; archery, 41, 48, 124; banquet, 41; Buddhist, 39, 48; capping, 40; of court nobles, xxi, 39; Dazai Shundai on, xiii–xiv, xviii–xix, xx, xxi, xxiii–xxiv, xxviii–xxix; drinking, 41, 45–47, 124; feasting, 41; interviewing, 41; marriage, 40, 44–45, 154; and the mean, 41; and music, xviii–xix, xxviii–xxix, xxi, 20, 38–40, 45, 48, 49–51, 59–60, 148, 149; Ogyū Sorai on, xviii–xix; and rightness, xxiii–xxiv, 43–44, 85–87, 145, 157; and the Six Classics, 3 n. 3, 180–181, 180 n. 24, 181 n. 25; transmission from China to Japan, 39; vulgar, 39, 43, 45; of warriors, xxi, 39;

Rituals of Zhou (*Zhou li*), 45 n. 7, 62–63, 62 n. 2, 68, 90, 181 n. 25

Roberts, Luke, xxxii n. 45

rōnin (masterless samurai), 14; Dazai Shundai's father as, xv

Russia, xxxv

Ryukyu: diplomatic relations with, 131, 131 n. 2; music of, 57; trade with, 189

sacrifices, 20–22, 20 n. 22, 119, 153

sage kings, xv, xvii, xix, xxi, xxii, 15, 133. *See also* Three Kings, Two Emperors, Way of the ancient kings, Way of the sages, Way of the Two Emperors and Three Kings

saibara, 33, 33 n. 64

samurai, xii, xvi, xxix, xxx–xxxi, 100–102, 104, 105, 107–109, 115, 116, 126, 128, 145, 158, 160, 163, 193, 194; and commerce, xii–xiii, xxix, xxxii n. 45, xxxiii–xxxiv; in the countryside,

Index

134–136, 163; Dazai Shundai as, xv; financial difficulties of, xii, xvi, xxix, 104, 172; masterless, xv, 14; as ruling class, xii, xvii, xx, xxxi, xxxiii. *See also* daimyo, feudal lords, warriors

Sang Hongyang, 117, 193, 193 n. 15

sarugaku ("monkey music"), 39, 53 n. 32; shogunal patronage of, 39 n. 2, 54, 54 n. 34; as vulgar music, 53–55, 59, 78

Satō Nobuhiro, xxxv–xxxvi

Sawada, Janine Anderson, xxx n. 41

scholar-officials (*shi*), 14, 30, 34, 47, 58, 86, 88, 145; adoption among, 152; effect of rice prices on, 100–101; marriage of, 45, 155

School of the Military, xxvii, xxviii n. 34. *See also* military learning, Sunzi

A Secret Plan for Unification (*Kondō hisaku*, Satō Nobuhiro), xxxv

Seigaku mondō. See Dialogue on the Learning of the Sages

Seiwa, Emperor, 78

sekkyō sermons, 55, 55 n. 40, 57, 57 n. 49, 60

Sengoku (Warring States) period, 26, 26 n. 47, 67, 144–145, 148; lingering effects of on Tokugawa-period practices, 67, 131–132, 145, 148

Sentence and Section Annotations on the "Great Learning" (*Daxue zhangju*, Zhu Xi), 4, 4 n. 6

shakuhachi end-blown flute, 51, 51 n. 22, 52 n. 23; and *komusō* monks, 52, 52 n. 24; original Chinese version of, 50–51; as vulgar music, 51, 58

shamisen, 55, 57 n. 45; as vulgar music, 57, 57 nn. 48–49, 58

Shang dynasty, 7, 7 n. 16, 11, 27 n. 51. *See also* Yin dynasty

Shang jun shu. See Book of Lord Shang

Shang Yang (Lord Shang), 19, 19 n. 20, 40, 60, 138–140

Shanhai jing. See Classic of Mountains and Seas

Shen Buhai, xxviii, 19, 19 n. 19, 40, 60, 139, 171

Shi jing. See Classic of Poetry

Shinto, xx; Dazai Shundai's criticisms of, xiv, xxviii, 162; Ishida Baigan's use of, xxx, 4 n. 7; Meiji-era, xxxvi

shirabyōshi, 53

Shiron. See A Discourse on Poetry

shogun, xiv, 8–10, 14, 25–26, 148; as "hegemon," xviii; as "king," xviii, 8–10, 10 n. 28; relationship to daimyo, xv, xxi, 70 n. 13, 71, 163, 163 n. 22; relationship to the emperor, xiv, xviii, 8 n. 23, 9, 26 n. 43, 70 n. 13

shogunal deputies (*kanrei*), 26, 26 nn. 45–46

shopkeepers, 30, 89, 118, 157, 161, 191. *See also* merchants, traders

Shōtoku, Prince: and Hōryūji temple, 51 n. 21; and introduction of Chinese court practices to Japan, xix, 66, 66 n. 6; and introduction of Chinese music to Japan, 50, 50 n. 18, 51

Shu jing. See Classic of Documents

Shun, Emperor, xxvii n. 33, 7, 7 n. 15, 17, 20, 33, 34, 35, 46, 60 n. 56, 61, 63, 72, 73, 77, 85, 87, 143–144, 161, 166, 172. *See also* Two Emperors

Shusun Tong, 38, 39 n. 1

silver. *See* silver currency

Sima Qian, 20–22, 133. *See also Records of the Grand Historian*

Six Classics, 3, 3 nn. 1–2, 18, 154, 180–182, 180 n. 24

Six Dynasties, 124

six ministers, 62–65, 68

The Six Secret Strategies (*Liu tao*), xxviii n. 34

Solitary Words (*Dokugo*, Dazai Shundai), xiv

Song dynasty, 4, 4 nn. 5–6, 95, 124; currency of, 110; dynastic name of, 11; music of, 51. *See also* Song dynasty Confucianism

Song dynasty Confucianism, xviii, xxiv, 4 n. 6, 5, 14, 43, 75. *See also* Chen Liang, Cheng brothers, Lu Xiangshan, Zhu Xi

The Spirit of the Gods (*Naobi no mitama*, Motoori Norinaga), xx n. 12

spirits, 75, 153, 162

Spring and Autumn Annals (*Chunqiu*), 3 n. 1, 63, 63 n. 3, 74, 151, 159 n. 19, 180, 181

stabilization granaries (*jōheisō*), xxxi, 101, 101 n. 23, 105, 106 n. 30

Sui dynasty, 124

Suiko, Empress, 66, 66 n. 5

Sunzi, 60, 60 n. 53, 127. *See also* military learning, School of the Military

surnames, 149; changing through adoption, 151–154; of rulers bestowed on subjects, 149–151

219

Index

Taika Reforms, 24 n. 37, 66 n. 7
Taira no Kiyomori, 53, 53 n. 30
Taira no Shigehira, 52, 53 n. 28
Taizong, Emperor (Tang dynasty), 100, 150
Taizu, Emperor (Song dynasty), 124
Takimoto Seiichi, vii
talent, xxv, 3, 27, 47, 123–126, 139, 186; cultivation through learning, 123, 124; use in official posts, xxv–xxvi, 66, 70, 125, 139, 159, 166
Tale of Genji (*Genji monogatari*), 51
Tale of the Heike (*Heike monogatari*): and *biwa* priests, 54–55, 54 n. 38, 55 n. 39; depiction of music in, 52–53, 53 n. 28
Tales of the West (*Seiiki monogatari*, Honda Toshiaki), xxxiv
Tang, King, xxvii n. 33, 7, 7 n. 16, 33, 60 n. 56. *See also* Three Kings
Tang dynasty: bestowing of ruler's surname on subjects during, 150; bureaucratic offices of, 65–66; calendar of, 78; Confucianism of, 3; currency of, 110; legal code of, 144; literary writing during, 124; rice prices during, 100; ritual and music of, 39, 50–51; taxation system of, 97
taxation: of agricultural production, xvi, xvii, 97, 100, 158; of commerce, 190, 192; exemption of Buddhist monks from, 158; expansion of, 191; of products of the sea, 97, 190; rates of, 98, 186, 190
temporary employees, 159–160
theater, 53–60, 161; as source of moral corruption, xiv, 54–60. *See also dengaku, jōruri, kabuki, kyōgen, noh, sarugaku*
Three Dynasties, 7, 23, 38–39, 50, 64, 65, 73, 80, 124, 133, 143, 175. *See also* Shang (Yin) dynasty, Xia dynasty, Zhou dynasty
three excellencies, 8, 8 n. 22, 34, 34 n. 71, 62–66, 68
Three Kings, xxvii, xxvii n. 33, 18–19, 60, 60 n. 56, 172, 175, 180. *See also* King Tang, King Wen, King Yu
Tillman, Hoyt Cleveland, xxvii n. 32
the times (*toki*), xxiv, 5, 23, 32, 35, 40, 164, 172; adapting ancient methods to, xxiii, 28, 36, 125, 172–173, 175
Tōhi mondō. See Dialogue of the City and Country

Tokugawa Ienobu, 125; and Arai Hakuseki, xxviii, 10 n. 28; and currency reform, 103, 112–113, 115; as "king of Japan," 9, 10 n. 28; and the Laws for Military Houses, 148 n. 1
Tokugawa Ietsugu, 125; and Arai Hakuseki, xxviii; currency policy during reign of, 103, 113
Tokugawa Ieyasu, xiv, xxi, 8 n. 21, 9, 9 n. 24, 12, 27, 27 n. 49, 27 n. 51, 27 nn. 53–55, 67, 122, 125, 150, 150 n. 7, 188 n. 7
Tokugawa Mitsukuni, 93, 93 n. 16
Tokugawa shogunate, xiv–xv, xx–xxi, xxxiii
Tokugawa Tsunayoshi, 76; and creation of new maps, 82; and currency debasement, 103 n. 25; promotion of Confucian learning by, 125; and reform of the calendar, 79; rice prices during the reign of, 101–103; and Yanagisawa Yoshiyasu, 150, 151 n. 9
Tokugawa Yoshimune: and the Kyōhō Reforms, xvi–xvii, xxx, 125 n. 7; and the Laws for Military Houses, 148 n. 1; use of the title *taikun* by, 9 n. 25, 10 n. 28
Toyotomi Hideyori, 8 n. 21, 27 n. 49
Toyotomi Hideyoshi, 8, 8 n. 21, 26, 27 n. 49, 144, 148, 150, 150 n. 6
trade, xvi, xxvi, xxxiii, xxxv, 87, 89, 113, 116; practiced by daimyo, xxxii, 188–194. *See also* barter, commerce
traders, 30, 89, 118, 157, 161. *See also* merchants, shopkeepers
A Treatise on the Way (*Bendōsho*, Dazai Shundai): Kokugaku criticisms of, xx n. 12; presentation of Confucianism in relation to Buddhism and Shinto in, xiv
tribute, 28, 80, 97, 99, 190
Two Emperors, xxvii, xxvii n. 33, 7, 18–19, 60, 60 n. 56, 175, 180. *See also* Emperor Shun, Emperor Yao

Urabe Kanetomo (Yoshida Kanetomo), 162, 162 n. 21
urban commoners, xvi. *See also* artisans, merchants
urbanization, xii, xvi
utility (*kōri*), xxvii, 18, 21

Index

Wadoku yōryō. *See A General Outline of Reading in Japanese*
Wakan rōei shū. *See Japanese and Chinese Poems to Sing*
Wang Anshi, 95–96, 95 n. 17
Wang Tong, 156, 156 n. 17
Wang Yangming, 4 n. 7, 5, 5 n. 8
Warring States period (China), xxvii, 19, 38
Warring States period (Japan). *See* Sengoku period
warriors: ceremonial guards and processions of, 131–132; customs of, 130, 135, 145; as farmers, 134–135; and fate, 174; government by, xx, xxi, 8, 8 n. 17, 11–12, 25–27, 67, 69, 76, 82, 121, 125, 130, 144, 148, 150, 158, 159; laws of, 144; practice of adoption by, 153; and profit, 101; and ritual and music, xxi, 39, 54, 78; Tokugawa samurai as, xvi, 135–136. *See also* samurai
Way, the. *See* Way of the sages
Way of the ancient kings, 3–5, 7, 87, 139, 166, 170, 180. *See also* Way of the sages
Way of Changes (*ekidō*), 172, 180–182. *See also Classic of Changes*
Way of Confucius, 3–5. *See also* Way of the ancient kings, Way of the sages, Way of the Two Emperors and Three Kings
Way of the sages, 7, 15; and commerce, xxxi–xxxii; and empirical reality, xxiii–xxv; and funerals, 121–122; governing as purpose of, xv, xxiii, 4, 5, 17–18; introduction to Japan, xix–xxi; and profit, 117; relationship to human nature, xxii, xxiv; relationship to non-Confucian methods of government, xxvii, 19, 44, 60, 138–139, 171; and ritual and music, 60, 181; and the samurai, xvii; universality of, 5, 180. *See also* Way of the ancient kings, Way of Confucius, Way of the Two Emperors and Three Kings
Way of the Two Emperors and Three Kings, xxvii, 19, 60, 60 n. 56, 180. *See also* Way of the ancient kings, Way of Confucius, Way of the sages
Wei dynasty, 11
well-field system, 97, 98 n. 20. *See also* taxation
Wen, Emperor (Han dynasty), 6, 88, 170

Wen, Emperor (Sui dynasty), 106
Wen, King, xxvii n. 33, 7, 7 n. 16, 18, 18 n. 14, 34, 60 n. 56. *See also* Three Kings
Wu, Emperor (Han dynasty), 21; economic policies of, 96, 193 n.15; promotion of Confucianism by, 50 n. 17, 170
Wu, King, 7, 7 n. 16, 18, 18 n. 14, 21
Wu Ding, King. *See* Gaozong
Wu Qi, 60, 60 n. 53

Xia dynasty, xxiii, 7, 7 n. 16, 11, 33, 61, 63, 175. *See also* Three Dynasties
Xiao, Duke of Qin, 19, 138
Xiao He, 169, 169 n. 9
Xiao jing. *See Classic of Filial Piety*
Xing Hongyang, 117
Xuan, Emperor, 101
Xuanzong, Emperor, 51
Xunzi, 137 n. 1

yamabushi, 158–159, 159 n. 18
Yamamura, Kozo, xvi n. 7
Yanagisawa Yoshiyasu, 151, 151 n. 9
Yao, Emperor, xxvii n. 33, 7, 7 n. 15, 17, 20, 33, 34, 35, 46, 60 n. 56, 61, 63, 72, 73, 78, 85, 87, 143–144, 161, 172. *See also* Two Emperors
Yasui Santetsu, 76, 79, 79 n. 19
Yellow Emperor. *See* Huangdi
Yi jing. *See Classic of Changes*
Yi li. *See Book of Ceremonies and Rituals*
Yin dynasty, xxiii, 33, 61, 63, 175. *See also* Shang dynasty
yin and yang, 172, 176–181
Yongle Emperor, 8
Yoshiwara, 161, 161 n. 20
Yu, the Great. *See* King Yu
Yu, King, xxvii n. 33, 7, 7 n. 16, 21 n. 28, 33, 33 n. 66, 60 n. 56, 79 n. 20, 80, 83, 166. *See also* Three Kings
Yuan dynasty, 79; coins of, 110; dynastic name of, 11, 11 n. 30
Yue jing. *See Classic of Music*

Zhangsun Ping, 106–107
Zhao, Emperor (Han dynasty), 100, 193 n. 13
Zhongyong. *See Doctrine of the Mean*

Index

Zhou dynasty, 7, 7 n. 16, 8, 11, 34, 60 n. 56, 151, 175; bureaucratic offices of, 34, 62, 63–65, 68, 80; decline of, xxvii, 18, 19, 38, 47, 166, 175; feudal system of, xxi, 12, 23, 28, 63–64; the hegemon during, xxvii, 18; rituals of, xxiii. *See also* Three Dynasties

Zhu Xi, xviii, xxiv, xxv, xxvi, xxvii, xxix, 4, 4 nn. 6–7, 75, 117; Chen Liang's criticism of, xxvii, xxvii n. 32; Dazai Shundai's criticism of, xviii, xxiv, xxv, xxvi, 28 n. 57; Ishida Baigan's use of, xxx; Lu Xiangshan's criticism of, 5, 5 n. 8; Ogyū Sorai's criticism of, xviii, xxiv. *See also* Song dynasty Confucianism

Zhuangzi, 60, 60 n. 54, 176

Zigong, 21, 136

zoku (vulgar, common, popular), xxi. *See also* vulgar music, vulgar ritual

Zuo Commentary (*Zuo zhuan*), 41 n. 5, 134, 156, 159, 159 n. 19; on arms, 21, 119, 133; on sacrifices, 21, 119, 153

CAMBRIDGE TEXTS IN THE HISTORY OF POLITICAL THOUGHT

Titles published in the series thus far

Aquinas *Political Writings* (edited and translated by R. W. Dyson)

Aristotle *The Politics and The Constitution of Athens* (edited and translated by Stephen Everson)

Arnold *Culture and Anarchy and Other Writings* (edited by Stefan Collini)

Astell *Political Writings* (edited by Patricia Springborg)

Augustine *The City of God against the Pagans* (edited and translated by R. W. Dyson)

Augustine *Political Writings* (edited by E. M. Atkins and R. J. Dodaro)

Austin *The Province of Jurisprudence Determined* (edited by Wilfrid E. Rumble)

Bacon *The History of the Reign of King Henry VII* (edited by Brian Vickers)

Bagehot *The English Constitution* (edited by Paul Smith)

Bakunin *Statism and Anarchy* (edited and translated by Marshall Shatz)

Bartolus of Sassoferrato *Political Writings* (edited and translated by George Garnett and Magnus Ryan)

Baxter *Holy Commonwealth* (edited by William Lamont)

Bayle *Political Writings* (edited by Sally L. Jenkinson)

Beccaria *On Crimes and Punishments and Other Writings* (edited by Richard Bellamy; translated by Richard Davies)

Bentham *A Fragment on Government* (edited by Ross Harrison)

Bernstein *The Preconditions of Socialism* (edited and translated by Henry Tudor)

Bodin *On Sovereignty* (edited and translated by Julian H. Franklin)

Bolingbroke *Political Writings* (edited by David Armitage)

Bossuet *Politics Drawn from the Very Words of Holy Scripture* (edited and translated by Patrick Riley)

Botero *The Reason of State* (edited and translated by Robert Bireley)

The British Idealists (edited by David Boucher)

Burke *Pre-Revolutionary Writings* (edited by Ian Harris)

Burke *Revolutionary Writings* (edited by Iain Hampsher-Monk)

Caliphate and Imamate: An Anthology of Medieval Muslim Texts on Political Theology (edited and translated by Hassan Ansari and Nebil Husayn)

Cavendish *Political Writings* (edited by Susan James)

Christine de Pizan *The Book of the Body Politic* (edited by Kate Langdon Forhan)

Cicero *On Duties* (edited by E. M. Atkins; edited and translated by M. T. Griffin)

Cicero *On the Commonwealth and On the Laws* (edited and translated by James E. G. Zetzel)

Comte *Early Political Writings* (edited and translated by H. S. Jones)

Comte *Conciliarism and Papalism* (edited by J. H. Burns and Thomas M. Izbicki)

Condorcet *Political Writings* (edited by Steven Lukes and Nadia Urbinati)

Constant *Political Writings* (edited and translated by Biancamaria Fontana)

Dante *Monarchy* (edited and translated by Prue Shaw)

Albert Venn Dicey *Writings on Democracy and the Referendum* (edited by Gregory Conti)

Diderot *Political Writings* (edited and translated by John Hope Mason and Robert Wokler)

The Dutch Revolt (edited and translated by Martin van Gelderen)

Early Greek Political Thought from Homer to the Sophists (edited and translated by Michael Gagarin and Paul Woodruff)

The Early Political Writings of the German Romantics (edited and translated by Frederick C. Beiser)

Emerson *Political Writings* (edited by Kenneth S. Sacks)

The English Levellers (edited by Andrew Sharp)

Erasmus *The Education of a Christian Prince with the Panegyric for Archduke Philip of Austria* (edited and translated by Lisa Jardine; translated by Neil M. Cheshire and Michael J. Heath)

Fénelon *Telemachus* (edited and translated by Patrick Riley)

Ferguson *An Essay on the History of Civil Society* (edited by Fania Oz-Salzberger)

Fichte *Addresses to the German Nation* (edited by Gregory Moore)

Filmer *Patriarcha and Other Writings* (edited by Johann P. Sommerville)

Fletcher *Political Works* (edited by John Robertson)

Sir John Fortescue *On the Laws and Governance of England* (edited by Shelley Lockwood)

Fourier *The Theory of the Four Movements* (edited by Gareth Stedman Jones; edited and translated by Ian Patterson)

Franklin *The Autobiography and Other Writings on Politics, Economics, and Virtue* (edited by Alan Houston)

Gramsci *Pre-Prison Writings* (edited by Richard Bellamy; translated by Virginia Cox)

Guicciardini *Dialogue on the Government of Florence* (edited and translated by Alison Brown)

Hamilton, Madison, and Jay (writing as 'Publius') *The Federalist with Letters of 'Brutus'* (edited by Terence Ball)

Harrington *The Commonwealth of Oceana and A System of Politics* (edited by J. G. A. Pocock)

Hegel *Elements of the Philosophy of Right* (edited by Allen W. Wood; translated by H. B. Nisbet)

Hegel *Political Writings* (edited by Laurence Dickey and H. B. Nisbet)

Hess *The Holy History of Mankind and Other Writings* (edited and translated by Shlomo Avineri)

Hobbes *On the Citizen* (edited and translated by Michael Silverthorne and Richard Tuck)

Hobbes *Leviathan* (edited by Richard Tuck)

Hobhouse *Liberalism and Other Writings* (edited by James Meadowcroft)

Hooker *Of the Laws of Ecclesiastical Polity* (edited by A. S. McGrade)

Hume *Political Essays* (edited by Knud Haakonssen)

Jefferson *Political Writings* (edited by Joyce Appleby and Terence Ball)

John of Salisbury *Policraticus* (edited by Cary J. Nederman)

Kant *Political Writings* (edited by H. S. Reiss; translated by H. B. Nisbet)

Ibn Khaldūn *Political Thought* (edited by Gabriel Martinez-Gros; translated by Anna Bailey Galietti)

King James VI and I *Political Writings* (edited by Johann P. Sommerville)

Knox *On Rebellion* (edited by Roger A. Mason)

Kropotkin *The Conquest of Bread and Other Writings* (edited by Marshall Shatz)

Kumazawa Banzan *Governing the Realm and Bringing Peace to All below Heaven* (edited and translated by John A. Tucker)

Lawson *Politica Sacra et Civilis* (edited by Conal Condren)

Leibniz *Political Writings* (edited and translated by Patrick Riley)

Lincoln *Political Writings and Speeches* (edited by Terence Ball)

Locke *Political Essays* (edited by Mark Goldie)

Locke *Two Treatises of Government* (edited by Peter Laslett)

Loyseau *A Treatise of Orders and Plain Dignities* (edited and translated by Howell A. Lloyd)

Luther and Calvin on Secular Authority (edited and translated by Harro Höpfl)

Catharine Macaulay *Political Writings* (edited by Max Skjönsberg)

Machiavelli *The Prince, Second Edition* (edited by Quentin Skinner and Russell Price)

Joseph de Maistre *Considerations on France* (edited and translated by Richard A. Lebrun)

Maitland *State, Trust and Corporation* (edited by David Runciman and Magnus Ryan)

Malthus *An Essay on the Principle of Population* (edited by Donald Winch)

Marsiglio of Padua *Defensor minor and De translatione Imperii* (edited by Cary J. Nederman)

Marsilius of Padua *The Defender of the Peace* (edited and translated by Annabel Brett)

Marx *Early Political Writings* (edited and translated by Joseph O'Malley)

Medieval Muslim Mirrors for Princes: An Anthology of Arabic, Persian and Turkish Political Advice (edited and translated by Louise Marlow)

James Mill *Political Writings* (edited by Terence Ball)

J. S. Mill *On Liberty and Other Writings* (edited by Stefan Collini)

Milton *Political Writings* (edited by Martin Dzelzainis; translated by Claire Gruzelier)

Montesquieu *The Spirit of the Laws* (edited and translated by Anne M. Cohler, Basia Carolyn Miller and Harold Samuel Stone)

More *Utopia* (edited by George M. Logan and Robert M. Adams)

Morris *News from Nowhere* (edited by Krishan Kumar)

Nicholas of Cusa *The Catholic Concordance* (edited and translated by Paul E. Sigmund)

Nietzsche *On the Genealogy of Morality* (edited by Keith Ansell-Pearson; translated by Carol Diethe)

Paine *Political Writings* (edited by Bruce Kuklick)

William Penn *Political Writings* (edited by Andrew R. Murphy)

Plato *Gorgias, Menexenus, Protagoras* (edited by Malcolm Schofield; translated by Tom Griffith)

Plato *Laws* (edited by Malcolm Schofield; translated by Tom Griffith)

Plato *The Republic* (edited by G. R. F. Ferrari; translated by Tom Griffith)

Plato *Statesman* (edited by Julia Annas; edited and translated by Robin Waterfield)

Political Thought in Portugal and Its Empire, c. 1500–1800 (edited by Pedro Cardim and Nuno Gonçalo Monteiro)

The Political Thought of the Irish Revolution (edited by Richard Bourke and Niamh Gallagher)

Price *Political Writings* (edited by D. O. Thomas)

Priestley *Political Writings* (edited by Peter Miller)

Proudhon *What Is Property?* (edited and translated by Donald R. Kelley and Bonnie G. Smith)

Pufendorf *On the Duty of Man and Citizen according to Natural Law* (edited by James Tully; translated by Michael Silverthorne)

The Radical Reformation (edited and translated by Michael G. Baylor)

Rousseau *The Discourses and Other Early Political Writings* (edited and translated by Victor Gourevitch)

Rousseau *The Social Contract and Other Later Political Writings* (edited and translated by Victor Gourevitch)

Seneca *Moral and Political Essays* (edited and translated by John M. Cooper; edited by J. F. Procopé)

Sidney *Court Maxims* (edited by Hans W. Blom, Eco Haitsma Mulier and Ronald Janse)

Sorel *Reflections on Violence* (edited by Jeremy Jennings)

Spencer *Political Writings* (edited by John Offer)

Stirner *The Ego and Its Own* (edited by David Leopold)

Emperor Taizong and ministers *The Essentials of Governance* (compiled by Wu Jing; edited and translated by Hilde De Weerdt, Glen Dudbridge and Gabe van Beijeren)

Thoreau *Political Writings* (edited by Nancy L. Rosenblum)

Tönnies *Community and Civil Society* (edited and translated by Jose Harris; translated by Margaret Hollis)

Utopias of the British Enlightenment (edited by Gregory Claeys)

Vico *The First New Science* (edited and translated by Leon Pompa)

Vitoria *Political Writings* (edited by Anthony Pagden and Jeremy Lawrance)

Volney *The Ruins and Catechism of Natural Law* (edited and translated by Colin Kidd; translated by Lucy Kidd)

Voltaire *Political Writings* (edited and translated by David Williams)

Weber *Political Writings* (edited by Peter Lassman; edited and translated by Ronald Speirs)

William of Ockham *A Short Discourse on Tyrannical Government* (edited by Arthur Stephen McGrade; translated by John Kilcullen)

William of Ockham *A Letter to the Friars Minor and Other Writings* (edited by Arthur Stephen McGrade; edited and translated by John Kilcullen)

Wollstonecraft *A Vindication of the Rights of Men and A Vindication of the Rights of Woman* (edited by Sylvana Tomaselli)

For EU product safety concerns, contact us at Calle de José Abascal, 56–1°,
28003 Madrid, Spain or eugpsr@cambridge.org.

www.ingramcontent.com/pod-product-compliance
Ingram Content Group UK Ltd.
Pitfield, Milton Keynes, MK11 3LW, UK
UKHW022136240226
468380UK00018B/332